Arthur A. Cohen graduated from the University of Chicago in 1946. From 1951–53 he was Fellow in Medieval Jewish Philosophy at the Jewish Theological Seminary of America and pursued studies in philosophy and the history of religion at Union Theological Seminary and Columbia University. In 1957 Mr. Cohen became a consultant to the project "Religion and the Free Society" of the Fund for the Republic, in which capacity he served until the project was completed in late 1961.

Mr. Cohen is a member of the Standing Committee on the Church and State of the New York office of the American Civil Liberties Union, the editorial advisory board of the Jewish Publication Society of America, the editorial board of the theological quarterly JUDAISM, and the Advisory Council of the Institute for Advanced Judaic Studies at Brandeis University. His writing has appeared in HARPER'S, THE CHRISTIAN CENTURY, COMMONWEAL, COMMENTARY, PARTISAN REVIEW, and other journals.

In addition to his calling as a theologian, Mr. Cohen has pursued a distinguished career in publishing, and is now Director of Religious Publishing for Holt, Rinehart and Winston, Inc.

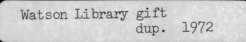

Gershon + Ann —
With affection + regards
Irving Levitas

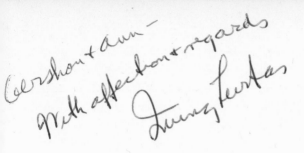

The Natural and the Supernatural Jew

ALSO BY ARTHUR A. COHEN
Martin Buber

EDITOR OF
Anatomy of Faith by Milton Steinberg

The Natural and the Supernatural Jew

An Historical and Theological Introduction

ARTHUR A. COHEN

PANTHEON BOOKS • NEW YORK

Library of Congress Catalog Card Number: 61–7455

Manufactured in the U.S.A.

FOR MY NATURAL JEWS, ELAINE AND TAMAR JUDITH

Contents

Whereas the peoples of Greece and Italy . . . have long since perished, these still survive, and, despite the endeavors of so many mighty kings who have over and over again sought to destroy them, as their historians testify and as it is easy to deduce by the natural course of things, they have nevertheless been preserved all through those many years (and their preservation was a thing foretold), and, stretching from the earliest to the latest times, their history embraces in its duration all others [which it long preceded]. PASCAL, *Pensées*

Those who find belief difficult seek a reason in the disbelief of the Jews: "If it was all so clear, say they, why would they not believe?" And they would almost have them believe, so as not to be held back by the example of their refusal. But it is just this refusal which is the foundation of our belief. We should be much less inclined to believe if they were on our side. We should then have a far more ample pretext. It is a wonderful thing to have made the Jews great lovers of things foretold, and great enemies of their fulfillment. PASCAL, *Pensées*

I remember how the materialist interpretation of history, when I attempted in my youth to verify it by applying it to the destinies of peoples, broke down in the case of the Jews, where destiny seemed absolutely inexplicable from the materialistic standpoint. And, indeed, according to the materialistic and positivistic criterion, this people ought long ago to have perished. Its survival is a mysterious and wonderful phenomenon demonstrating that the life of this people is governed by a special predetermination, transcending the processes of adaptation expounded by the materialistic interpretation of history. The survival of the Jews, their resistance to destruction, their endurance under absolutely peculiar conditions and the fateful role played by them in history; all these point to the particular and mysterious foundations of their destiny.

NICHOLAS BERDYAEV, *The Meaning of History*

Preface and Acknowledgments

Happily the preface to most books is written last, as it enables the author to anticipate the reader's questions and dissatisfactions by acknowledging the existence of his own. Surely this is the case here, for this book—written over a number of years—has often languished while I busied myself with other tasks. It is not diffidence which prompts me to warn the reader of my uncertainties; rather it is my conviction that any work, however tentative, is best sent forth to make its own way, while the writer retires to safer land to survey, with somewhat more detachment, what he has produced. In pushing this book away after nearly seven years of work, I have come, not to the end of one book, but to the beginning of many others which undoubtedly will modify and perhaps repudiate what is set forth here. With these caveats, *The Natural and the Supernatural Jew.*

The title of the present work, although considerably narrowed in application and statement, was employed in an essay which I wrote for *American Catholics: A Protes-*

tant-JewishView, which Sheed & Ward published in 1959. The concept of the natural and the supernatural Jew is not unique to me. It has a long, even if not explicit, history in Jewish thought, and its adaptation to the particular problems of assessing the relationship of Judaism to the Church was particularly apt for the purposes set forth by Philip Scharper, the editor of *American Catholics.* The essay for *American Catholics* was written in the midst of writing the present work. The concepts it employed had been in my mind from the very beginning of my work on the present volume, and so it seemed most appropriate to adapt the title of the earlier essay to the requirements of the larger and more intensive exposition which I have undertaken here.

I take particular pleasure in acknowledging the exceptionally detailed and critical reading which Dr. Gerson Cohen gave the first draft of this book. He is to be given credit for saving me from many errors of scholarship and interpretation; those that remain are of my own making. Portions of the manuscript were read by Dr. Nahum N. Glatzer, Rabbi Steven S. Schwarzschild, and Rabbi Everett Gendler. Their suggestions proved most useful to me.

אלול כב, תשכ״א

The Natural and the Supernatural Jew

Introduction: Some Existential Dogmas

The classic credos of Western religion conceal behind their verbal façade an edifice of argument which it has required centuries of disputation to construct. The passage of time, however, manages to spread over the seams and cracks of ancient controversy a tapestry of composure and equanimity. In this, history misrepresents the precarious situation of faith, for an illusion of wholeness and integrity, which conceals the knots and wormholes of disagreement and unbelief, is transmitted to the present and the future. Hopefully, the artificial peace is sometimes broken. At such moments believer and heretic, traditionalist and dissident—from whose disputation doctrine was originally fashioned—tangle once more.

The content of religious doctrine is founded on the presumption that God does not change. The endurance of religious doctrine, however, must presuppose that man changes, that his volatility is not mere caprice and inconstancy, but a response to the historical flux in which

God and man met once and meet again and again. Doctrine emerges, therefore, as the reflection of the constancy of God and the temporality and historicity of man.

Doctrine may be eternally true, yet die in history. It may continue to enjoy some abstract and remote validity, preserved pure and undefiled in apocalyptic enclaves, but it ceases to be a living force in history. History both authenticates and compromises the truth of doctrine. The process of authentication is truth become historical, liberated from its stony abstractness. The truth itself is not affected by the power of history: God continues to exist, hidden and secret. If he does not exist in history, however, he is as though he were dead. History is the medium through which God passes into human life.

To speak of religious doctrine is, therefore, to speak of history. We cannot even withdraw to the apodictic and compelling consolations of revelation to protect us from the ravages of history; since in revelation God's Word is as much in time and history as though he were present in all his immediacy. In no sense, therefore, can religious doctrine escape history.

Religious doctrine cannot escape history; Judaism cannot escape history. The day-to-day existence of Judaism is wholly historical. It may transmute the events of time, wrenching them out of the orbit of the routine and elevating them into a new time. By so doing it does not negate time. It only succeeds in giving to temporal events a symbolic and sacramental status. The commandments of Judaism, wherein time is sanctified, project the image of the end of time. The commandments are the constant symbols of Jewish redemption. They anticipate the end of time, for they are so consciously refusals to take normal time and natural history for what they are: the subverters of redemption. The performance of each commandment carries with it the injunction to think upon the meaning toward which time and history point. The hallowing of time and history consists in the prescient recognition that they are linked to the *beyond-time* and the *beyond-history*. Sanctification is symbolic, and holiness, wherever it exists, is little more than an anticipation amid creation of what it is that God prepares as the fulfillment of history.

The confession with which I begin is a statement of existential dogma—that is, what *I* say here *I* must believe, because without it there is nothing I consider *ultimately* relevant or meaningful to believe.

I feel obliged, however, to qualify immediately this assertion of dogma. Obviously the dogmas I shall define are not dogmas of tradition nor even formulas founded upon the reworking of inherited principles of Jewish faith. They are, rather, evocations of meaning implicit in the "dogmatics" set forth during earlier ages of Jewish faith; but even this historical foundation does not permit me to make claim for their being authentically Jewish. The dogmatics I employ has primarily a *heuristic* value, for it enables me to define the ground from which my investigation will depart. My dogmas are conclusions drawn from my understanding of the actual situation of the Jew—in this sense they are *empirical;* they are also judgments upon the events of Jewish history which transmit meaning and instruction regarding the predicament of the Jew amid the nations—in this sense they are *historical;* and lastly they define a view of the Jew's involvement with ultimate reality, his connection with a destiny which commands him, with that which makes him, in fact, Jewish—in this sense they are *transhistorical,* possibly metaphysical, and certainly theological.

The thing to remember, however, is that I do not consider these dogmas to be necessarily valid for all time. They may be, but they need not be. What is crucial is that they serve me and assist in clarifying my understanding of the times in which we live. They are, I believe, properly termed existential dogmas.

The dogmas are these:

One: There is a distinction between the natural and the supernatural Jew. The natural Jew is a creature situated in nature and activated by history. His natural environment shapes his physical person and his contingent personality and disposition; the interaction of his natural environment and the events which come to form his personal history—his country of birth, the language he speaks, the wars in which he fights, the national culture he espouses, the work he does—define a nexus which is fatalistically limited. Only if he exercises his freedom to intend transcendence, to become conscious of the limitations to which environment and personal history compel him to submit, is he able to break out of fate into destiny. In a community such as that of the Jew, which believes itself not only open before God, but the one to whom God has opened himself, one can speak of a supernatural community. God has covenanted with the Jewish people that it shall transcend nature and history to him alone. He has confirmed in the Jewish people the possibility (which all men possess) of *intending* its transcendence. Moreover, God has converted the fatality of nature and history into the destiny of the Jew, that he transcend his natural situation to Him. Without the command to sustain one's supernatural vocation (that is, the belief that God has called the Jew to Himself) to call oneself a Jew is but a half-truth—a mere designation without ultimate meaning.

Two: The consciousness of supernatural vocation, as a condition of Jewish existence, is made doubly important by the continuing significance of the Exile. The Exile, as I understand it, is not an accident of history, remedied by security within the Diaspora or national fulfillment in the State of Israel. It is not only an historical predicament, but a theological category. The Exile is the historical coefficient of being unredeemed.

Three: Since the Exile is the coefficient of being unredeemed, the purpose of the supernatural vocation of the

Jew is to make all history alive to its incompleteness. This is no more than to reaffirm that the Jew is a messianic being for whom there is *no* redemption until *all* history is redeemed.

Four: Although the Jew is a messianic being, he cannot be a messianist in isolation from the community of Jews and the whole of mankind. If he remains single, isolate, and alone he compromises the demanding assumption of his supernature, that not in solitude but in community was he joined in covenant to God. God elects, not the single Jew, but the Jewish people. The obligation to engage in concert in the work of redemption joins the people of Israel to the fortunes of all peoples. The Jewish people has not itself alone to redeem.

Five: Insofar as the Jewish people has both a natural and a supernatural dimension (and it is understood that neither can exist distillate and pure) it is obliged to acknowledge that its situation at any given moment is fashioned not only by God but by the events of time and history. It has law and tradition, teaching and belief, *halachah* and *aggadah,* but these are involved—as is all else—in the dialectical contrariety of divine prescription and historical freedom. It does as much violence to our supernature to trivialize our lives in submission to the accommodations which time and history may recommend as it does violence to our human condition amid time and history to pronounce the Word of God, as once stated, to be final.

The preceding assertions, complex though they may be, are unqualified. They define something infinitely more precious than the triumph of thought and argument. They are what enables me to understand myself as a Jew. Such affirmations are not, however, without their correlative intellectual imperatives, for they do not enjoy a merely subjective status in my thought.

There is little question that my reflections on history have no resemblance to the formal discipline of the historian, but this does not mean that my reflections are therefore false. Every man who confronts his world with the question of meaning is raising a fundamentally historical question. He is not only asking whether an event occurred; he is asking why it occurred. The question of "why" is rarely a dispassionate question. It is asked not only because man has curiosity about his past, but because he has concern about his future. The search for meaning in history may be the modest effort to enrich self-understanding (which is, after all, what R. G. Collingwood considered the sufficient purpose of historiography) or it may be the grander and more unscientific effort to fathom a unity and to define a purpose immanent within history, or to locate an end-point toward which history is directed and through which it is fulfilled. The variety of meanings which have been discerned in history, whatever their questionable status as scientific truth, may have the value of illuminating the life of reflective men, of strengthening character, of shaping conviction, of giving to each new moment a quality of excitement and expectation which otherwise it might lack. It is true that such metaphysicians of history might well be satisfied with meanings discerned *within* the flow of historical events. However, a partisan of existential dogmatics might add something more: no longer do we know the end for which we strive; but if, indeed, there is an end, each moment prefigures something of it. Each moment becomes a prism through which the murky light of history and the clear light of God become one. This is, perhaps, all that eschatology can say to history, for any doctrine of the last event seems captious and gratuitous while we stand amid the agonies of actual history.[1] We may be assured of the beginning of history and we may demand its end, but all we have is the present and it is in the present, *the time between creation and redemption*, that we must live. It is for these reasons that any dog-

[1] Arthur A. Cohen, "The Past and Future of Eschatological Thinking," in Harold Stahmer, ed., *Religion and Contemporary Society* (New York, Collier Books, 1963).

matics is unavoidably existential, because its truth and power arise out of a decision with respect to *our history* and *our eternal task*.

If the dogmas which I have affirmed are authentic Jewish dogmas they must have been latent in the past against which Jewish thought developed and matured. It is obviously of little interest to project a view of Jewish destiny so at variance with possibilities present in Jewish history as to be ludicrously implausible and tendentious. Undoubtedly my view is a harsh view. However, I am afraid less of harshness than of inauthenticity. I am afraid less of abnormalizing the Jew than of normalizing him. This is so because my concern is less with Jewish history as such, with the works of the Jewish mind, with the identification of its peculiar cast and accent, its spirit and force, than with a specific phenomenon: the Jewish mind as it has thought and continues to think about its supernatural vocation.

1

The Century of Uncertainty

The expulsion of the Jews from Spain in 1492, an event which affected the lives of Jews throughout the Christian and Islamic worlds, marked the end of the cultural and intellectual exchange of medieval Judaism and Christianity. The destruction of the most elegant and cultivated Jewish community of the Middle Ages carried with it, as well, a symbolic end, for it severed the link which bound the Jews of Europe to the Jews amid Islam. The Jewish *oikoumene* ended. The unhurried and leisurely exile of the Jews—which took more than a millennium to accomplish—was now accelerated by a most violent dispersion.

The rapid destruction and dispersion of the Iberian Jewish community made necessary an attitude of cultural containment and self-defense which lasted more than three centuries until the emancipation of European Jewry.[1] The Jews of Europe felt their way through dark

[1] This description has been called a false generalization, a gloss and distortion of Gershom Scholem's description of the impact of the Expulsion on Spanish Kabbalism. However, in spite of the fact that in Renaissance Italy cultural communication between Judaism and Christianity continued to flourish after the Spanish exile, what must

centuries which saw the decimation of Europe by religious and dynastic wars, the decline of the papacy, and the expansion of nationalism and capitalism. Still bound by medieval law to ghetto enclosure, marked off by badge and dress, subject to economic, political, and social restrictions, they developed the sight of the blind and learned to live in the joy of their familiar hegemony and the splendid isolation of their self-administered communities. Until the eighteenth century the Jew accommodated to his portion, understood as best he could the torments of the times, and cultivated the mysteries of his past glory and his future redemption.

In the late eighteenth century the communal and religious unity of the Jewish community was disrupted and a painful uncertainty began to afflict the members of this previously stationary and immobile society. The Jew was no longer certain of his position nor his place. Neither the Church nor its secular arm the State possessed sufficient power any longer—except in countries where medieval precedent endured—to fix the privileges and limits of the Jew. The Jew was forced into the modern world at least a century before he coveted its benefits. European society, in transition from the hierarchic organization of the Middle Ages to the competitive heterogeneity of the modern world, found Jewry unprepared. The Jew could no longer anticipate from which quarter threat might come—whether from Church, merchants, peasantry, landlords, or any of the other clusters of power and self-interest that an aggressive and fluid society displays. Having routinized and, to a degree, desiccated the faith and discipline which gave him surpassing pride before the ancient and the medieval world; having accepted as just the conditions of secular life before being formally admitted to its precincts, the Jew was unprepared to

---

be emphasized is that the intellectual life of Judaism as a whole went into a decline, exploration in philosophy and theology all but ceased, and Jewish religious life redirected itself to the tasks of conservation and exegesis.

combat the irrational hostility of secular society. It was possible for him to understand the theological animus of medieval Christendom and to combat it with argument or silent contempt. But his social exclusion from the already secular European society of the eighteenth century was thoroughly unintelligible. It was therefore all the more devastating. Lives were not lost—Jews fell no longer before Crusader and Inquisition; but Jewish society was decimated nonetheless. What the tyrannies of a powerful faith had failed to achieve, the insinuations of secular society began to accomplish on a grand scale.

I. SOLOMON IBN VERGA (LATE 15th–EARLY 16th CENTURY)

It was the expulsion of 1492 which first moved a Spanish Jew, who had fled to Italy in the early sixteenth century, to meditate upon that most difficult of questions: Why do men hate the Jews? [1] This was a question asked of history. Solomon Ibn Verga did not pose it as a theological question, although he could not resist an ultimately theological answer. Rather Ibn Verga reflected, in his *Rod of Judah* (*Shevet Yehuda*), upon the history of the Jews from the days of the Roman conquest of Palestine [2]—those first days of exile and destruction—

[1] Yitzhak Fritz Baer, *Galut* (New York, Schocken Books, Inc., 1947), p. 79. See particularly Solomon Ibn Verga, *Shevet Yehuda* (in Hebrew), ed. by Yitzhak Fritz Baer and Azriel Shohet (Jerusalem, The Bialik Institute, 1947), pp. 46–48. For an indispensable critical edition of this work, other than the Hebrew text and notes edited by Professor Baer, see M. Wiener, *Das Buch Schevet Jehuda* (Hanover, Orient-Buchhandlung Heinz Lafaire, 1924); also (Yitzhak) Fritz Baer, *Untersuchungen über Quellen und Komposition des Schebet Jehuda* (Berlin, C. A. Schwetschke & Sohn, 1923).

[2] Ibn Verga, *Shevet Yehuda*, pp. 19–20; p. 166. Baer questions the historical accuracy of Ibn Verga's account of the persecutions of the Jews under Emperor Antoninus, suggesting rather that it is a re-

to the expulsion of the Jews from Spain and Portugal. He recounts first, with terseness and unembarrassed frankness, the backslidings of the Jews, their sufferings at the hands of emperor, caliph, or king, their capitulation to various ultimatums of "conversion or death," their apostasy or their massacre, the remission of their condemnation under a compassionate ruler, and their return or final apostasy.

Beneath the matter-of-fact reckoning of persecution and attrition there runs the abiding question: Why? Unlike his predecessors, Ibn Verga is not content with a recital of his people's sins; though he acknowledges these, he numbers among them the sins of passivity, undue pride, and excessive trust in God. Casting themselves upon God's mercy, the Jews neglected their natural strength; nourished by the spiritual strength of obedience and hope, they neglected, as Maimonides had already suggested, the virtues of military skill and political craft. Thus "twice naked," they were open and exposed to the ravages of exile.

Ibn Verga, unlike those who preceded him in his reflections upon the Exile, concentrated upon its natural causes. Though he readily admitted, orthodox Jew that he was, that the hand of God was visible in the destiny of the Jew, he stressed the primacy of natural causes and historical events as determinants of character and action. In the dialogues that form the major part of *Rod of Judah*—dialogues between rabbis, councilors, bishops, and kings—a catalogue of intellectual and political defects are set forth (the refusal to recognize a plurality of religious beliefs, the countenancing of outrageous superstition and legend, the manipulation of popular prejudice in the interests of power) which cause the Christian to be intolerant and the Jew unaccommodating. The primary agents of persecution, Ibn Verga believes, are

---

working of material found in *Josippon,* an historical work based on the writings of Josephus, which is thought to have been composed in Italy in the tenth century.

the masses whose poverty and stupidity are easily canalized by fanatic priests, often in defiance of equally intolerant but clever princes who would have preferred to plunder rather than to kill the Jews. Ibn Verga's phenomenology of anti-Semitism is not restricted to a cool exposition of the feints and libels which a collusion of Church and State enforced, but includes a realistic appraisal of the Jewish character. Unlike the medieval elegists (*paytanim*) and apologists, Ibn Verga is already too much a man of the Renaissance to be unsettled by an enthusiasm emboldened by extremity. The Jew is degraded in his own eyes, a mere caricature of his elect self. Those defects that were small and imperceptible in the days of Jewish unity and nationhood on the soil of Palestine—are now grotesquely magnified in the Exile: the passivity and supineness of the Jew.

This pastiche of history and fantasy, mythology and real event is undoubtedly conscious. Ibn Verga did not intend merely to write history. He was a predecessor of the moderns, for he sought in history an underlying motif which would define and interpret a specific reality—the Jew in Exile. Although he is reasonable and ironic, sad, and filled with unexhausted despair (for his narrative, open throughout and endlessly sprawling in construction, need not have been restricted to the sixty-four persecutions he describes), he is content to close his narrative with his own day. And yet, though he acknowledges the defects of his people, though he encourages the princes to liberality and tolerance, though he cautions all nations against believing their relative and finite viewpoints to be absolute, and abjures religious pretensions to superiority (when all beliefs in fact propagate the truth of the unproved and the fantastic), he ends with a characteristic expostulation: "The Day of the Lord is near. . . . Speak, Lord. Arise and fulfill your vows, for salvation is from the Lord. Amen! Amen!" [3]

[3] *Ibid.*, p. 164.

Solomon Ibn Verga anticipates the style of the enlightenment to come—an enlightenment which is within Judaism but between cultures, attached to tradition and the theology of tradition and yet conversant with the ways of the world and the realities of an ungracious environment. He acknowledges that the Exile is ordained, yet he perceives that although God may shape history, forming its possibilities and disclosing its lines of fulfillment, he cannot command it. Men must live through events which, though partially expressing the judgment of God, more often expose the corruptions, pettiness, and avarice of man. The Jew—undeniably Jew—is seen as well, through the cloaks and velvets of this Renaissance understanding, as a creature of will, passion, and power. The Jew is not different from man (or rather, as an older, more ethnocentric Judaism might have it, the humanity of man is the Jewish component in all men), but rather the Jew is a species of man and still, notwithstanding, a servant and beneficiary of God's justice and mercy. For the first time we have a vision of the man and the Jew confronting realities and bestriding them, assessing the natural life of both man and the Jew but keeping faith with the eternal promise of God.

The Jew was an accidental beneficiary and victim of the rise of nationalism and the diffusion of the spirit of enlightenment throughout Western Europe in the eighteenth century: *beneficiary* in that the irrepressible logic of revolutionary egalitarianism could not help but include, and therefore, however reluctantly, liberate the Jew; and *victim* in that the price which was demanded for the Jew's free entry into European society was that he divest himself of all that he had cultivated to protect and rationalize his exclusion. It has been incorrectly thought that Jewry relished the Emancipation and coveted its privileges.[4] This is not to suggest that Jewry

[4] Salo Baron undoubtedly led the way in the reassessment of the relation of the Jew to pre-Emancipation society. See his *A Social and*

had previously welcomed exclusion, although to be sure ritual separatism has been a characteristic of Jewish religion. Voluntary separation and distinction is vastly different, however, from obligatory exclusion. The Jew amid Islam was, to be sure, restricted by his membership in a presumptive religious nationality, but his cultural, intellectual, and social penetration of Islamic society was vastly freer than is commonly thought. Christian society was considerably less fluid than that of Islam: its intimacy and competition with Judaism was more intense; the Jew personified for popular Christian religious imagination a species of demonic miscreancy and betrayal unparalleled in history; the Jew's presence amid Christian society was tolerable only on condition of rigid and unyielding restrictions. The Christian excluded the Jew and the Jew accepted his exclusion, being still better off than many other sectors of medieval society. Though he enjoyed a degree of latitude and freedom in some areas of Christendom, notably Italy, southern France, and Spain, such clement conditions were disturbed by the publication of the anti-Jewish legislation of the Fourth Lateran Council in 1215,[5] the persecution of the Albigensians in Provence and the terrorization of Provençal centers of Jewish learning, and finally the reconquest of the Iberian Peninsula by Christian armies. The Jew no longer had an exit from Europe—he could be driven from Christian land to Christian land, but he no longer enjoyed the leverage of being a mediate culture poised between Christianity and Islam.

From the fifteenth to the eighteenth century the history of Judaism was a history of conservation, the pruning and weeding of a private garden of law and tradition,

Religious History of the Jews, 1st ed., Vol. II (New York, Columbia University Press, 1937); "Ghetto and Emancipation," *The Menorah Journal*, June, 1928, pp. 1–18; "Newer Approaches to Jewish Emancipation," *Diogenes*, Spring, 1960, pp. 56–81.

[5] Solomon Grayzel, "The Policy of Degradation," in *The Church and the Jews in the Thirteenth Century* (Philadelphia, The Dropsie College Press, 1933), pp. 41–75.

observance, and expectation. To accommodate convenience and ensure control and submission, Christian princes found it expedient to grant Jewish communities in their midst a high degree of autonomy—courts, police, civil administration. The Jews often took the opportunity of such autonomy to strengthen the dominion of the Torah and to repel divisive cultural and intellectual influences.

In the aftermath of the expulsion of the Jews from Spain liberalizing influences did find their way into selected Jewish communities. More sophisticated and cultured families of Portuguese and Spanish Jews—often marranos who reverted to Judaism after their escape from Inquisitorial jurisdiction—made their way, for example, to the Italy of the Renaissance, to Amsterdam, and to the Huguenot strongholds of France; and in the course of the following two centuries established flourishing communities which enjoyed a degree of intellectual communication with their Christian neighbors as yet unknown in Germany, northern France, or Eastern Europe.[6] Although such communities as that of the Jews of Amsterdam were legally separate and autonomous, being ruled by strict and pious *parnassim,* they were surrounded by a hospitable population. Liberality and tolerance have the magnificent capacity to undermine authority founded upon fear. Jews wishing to temporize or to escape their Judaism found Amsterdam a congenial environment. Unlike Berlin, Amsterdam did not require a formal Jewish movement of enlightenment, nor did it engender the wave of apostasy, assimilation, and reform which came in the wake of the German Enlightenment.

It is against this background that we must draw a preliminary and basic distinction between the movement of enlightenment and the movement of emancipation.

[6] Cecil Roth, *The Jews in the Renaissance* (Philadelphia, Jewish Publication Society of America, 1959); also *A Life of Menasseh Ben Israel* (Philadelphia, Jewish Publication Society of America, 1934), particularly pp. 1–27; pp. 140–75.

Though they are connected, indeed interdependent, movements, they arise from differing impulses and requirements.

Many Jews desired enlightenment who had no interest in emancipation; many Jews desired enlightenment the better to serve the classic preoccupations of Israel (Moses Mendelssohn, Naḥman Krochmal, and Samson Raphael Hirsch are among these—though vastly different from each other), while others sought enlightenment that they might be liberated from Judaism (Solomon Maimon, David Friedlander, and many members of the original Society for the Culture and Science of the Jews). The forms of enlightenment were various and the movement for enlightenment pressed forward supported by many different and otherwise incompatible allies: by communal leaders such as Cerf Berr and his descendants; by ambivalent, satiric, and self-contemptuous writers like Heinrich Heine and Ludwig Börne; by salon leaders like Henrietta Herz and Rachel von Varnhagen; by second-rate Kantian philosophers like Marcus Herz and Lazarus Ben-David; and by enthusiastic but leaden-tongued Hebrew poets and journalists like the *Meassefim.*

The Enlightenment was a mixed dream. The passion to reason, an old Jewish passion, was rediscovered as though Jews had never known the discourse of reason. Solomon ben Joseph of Lithuania, for example, was so overcome by his discovery of Maimonides' *Guide for the Perplexed* that he took as his surname Maimuni; and Naḥman Krochmal, of whom we will speak later, entered into vigorous controversy with S. D. Luzzato, who had disagreed with his reading of the philosophy of Ibn Ezra. However, where the latter was to devote his life to a rational exegesis of Jewish history, the former was to embrace Maimonides as but an interlude on his way to intellectual independence from Judaism.

The impetus to emancipation, however, was not dependent upon the Enlightenment. Emancipation was a phenomenon of the rising European middle class, a business and professional revolution directed against an entrenched aristocracy and church. Although the first weapons of emancipation were the pens of the enlighteners, enlightenment was restricted to the educated who had been practicing the arts of humane debunking well before the French Revolution, the equalitarian despotism of Napoleon, and the revolutions of 1848. The Jewish preoccupation with enlightenment arose from within—it was first a desire for self-education and self-ennoblement; it became, however, a movement of emancipation when the "enlightened" discovered that learning, manners, and a mastery of French or German were not enough to qualify them for a position in civil society. At this moment, some fifty or more years after the Jewish *Aufklärung* began, emancipation became a vastly more popular, diffused, and communal enterprise. It outstripped the Enlightenment as a cause, uniting under its call to freedom many Jews who were otherwise indifferent to the importance of secular learning.

All of these currents, those which preceded the Jewish Enlightenment and those which stemmed from it, pass through the figure of Moses Mendelssohn, the epitome and *epigone* of the German Enlightenment.

II. MOSES MENDELSSOHN (1729–1786)

The fame which Moses Mendelssohn came to enjoy within but a few years of his appearance on the German intellectual scene testifies less to the power of his word and example than it does to the ripeness of the times which he addressed.

The German Enlightenment, no less than the French before it, was anxious to divest itself of the confining influence of Christian religion, indeed of all religions—including Judaism—which depended for their truth upon the irrational graciousness of a revealing God. A religion of revelation, carrying with it, as it had, the union of State and Church, an interdependent politics and ecclesiology, intellectual censorship, rampant superstition, and the discouragement of free inquiry, only inhibited the growth of a transnational and transreligious humanism. The Enlightenment which Montaigne, Fontenelle, La Bruyère, and Montesquieu had shaped, and Voltaire and Diderot were to propagate, became for Lessing and later for Goethe not only a doctrine but a mode of politics. Intolerant supernaturalism had first to be disdained before the reign of reason and humanist culture could be realized. The humanism of the eighteenth century was undoubtedly a different humanism than that of the Renaissance—the former was closer to a humanitarianism liberated from dogmatism, the latter to a union of classicism and Christianity in which the learning and culture of the former were joined to the formalism and theology of the latter in hopes that each would make the other acceptable. The humanism of the eighteenth century had, however, various faces. Whereas it was fiercely inhospitable and polemic toward religion in its French phase, in the period inaugurated by Lessing and extended by his followers, including Mendelssohn, it had a different cast. The German Enlightenment was based upon the desire for an interconfessional community whose cultural ties transcended, and thereby rendered secondary, ecclesiastical differences.[1] This inter-

[1] Julius Guttmann, *Ha-Pilosophia shel Ha-Yahadut* (in Hebrew), (Jerusalem, The Bialik Institute, 1952), pp. 261 f. For a remarkable extension of the same argument see Yehezkel Kaufmann, *Golah v'Nechar* (in Hebrew), (Tel Aviv, Dvir, 1930), Part 2, pp. 22–42. It should be noted that the supraconfessional emphasis, the religious concern with the abolition of religious difference and the achievement of a rational religion, is peculiar, in its stolid seriousness, to the German Enlightenment. Germany had a confessional problem, whereas France had not. It was easier for Voltaire, for instance, to pronounce upon the necessity of a regulative divinity to coerce the conduct of man (Peter Gay, *Voltaire's Politics* [Princeton, N. J., Princeton University Press, 1959], pp. 259–72; particularly p. 286

pretation is clearly confirmed by the career of Moses Mendelssohn, for Mendelssohn was uninterested in building his reputation upon the primacy of Jewish interests; yet it is true that the more he achieved as a European—the more his poetry delighted, his use of German fascinated, his essays on aesthetics and metaphysics persuaded—the more he was praised as a Jew.

Although he was educated in the Berlin ghetto and well trained in Talmudics, it was Mendelssohn's early contact with Lessing which defined a division of secular and religious preoccupation which, however successfully he was to contain it, those who came after (those who in Graetz's exaggeration were to become "little Mendelssohns" [2]) were soon to ignore. Mendelssohn had no wish to compromise his Judaism by entering upon a fatal comparison of Judaism and Jewish culture with European society and culture. He would have been quite content to be, as J. L. Gordon was later to describe it, a Jew in his tent and a man abroad; [3] keeping privately the civil ordinance of the Jewish faith (for it was as constitutional law that Mendelssohn was to interpret the *halachah* in his *Jerusalem*) and advancing his metaphysical

passim) and at the same time ridicule Catholics, Protestants, and Jews, than it was for any figure of the German Enlightenment. The latter could not hope to establish the superiority of an enlightened humanism to revealed religion unless they could bypass the divisions and pieties of innumerable sects while strengthening the common national tradition which, to their view, was obviously a superior bond. This is at least one reason why the German Enlightenment came to see itself as more elevated than the French. Heinrich Graetz, among Jewish historians, continually acknowledges that France offered more, and more quickly, to the Jews than did the Germans; nevertheless he condemns the frivolity and captiousness of Diderot and Voltaire while praising German seriousness.

[2] Heinrich Graetz, *History of the Jews*, trans. by Bella Loewy, Vol. V (Philadelphia, Jewish Publication Society of America, 1895), p. 334; Shalom Spiegel, *Hebrew Reborn* (New York, The Macmillan Company, 1930), p. 56.

[3] See the excellent discussion of the problems posed by Gordon's formulation in Spiegel, *Hebrew Reborn*, p. 62 *passim;* p. 445, note to p. 63. See also Yehezkel Kaufmann's comment on Gordon, *Golah v'Nechar*, p. 17.

and literary interests in public. Indeed, it might be said that precisely because Mendelssohn did not force the issue of his Judaism upon the attention of his public, but allowed it to emerge as a consequence of attacks by anti-Jewish polemicists, his Christian and Jewish supporters were encouraged to proclaim him. Mendelssohn became the supreme example of the European Jew by *force majeure,* that *force majeure* being the inherited disinclination of European society to imagine that a Jew might master general culture, much less contribute to it.

It should not be thought that Mendelssohn's notoriety was only a fortuity. It was fortuitous in that others more profound than Mendelssohn would have been less well received had they appeared in the Berlin of the eighteenth century. Naḥman Krochmal[4] would not have thrived in Berlin; his Jewish learning and historical sense were too intense, his intellect too complicated, and his vision too imperiously Jewish to have been welcomed by European humanists, who wanted the cultured Jew around merely to prove a point: namely, that that most alien, self-centered, separatist, and "backward" of communities, the nation of Israel, could become master of a European tongue, indeed become European, if Europe would condescend to educate, ennoble, and refine it. However much we may approve the humanitarian sentiments of Lessing or the apologia of Christian Wilhelm Dohm, *Upon the Civil Amelioration of the Condition of the Jews* (1781), we may detect in them both a note of patronage and charity founded upon a judgment of Jewish cultural retardation. For Lessing to satirize the intolerance of German Christians by making a Jew the epitome of refinement, tolerance, and humanity, and for Dohm to couple his appeal for Jewish emancipation with a practical program for the moral elevation of the Jewish community, was to assume, as European culture did, that the Jew was only as bad as Christian society and Jewish

[4] See pp. 29–39.

superstition had made him. Christian society could afford to disdain and condescend, having determined that what was human about the Jew was separable from and independent of what was Jewish about the Jew.

The major achievements of Mendelssohn confirm rather than mitigate the dreadful cleavage which had come to divide the relation of the Jew to humanity and that of the Jew to Judaism, for Mendelssohn's distinction to our mind rests upon his having vindicated Judaism before Christianity on the grounds of reason independent of revelation and, in spite of his observant orthodoxy, of having first formalized the distinction of Judaism as a religion from Judaism as the community of the Jewish people.[5]

[5] We cannot really endorse the estimate of Mendelssohn's accomplishments which Leo Baeck presents in his essay, *Von Moses Mendelssohn zu Franz Rosenzweig* (Stuttgart, Kohlhammer Verlag, 1958), pp. 15–24 (trans. by H. C. Stevens, in *Judaism*, Vol. IX, Nos. 1 and 2 [1960]). Baeck is rather too enthusiastic about Mendelssohn's achievement, conceiving it as a triumph of individuality rather than what to our view it really was, namely, the juncture of a remarkable and talented human being and the appropriate historical moment. It is unquestionably true, as Baeck says, that "without him the Judaism of our day and of days to come would be unthinkable," but this is not to judge those days good nor is it to contest the possibility that Mendelssohn merely anticipated the forms which Jewish enlightenment, emancipation, and assimilation would ultimately take. In this context one may note the unquestionably radical, but fascinating, argument of Hans Joachim Schoeps, who sees Mendelssohn's argument with Lavater as the first example of modern, post-Enlightenment Jewish apologetics. As a Jewish thinker strongly influenced by neo-orthodox Protestantism, Schoeps is rather critical of Mendelssohn's view. Schoeps's realism has, however, more to commend it than the somewhat sentimental interpretation of Baeck. See Schoeps, *Juedisch-Christliches Religionsgespraech in neunzehn Jahrhunderten* (Frankfurt am Main, Atharva-Verlag, 1949), pp. 95–105; particularly p. 98. See as well the splendid essay of Isaac Eisenstein Barzilay, "Moses Mendelssohn (1729–1786)," *The Jewish Quarterly Review*, July, 1961, particularly p. 72, where he writes: "This policy [a reference to Mendelssohn's dual use of German and Hebrew] was actually an overt expression of a deeper dualism, which characterized his life and philosophy, the dualism of worldly culture on the one hand and of Judaism on the other hand, of a humanist universalism versus a conservative irrational particularism."

In the French translation of Mendelssohn's first celebrated work, his *Phaedon or Conversations on the Spirituality and Immortality of the Soul,* the translator comments that the work is all the more remarkable if one considers that it was written by one "born and raised amid a nation which stagnates in vulgar ignorance." [6] Authored as it was by one just emerged from the society of "vulgar ignorance," its moral earnestness, felicitous style, and classical, non-Biblical setting proved more impressive to the intelligentsia of Europe than its unexceptionable and pedestrian rendering of the arguments for the immortality of the soul.[7]

It was the publication of *Phaedon* which moved John Caspar Lavater, a Swiss Protestant minister and later Jesuit, to dedicate to Mendelssohn his German translation of a slight and insignificant Christian apologia by a Geneva professor, Charles Bonnet. This dedication is rhapsodic in its praise of *Phaedon* and presumptuous in its conviction that Mendelssohn might succumb to Christianity with the same degree of reasonableness and objectivity with which he permitted his Socrates to convince Phaedo of the immortality of the soul. The challenge of Lavater, later disclaimed by Bonnet, served to draw Mendelssohn out, to effect an explicit union of his public career and his private religion. In his open letter to Lavater (1769), Mendelssohn affirms his unalterable attachment to Judaism, and in the fourteen years which follow the controversy and culminate in the publication of his *Jerusalem or Upon Religious Power and Judaism* (1783), the dominant characteristics of Mendelssohn's religious position emerge.

Mendelssohn's Judaism is formally indistinguishable from the Judaism developed in earlier centuries. The con-

[6] Moses Mendelssohn, *Phédon,* trans. by M. Junker (Paris, 1772), pp. 1 f.

[7] Guttmann notes that Mendelssohn's arguments were by and large identical with those which had been offered for centuries by Jewish scholastic philosophy. Guttmann, *Ha-Pilosophia shel Ha-Yahadut,* p. 264.

formation of Mendelssohn's doctrine to that affirmed by medieval rationalism should not, however, obscure the fact that for Mendelssohn—as earlier for Maimonides—a significant distinction has been drawn between the judgments of reason and the traditions of faith. Moreover, in the same manner as Maimonides distinguished between the internal rule of reason and the external compulsion of the law, so Mendelssohn was to distinguish between Judaism, as the pre-eminent religion of reason, and the commandments, as divine directives to conduct. Whatever their seeming likeness, the differences between Maimonides and Mendelssohn are crucial. Whereas Maimonides considered reason to be most pure and uncorrupt where it approaches prophecy and viewed the *halachah* as the regimen which assists the unreasoning to a life pleasing to God, Mendelssohn was to reverse the order, making its reasonableness that which commends Judaism to all men, while reserving the *halachah,* with all its irrationality, for that sectarian expression which differentiates Jew from non-Jew. The reversal of inner and outer, private and public, rational and irrational, prophetic reason and political necessity, underscores the differences between Maimonides and Mendelssohn.

Mendelssohn, as is evident from the order of argument in both his open letter to Lavater and his *Jerusalem,* proceeds from a consideration of the public problem of the Jew to an explanation of his private religious convictions. It is necessary first to demonstrate that essential Judaism is rational, nondoctrinal, and directed toward the instruction of conscience. The Jew, in effect, is rational in all things pertinent to the obligations of citizenship—he is tolerant of others, attentive to the promptings of conscience, and obedient to any law which is designed for the common good. Only in those private domains where the State is not qualified to intrude—the relations of man to God—does he believe that individuality and nonconformance should be respected. Mendelssohn's argument on behalf of religious toleration and enlightenment was based, not upon a toleration which has something obdurate and unyielding to tolerate (for tolerance is always an attitude toward the unyielding and unpopular), not upon the acceptance of the ineradicable differences between Jew and Christian, but upon the common commitment of rational Christians and rational Jews to an ethical and religious ideal which unites both in supraconfessional loyalty. At the same time that Mendelssohn could express his conviction of the superiority of Judaism to Christianity on grounds of its uncompromising rationality—"Blessed be the Lord who has given us a true Torah. We have no dogmas which are opposed to reason or above it"—he could affirm to the Duke of Braunschweig that when Christianity is properly explained (meaning when its irrationalities and mysteries are discarded) a common faith for Jew and Christian may become possible.[8] In effect, the universal in religion—its metaphysical and moral teaching—is sustained by reason independently of faith. The specific injunctions which comprise the body of Jewish law, the particularities of revelation, are *regulative* in that they are the ordinance of Jewish society and *directive* in that they enforce and strengthen the law of reason. The law writes large the moral injunctions for the foolish who cannot understand, while at the same time it links the common believer and the philosopher in a single communion.

Mendelssohn transformed the argument which Judaism offered to the nations. The transformation was inevitable, because the politics of Jewish existence had changed from one of stubborn unbelief before Christianity and self-confident perseverance in the Jewish way to acquiescence before the opportunity of cultural acceptance and full participation in the "messianic" universalism of European society. In the past, where nationhood

[8] Jacob Agus, *The Evolution of Jewish Thought* (New York, Abelard-Schuman Limited, 1959), pp. 371–87. See particularly p. 382.

and faith were inextricably united—there being no exit from one without the abandonment of the other—it was impossible to conceive of a distinction between nation and culture, as both were vital developments of the religious covenant. The age which Mendelssohn epitomized, however, made possible for the first time the real distinction of the public and the private. The public domain ceased to be, as it had been earlier in Jewish tradition, the sphere of communal responsibility and became the secular and neutral. It ceased, however, to be the domain of visible religion for Christian as well as for Jew. As passionately as Mendelssohn sought to explain the Jew who could be both cultured European and religious Jew, so the weight of the European Enlightenment was turned toward the secularization of the public order. Mendelssohn is but a Jewish moment in the history of the secularization of European society.

I. M. Jost, the precursor of Heinrich Graetz as an historian of the Jewish people, is probably correct in viewing Mendelssohn as an implicit opponent of rabbinism, as an innovator who prepared the way for establishing Judaism on a different basis than tradition had envisaged. But where Jost approvingly conceives Mendelssohn as a covert reformer, Yehezkel Kaufmann is closer to the mark in his conviction that Mendelssohn sought to substitute "the culture of the nations" for "the culture of Torah." [9] This is only to say that Mendelssohn could no longer believe that the Torah contained everything, that the Torah was in fact a complete culture. Mendelssohn, more than having inaugurated a new era, symbolized the irrevocable end of an earlier one. Henceforward, the union of the natural and the supernatural Jew would be both occasional and exceptional, an aber-

[9] For an excellent summary of the variety of views which have been adopted toward Mendelssohn in Jewish literature, see Azriel Shohet, *Im Hilufei Tekufot: Reshit Ha-Haskalah b'Yahadut Germanya* (in Hebrew), (Jerusalem, The Bialik Institute, 1960), pp. 242–60; pp. 330–36. Also Kaufmann, *Golah v'Nechar,* pp. 44–54.

ration and self-conscious dissent from that deep division to which the modern Jew has testified so profoundly and so tragically.

The modern Jew who succeeded the age of Mendelssohn was a European according to nature and history and a Jew according to God. It was, however, patently impossible for one to be a Jew according to God without sustaining the vision of God's intimate connection with history. The God of Israel became a confessional God, and Mendelssohn became, as Kaufmann has called him, the Jewish Luther, who sundered the living connection of the faith and the people in order to return the people to the pristine condition which preceded its involvement in world history. But such a reform and a reversal could not be achieved without profound consequences. One consequence—and it is one from which the Jews of the Diaspora have never ceased to suffer—is that the interconnection of faith and people ended. Henceforward one's culture was that of one's nation and language and one's faith was directed toward a God no longer covenanted to a specific people. It is no surprise that the earliest reformers—Israel Jacobson, Jacob Herz Berr, Abraham Geiger, and Samuel Holdheim—should have rejected a personal messiah, denied the centrality of the Land of Israel, abandoned the Hebrew language, and transformed the historical monotheism of tradition into ethical idealism. The messianism of the classic Jew disappeared and the new European messianism—culture, emancipation, and equality—were substituted.

The ways of reason are fortunately many. The formalism of eighteenth-century reason—its empiricism on the one hand and its bloodless, unyielding abstractness on the other—was soon to pass as the innovations inaugurated by Kant and extended by his disciples, Fichte, Schelling, and Hegel, became influential. The second-rate rationalism of Mendelssohn, unequal as it was to the daring empiricism of the French Enlightenment or the imaginative, indeed ingenious, formulations of the

German idealists, passed into insignificance. Mendelssohn the thinker was quickly forgotten, although Mendelssohn the exemplar of Jewish culture survived and continued to prove unpredictably influential. Clearly the influence of Mendelssohn the thinker derived from the fact that his thought was unintentionally political. This is not to say that Mendelssohn was a politician. It is rather to say that the peculiar accent and emphasis of his thought—its sublime and admitted ignorance of Jewish history, its disastrous separation of law and teaching (those two inseparable senses of the concept of *Torah*), its uncompromising commitment to the superiority of natural reason over revelation—gave birth to a modern phenomenon, natural religion. Natural religion served most particularly the political ambition of the Jew. The thought of Mendelssohn is undistinguished; but the political impact of a Jewish thinker who represented the cultural ideals of an already secular humanistic intellectual class was enormous. Mendelssohn made credible to Europe the existence of rational Judaism and the possibility of the de-Judaized Jew.

III. NAḤMAN KROCHMAL (1785–1840)

While the emergent Berlin *haskalah* [1] was organizing its salons and literary journals, mastering German and French, perfecting its social graces, and working out the agonies which attended its passage from Jewish society—of whose usages and history it was often ignorant—to the European society whose usages and history it uncritically embraced, Naḥman Krochmal, who lived and

[1] Isaac Eisenstein Barzilay, "The Background of the Berlin *Haskalah*," in Joseph L. Blau *et al.*, eds., *Essays on Jewish Life and Thought* (New York, Columbia University Press, 1959), pp. 183–97; Spiegel, *Hebrew Reborn*, pp. 49–72, particularly pp. 59–72.

died amid the small provincial Central European world of Galicia, was quietly and undramatically laying the foundations for the survival of Judaism.

Krochmal was not indifferent to the challenge which the Europeanization of Western Jewry was posing. If we may judge from his correspondence with his friends and the reminiscences of S. J. Rapoport, Meir Halevi Letteris, and Leopold Zunz, he was acutely aware of the intellectual bankruptcy which compromised the enlighteners and the militant anti-intellectualism with which official orthodoxy sought to counter them. The unknowing hostility of the enlighteners and the unknowing obstinacy of the orthodox revealed to him, more even than did the mounting threat of Jewish apostasy and assimilation, the real malady of Jewish life: its ignorance of history. It could not be otherwise than that educated Jews of the West should be repelled by Judaism, when Judaism continued to be represented as an undifferentiated amalgam of high truth and parochial superstition. On the other hand, Krochmal could be equally unyielding to those *maskilim* (the enlightened) who smugly passed judgment upon Judaism without attempting to discern its enduring character beneath its changing surface. Europe was not the problem of the Jew, nor was enlightenment a threat where the Jew had self-consciousness, an awareness of the historic links which defined his connection with an unfulfilled yet absolute destiny.

It is against this background that Krochmal set forth to make a new beginning for the Jew, to demonstrate that the history of the Jew and the metaphysics of history are intimately connected, that the Jew, far from being displaced by the history and predominance of the nations, was still at the center of history.

It is hopeless to attempt a summary of Krochmal's single work, *The Guide for the Perplexed of the Time*, for it is complex, diffuse, and incomplete. It is hard to see how it would ever have been a complete work, even had Krochmal lived to write the many chapters which he had promised. The very structure of the work defies completion, for its method of scientific investigation and philosophic reflection is not patterned upon a closed and abstract schema, but is constantly open to the discoveries of historical research and the refinements of new evidence. It is more proper to describe this *Guide* as a private philosophical and historical journal in which general order is imposed by the system of ideas which are its tools of analysis, but whose subjects of investigation are endless and inexhaustible.

It has been observed [2] that Krochmal's adaptation of the title of Maimonides' most famous philosophic work is not casually intended. Indeed it is even possible that *The Guide for the Perplexed of the Time* was not the work's original title, although it seems hardly likely that Leopold Zunz (who edited the work with the aid of Moritz Steinschneider) would have used this suggestive title had there not been explicit instructions to do so. Nevertheless the subtitle with which the work was published, *The Guide to Pure Belief and the Teacher of the Wisdom of Israel,* enforces its fundamental intention. The perplexed of one age are not the perplexed of another, for perplexity is not only the condition of intellectual unclarity and philosophic ignorance, but the absence of a sense of history. It is history that permits the category of time to emerge and it is history which makes time pre-eminent. How should there be "pure belief," and how should the "wisdom of Israel" be taught, if, as the orthodox would insist, there is no meaningful function to the category of time (there being "no early and no late" in Torah) ; and if, as the moderns insist, all of Judaism is judged wanting before the bar of timeless reason? Only if the category of time is restored to history and history

[2] Simon Rawidowicz, *Kitbay Rabbi Naḥman Krochmal* (London and Waltham, Ararat Publishing Society, Ltd., 1961), p. 101; Solomon Schechter, *Studies in Judaism,* First Series (Philadelphia, Jewish Publication Society of America, 1945), pp. 67–68; Spiegel, *Hebrew Reborn,* p. 108.

itself made the pilgrimage toward truth does it become possible to discriminate between the essential and the accidental, the important and the vulgar, the primary and the marginal. Only if a method of investigation is devised which will allow the phenomena of Judaism to be sought out, revealed, and established "in and through the actual period of their origin"[3] can the contemporary perplexed be illuminated. The Judaism that is known to both *maskilim* and orthodox is a Judaism without history—frozen and timeless. Such a Judaism cannot hope to survive the assaults of those who have mastered the weapon of historiography put into their hands by others as unknowing as they of the history of Judaism. The *maskilim* attack Judaism with a weapon fired at foreign forges, and the orthodox, uninformed by the historical sense, are powerless to defend themselves except by the calumny and anger which confirm the justice of the attack. The contemporary perplexed can be enlightened and pure belief can be taught only when the relation between history and truth is defined, the connection between religion and philosophy is established, and, in consequence, the high mission of Judaism to reveal the fullness of the absolute spirit is accomplished.[4]

It was not enough for Krochmal to examine the historical inaccuracies which interrupt the proper narration of the history of Israel, to correct naïve historical judgments, to evaluate the proper relations of aspects of Jewish literature, to place in perspective the roles of philosophy and mysticism, *aggadah* and *halachah,* in the unfolding of Jewish religion. To be sure, these are au-

[3] Rawidowicz, "Moreh Nebuchei Ha-Zeman," in *Kitbay Rabbi Naḥman Krochmal,* p. 5.

[4] "At both extremes there is a lack of true faith in our time. Both extremes are alike in believing that religion is what they used to believe in childhood; and the difference between them is only this: that some rejoice when they can find an opportunity to cast suspicion and doubt upon that faith, while others (and they are in the majority) endeavor to strengthen and sustain faith with fantasies and various exaggerations—futile measures in an age where knowledge is widespread." *Ibid.,* p. 6.

thentic problems of Jewish religious history, and Krochmal, singlehanded, established the criteria and procedures with which the encyclopedic historians of Judaism would shortly begin to work. But the work of historical investigation, the establishment of events "in and through the actual period of their origin," is subsidiary, indeed tributary, to his primary concern. The perplexed are not illumined simply by the knowledge of history. They are illumined, their belief purified, their wisdom elevated, only if the knowledge of history is firmly set into the context of metaphysical truth. The accurate understanding of history will not strengthen belief if history and belief are estranged, if history is not made indispensable to the apprehension of truth.

It is therefore crucial that the opening chapters of *The Guide for the Perplexed of the Time* commence with a statement—often oblique and obscure—of Krochmal's metaphysics of history. Krochmal learned well from German absolute idealism, but his learning was eccentric, determined as it was by a prejudgment which placed greater stress upon ensuring the continuity of Jewish philosophic speculation from the Middle Ages to his day than upon a slavish obedience to the historical predispositions of his teachers, Kant, Fichte, and particularly, Schelling and Hegel. German idealism supplied him with a vocabulary and a doctrinal impetus, but it could not possibly dictate the content of his doctrine, which would be radically dissimilar, radically Jewish.

Krochmal's axiom of faith—elusively articulated and expressed, but clear throughout—is a reversal of Hegelian doctrine. All that was rational was not real, but quite definitely all that was real was rational and all that was real in the history of Judaism was significant in the unfolding of Jewish destiny. The history of Judaism is not to be accounted an accidental configuration of persons, teachings, and events. Such an account, proper to a historiography lacking metaphysical and religious presentiments, is improper to Krochmal. The events of Jewish history are meaningful over and beyond their immediate significance because they disclose a fundamental characteristic of all life—the progress of human consciousness from its rooting in nature to its identification with absolute spirit. Paganism cannot move beyond the objectification of the spirit in its myths and idols. Biblical religion, first and pre-eminently, removed the spirit from the confinement of space to the unlimited hegemony of time, freed spirit from artificial limitation to objects of nature, and permitted religion to become the movement of consciousness toward its fulfillment in spirit. Judaism—divested as it is, in Krochmal's view, of every aspect of natural religion—is turned only toward the absolute spirit which is absolute truth. Its destiny is to bring those who adhere to it into union with the spirit, to expand their consciousness, to refine their beliefs, to transform their incomplete and partial apprehensions into full and complete knowledge. The history of Judaism is thus properly the history of the education of consciousness.

It must be noted here that Krochmal did not oppose religion and philosophy, faith and reason, in order to polemicize against one from the unassailable fortress of the other. He would not have been moved, as have far too many contemporary Jewish thinkers, by Pascal's ecstatic opposition to the "God of the philosophers." Moreover, he would argue that Judaism is not simply a religion, but rather the total history of the unfolding of Jewish consciousness toward God. Judaism is both religion and philosophy; moreover, only insofar as philosophy purges and refines religion is the true role of religion fulfilled. Religion apprehends the truth through the imagination, defining to itself the nature of God through image and representation; whereas philosophy depends upon the pure concept alone. Philosophy works upon the matter of religion, penetrating its images to the concepts which they mask. Philosophy works upon religion to purify it, but—and there is no ambiguity here—both are indispensable, however unequal, means of bringing the individual into communion with God. Without pressing Krochmal's doctrine further, it can be seen why history and historical research proved so enormously important. History is the confirmation of the mission of Judaism,[5] for history testifies to the struggle of Judaism to purify and perfect its apprehension of God.

Krochmal's division of Jewish history into cycles of growth, maturity, and decline, although undoubtedly influenced by Hegel's dialectic of history, is indifferent to the latter's formal rigor and content. Krochmal was not interested in describing the moments through which the spirit passed on the way to its historical consummation. Rather he introduced his concept of cycles in order to permit a sorting-out of Jewish history and literature and to avail himself of a more graphic device of indicating that Jewish history is a continuing and meaningful struggle to clarify itself to itself. By his cyclical theory Krochmal is afforded an artifice for demonstrating the origin and emergence of texts and ideas: in a period of growth, for example, concepts which display high sophistication and refinement could not—as inherited tradition often has it—exist side by side with naïve and unweathered ideas. On the other hand, although his cycles appear to be but literary devices for organizing his historical inquiries more effectively, it should not be forgotten that Krochmal was primarily concerned with demonstrating the interrelation of religion and philosophy in Jewish history. His doctrine of cycles only serves to underscore the progress and backslidings of Jewish consciousness toward a clearer apprehension of God. Whatever their artificiality, Krochmal's cyclic divisions

[5] It is interesting that in his use of the idea of the Jewish mission, Krochmal undoubtedly influenced Jewish Reform. However, Krochmal did not consider the Jewish mission to be the demonstration of the ethical high-mindedness of Jewish teaching, but rather the direct education of the Moslem and the Christian, whom he considered to have departed from the truth which Judaism had given them.

suggest that he sought a morphology in Jewish history, a mode of development and unfolding which strengthened the intimate connection of the realities of history with the spiritual education of Jewish man.

Naḥman Krochmal was an unalterably pious Jew, uncompromisingly orthodox in practice and conviction. His rarity consists, however, in the more subtle fact that he was able to combine, as perhaps none other after him, the intellectual doctrine of medieval rationalism with a profoundly modern understanding of the supreme importance of history. Where the medievals were overwhelmingly indifferent to history, employing the rational construct as a substitute for historical inquiry, the suggestions of German absolute idealism had enabled Krochmal to establish a connection between reason and history, to revive the supremacy of reason without undercutting the requirements of faith, to develop a view of the interplay of history and reason which permitted both faith and knowledge to retain their viability.

It should be noted that the question which continues to snap at the heels of Jewish doctrine, the question of messiah and the consummation of history, is all but irrelevant in Krochmal's teaching. For Krochmal the unity and character of history are defined by the immanence of absolute spirit, the fact that history, at least in principle, can be brought to perfection by the union of consciousness and spirit. With such a view it is clearly impossible to give meaning to any eschatological teaching regarding the end-moment of history. In Krochmal's view, history does not require an end, for its structure, purpose, and meaning are implicit at every moment. Such an idealist view of history, at the same time as it marks a renascent concern for the activity of Jewish historiography and the philosophic meaning of historical events, is wholly confined to the operation and movement of nature and history. Krochmal succeeds in restoring the connection between reason and history (and in much the same fashion as Maimonides esteems prophecy the highest example of their connection), but the eschatological dimension of Jewish prophecy is minimized. The natural order in which God and reason are present within history is well articulated, but the tension and opposition between God and history which make the eschatological question relevant are all but obliterated.

It is unfortunate that those who learned from Krochmal divested his historical method of its metaphysical foundation. Schechter has rightly observed that every historical suggestion which Krochmal made has been the source of later research; his metaphysical inquiry, however, has been almost wholly neglected. His method of historical realism, shorn of its metaphysic, survived to influence and assist the inquiry of *Wissenschaft des Judentums*—Science of Judaism. It is sad to reflect, however, that much which preoccupied the Science of Judaism would have been considered by Krochmal to be beside the point. History without spirit is as unavailing as spirit divorced from history. The techniques of inquiry, the patient and unprecedented research, the passion for historical accuracy—these traits of Krochmal's historiography—shaped modern Jewish historical science. Divested, however, of the grounding of historical events in the history of the divine spirit and the evolution of human consciousness, history does not resolve the dilemmas of the perplexed of the time. The perplexity which set Krochmal to his lifework had two intimately conjoined aspects: the irrelevance of Jewish history to the demands of life and the consequent meaninglessness of Jewish life. Krochmal adumbrated a doctrine whereby Jewish life became not only meaningful but the source of all meaning; he supported that view by melting the glacial monument of Jewish doctrine and literature and releasing the living waters which it contained.

Whether Krochmal's doctrine is satisfactory or not—and we have not attempted a critical assessment of it—it is undeniably rich and allusive. Unsentimental, hard, and unromantic doctrine that it is, it is nevertheless profound in its quality of hope, for it takes its stand upon a rigorous separation of natural religion from religion informed by revelation (which Krochmal affirms without equivocation) and of popular belief from philosophic belief. Both the informed belief of the prophets—who come the closest of religious men to having knowledge by concept—and the pure belief of philosophers who apprehend by concept what is denied to them by imagination, teach Judaism and catalyze its development. But Krochmal is fully aware that although the prophet and the philosopher are rarities, every man apprehends by both imagination and concept, by both faith and reason. Both prophet and philosopher are indispensable to Judaism. Without them the history of Judaism would not be the unfolding of consciousness toward God.

The Judaism of the Enlightenment learned inadequately from Krochmal's teaching, and the Judaism of orthodox tradition learned little or nothing at all. The scientific investigation of Jewish history, though inspirited by Krochmal's example, embodied neither Krochmal's metaphysical passion nor his unqualified commitment to the future of Judaism. Its strength would indeed be lasting strength, but its deficiencies would prove equally monumental. In the space of but fifty years the scientific study of Judaism would engage numerous scholars who would set themselves the task of organizing, assessing, and preserving for posterity the long and complicated history of the Jews. What it could not achieve—what the historian can but rarely achieve—was the conjunction of historical precision and philosophic conviction. Historiography, fashioned as it was by principles of quasi-scientific sanctity, replaced theology and philosophy. And what remained? To be sure there remained the virtues of historical science: a sense of the continuity of events, an attention to fact, a genius for construction, a shaft of intuitive illumination, an adumbration of the whole. But the historian's "whole" can only be the "whole" of the past. However conditioned by an optimism for the present (as in Abraham Geiger's Reformist historical research) or by a pessimism for the present (as in Leopold Zunz's certainty that Judaism was really finished), the historian's "whole" rarely sustains a continuity with the future. To affirm a future—to speak as Krochmal did—is to risk a censure such as Graetz imposed upon Krochmal when he asserted that Krochmal was more interested in "general and encyclopedic studies," details serving him only as confirmation of theory.[6] Graetz's inability to understand the intention of Krochmal's grand theorizing and Graetz's hostility to Zunz's Hegelianism—little understood by Graetz and but artificially employed by Zunz—disclose the profound difficulty of Jewish scholarship. Jewish scholarship was pursued independently of both the living faith and the living people. It was pursued as a science—a science which the religious scholar could rationalize as pursued "for the sake of heaven" and the secular scholar could rationalize as pursued for the sake of truth; however, the heaven of the religious and the truth of the secular no longer lived in the midst of the people.[7]

IV. THE SCIENCE OF JUDAISM: LEOPOLD ZUNZ (1794–1886) AND HEINRICH GRAETZ (1817–1891)

The Science of Judaism supplied an indispensable moment of respite amid ferment. It was not a new begin-

[6] Although Graetz considers Krochmal the founder of the scientific study of Judaism he does not moderate his criticism of him. Graetz, *History of the Jews*, p. 618.

[7] *Wissenschaft des Judentums* was submitted to a different, but compatible, form of attack than we have defined, by Gershom Scholem in *Mitoch Hirhurim al Chochmat Israel* (Tel Aviv, Luach Haaretz, 1944). See further bibliography of criticism of *Wissenschaft, Yearbook II*, Leo Baeck Institute (London, East and West Library, 1957) p. xxv, note 1.

ning of Judaism, but it interrupted a progress toward a conceivable end. Born out of Jewish neurasthenia, it lived to provide a new occasion for Jewish "health."

It may well be tendentious romanticism for Heinrich Graetz to have characterized the history of the Jews as a history of "sufferings and scholars." That he should have chosen these recurring phenomena of Jewish history to define the continuity of his great history is indicative of the perspective from which he wrote. Fortunately he completed his history with events which transpired shortly before his death in 1891. His immediate past—now nearly a century ago—was also his own proximate present. What transpired in the fifty years during which he constructed and wrote his history was less the history of "sufferings and scholars" than the history of the discovery of history.

Graetz, perhaps like every historian, is weakest in his narration and accounting of his own times, for the history of the Jews of his day was formed, not by disaster and the sequestration of scholars, but by the *reaction* of the masses of Western Jews (of whom Graetz was a sympathetic representative) to both sufferings and scholars. The Jews who deserted the *Yeshivot* of Germany and Western Poland in the late eighteenth and early nineteenth centuries, who entered mercantile trades and strove—by and large unsuccessfully—to enter the professions, who identified their aspirations with the aspirations of the European bourgeoisie, who accepted fully the transnational liberalism of the day, who adopted anticlericalism and tolerated generalized forms of anti-Semitism, who considered Christianity but a social (indeed humanitarian) community whose aids to advancement and self-liberation outweighed the guilt of baptism—these Jews, the undistinguished but articulate mass of "enlightened" Westernized Jews, brought about the crisis of European Jewry. To be sure, the rescission in 1815 of liberties granted under Napoleon and the outbreak of anti-Semitic violence throughout Germany and other parts of Europe in 1819 supplied an external stimulus of suffering to awaken the conscience of Western Jewry, but it cannot be imagined that the movement toward a religious and intellectual reappraisal of Judaism which began with the formation of the Society for the Culture and Science of the Jews (1819–1824) can be attributed to such a familiar *volte face* in European politics.[1]

The politics of reaction and emancipation encompassed more than the Jews. It involved all Europe and threatened all ideologies but the most conservative. The real problem—which Zunz vividly described—was that the mass of Jews who had embraced the Enlightenment and sought emancipation had given over all trust, dignity, and hope to the charity and solicitude of the non-Jew.[2] The movements of emancipation, though they might enjoy the services of a Gabriel Riesser or the devotion of sundry Jewish militiamen, were dependent upon ideologies to which the Jew had made little contribution and whose course he could not direct. When the tide moved toward general emancipation—as under Napoleon—the Jew was exultant; but when the tide turned after the Congress of Vienna, the Jew was in despair. In neither case did his elation or despondency draw upon the reserves of his Jewish past.

[1] This point is stressed because Graetz seems to take Eduard Gans's reasons for founding the *Verein* at face value. (Heinrich Graetz, *History of the Jews,* Vol. V [Philadelphia, Jewish Publication Society of America, 1895], p. 583). Zunz, likewise, with vastly more sinuous subtlety, argues that the *Verein* would aid in restoring the dignity of the Jewish people, but Zunz did not imagine that persecution was the impelling motive to the loss of dignity. See Luitpold Wallach, *Liberty and Letters: The Thoughts of Leopold Zunz* (London, Leo Baeck Institute, East and West Library, 1959), p. 6.

[2] One has but to recall the almost embarrassing appreciation with which Graetz welcomes, in his *History,* the appearance, throughout the eighteenth and nineteenth centuries, of Gentile replies to anti-Semitic propaganda, even though many of these replies were in their own special way uninformed and prejudiced.

The Society for the Culture and Science of the Jews, founded in Berlin in 1819 by Eduard Gans, a brilliant but erratic thinker, Moses Moser, a stolid mathematician, and Leopold Zunz, then a young historian, had as its ostensible purpose the investigation of Jewish culture in such a way as to display its intrinsic richness, its comprehensive scope, and its compatibility with standards of European culture. Their presumption, founded upon an unoriginal reading of Hegel's philosophy of culture, was that a scientific rendering of culture was only possible in a free state; however, since a free state is dependent upon the level of culture which its citizens can achieve, if one elevates one's citizenry one prepares the way for freedom. Transposed into the Jewish idiom, the task of the Science of Judaism was to rediscover the authentic and undebased traditions of the Jews in order thereby to attract enlightened Jews to an enlightened Judaism. The publicist talents of Gans managed to bring into the Society the peripatetic services of a strange motley: the elderly rebel of the Mendelssohnian era, David Friedlander, the pedestrian Kantian Lazarus Ben-David, I. M. Jost, Heinrich Heine, and others. The experiment proved disastrous. On the one hand its aims were too serious and its members too young to command popular support; on the other hand—with the exception of Jost and Zunz—its interest in Judaism and Jewish scholarship was largely political and rhetorical. The Society collapsed in 1824, and many of its members went the way of baptism or anonymity.[3]

In its short life the Society published under Zunz's editorship one volume of its journal, *Zeitschrift für die Wissenschaft des Judentums*. In the first number, Im-

[3] H. G. Reissner, "Rebellious Dilemma: The Case History of Eduard Gans and Some of His Partisans," *Yearbook II*, Leo Baeck Institute (London, East and West Library, 1957), pp. 179–93; Wallach, *Liberty and Letters*, pp. 5–32; Graetz, *History of the Jews*, pp. 582–88.

manuel Wolf undertook to define the scope of the Science of Judaism.[4]

His essay, a model of opacity and pretension, nevertheless cues the movement which will arise, for Wolf repetitively stresses the following: the *religious idea,* conditioning all the multifarious developments of Judaism, is "unity"—the unity of God, the unity of man, and undeniably the unity of knowledge and science. Since the idea of Judaism, so defined, is a spiritual idea, it required centuries of struggle and purgation to be refined; when the commonwealth of Judaea passed and the Jews were cast adrift amidst the nations, the *idea* alone sustained them; throughout its sojourn in the Moslem world and until the advent of Christian persecution Judaism maintained the creativity of its idea. It is only in the modern world—that world which begins, according to Wolf, with the expulsion of Spanish Jewry in 1492—that the cultures of the nations overwhelmed and humbled Judaism into submission and isolation. What then of the Jewish idea in the modern world? It has survived all vicissitudes. If so, this idea must be of the "essence of humanity itself and thus be of the greatest significance and importance for the thinking spirit." [5]

The task of the Science of Judaism is to manifest the patent and obvious dispassionately and objectively; to display the Jewish spirit in such a fashion as to demonstrate not only its inner authenticity (for this, the study of its historical and literary documents) but its relevance to the struggle of all mankind for liberty and justice. The Science of Judaism thus becomes a province of all science and Jewish knowledge a particular manifestation—which must be examined in order that all knowledge may

[4] Immanuel Wolf, "On the Concept of a Science of Judaism (1822)," trans. by Lionel Kochan, *Yearbook II*, Leo Baeck Institute (London, East and West Library, 1957), pp. 194–204; Wallach, *Liberty and Letters*, pp. 12–13.
[5] Wolf, "On the Concept of a Science of Judaism (1822)," p. 200.

be increased. Lastly—and indeed it is a painfully romantic coda to an otherwise stolid orchestration—"the Jews must once again show their mettle as doughty fellow workers in the common task of mankind. They must raise themselves and their principle to the level of a science, for this is the attitude of the European world. This attitude must banish the relationship of strangeness in which Jews and Judaism have hitherto stood in relation to the outside world. And if one day a bond is to join the whole of humanity, then it is the bond of science, the bond of pure reason, the bond of truth." [6]

Wolf's announcement of the program and objectives of the Science of Judaism has been correctly described as "an unusual formulation of Jewish universalism divorced from authentic religious or theological foundations." [7] The overarching grandeur and comprehensiveness of the idea of total history to which particular histories are but tributary conduits, the definition of dispassionate science, and the commendation of history as the weapon of Jewish emancipation and humanitarianism all suggest an irresponsible intellectualism. It was, however, neither Wolf nor Gans who was to embark upon the fulfillment of the Society's program. That task was assumed by Leopold Zunz.

Leopold Zunz (1794–1886) was both an historian and an antiquarian. Although the younger historian Heinrich Graetz was to complain that Zunz's work amounted to little more than a revealing collection of notes striated by the complicated lines and divisions of Hegelian nomenclature, and Hermann Cohen was later to dismiss him as one who might have been a great historian but succeeded in being little more than an antiquarian,[8] the

[6] *Ibid.*, p. 204.

[7] Max Wiener, *Jüdische Religion im Zeitalter der Emanzipation* (Berlin, Philo-Verlag, 1933), p. 194; Robert Weltsch, "Introduction," *Year Book II*, Leo Baeck Institute (London, East and West Library, 1957), p. xxv.

[8] Heinrich Graetz, *History of the Jews*, Vol. V, Preface; Hermann Cohen, *Jüdische Schriften*, ed. by Bruno Strauss, intro. by Franz

truth is more complex. Zunz was undoubtedly dull and plodding. One cannot read his *Die Namen der Juden* or his *Zur Geschichte und Literatur,* for instance, without wearying of their diffuse and seemingly unconnected presentation of historical fact. But Zunz was not embarrassed by such criticism; indeed, he recognized and justified the importance of his offending antiquarianism.[9] One could not write Jewish history, he contended, unless one had first established, classified, and connected its materials. The antiquarian precedes the historian—without him the historian cannot write history.

The history of the Jews, according to Zunz, is a particularity of world history. The laws of world history are *its* laws; the political, legal, and social institutions which constitute the external matter of history have been formed by *its* presence; the goal to which history strives —that perfect society in which Right and Freedom will be harmoniously balanced—is *its* goal. The Jews had enjoyed but one brief moment in their history—during the days of the ancient Jewish commonwealth—when inner spirit and external form were conjoined. With the destruction of the Jewish state and their expulsion from the land of Israel, the Jews' external fate was delivered into the hands of the nations among whom they lived; their internal history became "a history of ideas." The external history of the Jews among the nations became a history of suffering;[10] the internal history of the Jews became the source of ideas—literature, poetry, philosophy, instruction.

The perspective from which Zunz wrote Jewish history is essentially de-Judaized. This is not to say that Zunz was not capable of enormous compassion, affection, and understanding for the events and persons of Jewish his-

Rosenzweig (Berlin, C. A. Schwetschke & Sohn, 1924), p. xxii, "Anmerkungen zur Einleitung," p. 332; Wallach, *Liberty and Letters*, pp. 94–95.

9 Wallach, *Liberty and Letters*, pp. 94–95.

10 Leopold Zunz, *Die Synagogale Poesie des Mittelalters* (Berlin, 1855), Chap. 2; Wallach, *Liberty and Letters*, p. 105.

tory. Indeed he was! But his research was more in the manner of those technicians at a waxworks museum who are painstaking in their efforts to catch and define each nuance, idiosyncrasy, and distinguishing mark of the subject to be preserved. Zunz's attitude—Hegelian throughout—was that Judaism, this "religion of sublimity," had been overwhelmed by history, that its remaining task was to habilitate its credentials that it might pass away with dignity and honor. The real goal, the goal toward which world history had moved for centuries, was approaching fulfillment. A new nation and a new society, bound by laws, guaranteed in freedom, and administered in equity—though it would not come, Zunz felt, in his lifetime—would soon be born. What need had the Jew, to whom such a messianic consummation was offered, for his sects and creeds, his rabbinism and Talmudism? All such partialities and incomplete moments in the history of the Idea could be put aside. But first—and it was a crucial and revealing first—it was the obligation of the Jew to demonstrate that he had contributed to the coming of this political parousia. This was the task of the science of history.

The ambiguous legacy of the Science of Judaism cannot be laid to the paternity of Zunz. Zunz was clear and unambiguous. He left no doubt that he believed the course of Judaism was nearly over; that the Jewish historian had the task of transferring the legacy of the Jewish idea to world history; and that henceforward the Jewish people would join with other peoples to celebrate a community sustained beyond confession and ecclesia.

The essential defect of the Science of Judaism, the defect which looms particularly large with its twentieth-century critics, was that Jewish culture was consistently subordinated to the requirements of general culture. The Science of Judaism was conceived, not as a Jewish discipline directed to the ends of Jewish learning and community, but as a general discipline. Put another way, the primary objection of contemporary critics of *Jüdische*

Wissenschaft is that its researches were not tied to an ideology of independent Jewish survival. Radical Zionists —those for whom Jewish nationality is possible without Jewish religious culture—will accuse the Science of Judaism with having provided the foundations for accelerating, rather than arresting, Jewish assimilation. Cultural and religious Zionists will adjudge its deficiency to be the emphatic disjunction, enforced by the Hegelian disciples of Jewish scholarship, between the national history of the Jew and his ongoing religious destiny. We should incline to yet a third criticism, one which assumes the condition of the Exile, but is yet unwilling to accept the conclusion of Zionists or assimilationists that no Judaism is really possible in the modern Diaspora.[11]

The Science of Judaism had the opportunity of defining the reality of Judaism—its historic past and future —without abandoning Judaism to Western culture. It did not seize this opportunity, because it considered the task of Jewish history to be related to the general liberal ideology of European emancipation and conceived its function to be the demonstration that Jews, far from having an uncreative and dependent historical past, were independent, creative, and therefore eligible to enjoy the same rights and privileges for which their neighbors struggled. The fact that it had only the most naïve notions of the recidivist character of anti-Semitism, that it understood little or nothing of the social and political uses of prejudice among Gentile liberals, socialists, and

[11] Witnessing as Shneour Zalman Shazar and Gershom Scholem did the lamentable unpreparedness of European Jewry for the fate that would overtake it (a fate which they both limned), their attack against *Wissenschaft* as a scientific rationalization of Jewish assimilation made sense. Without the fulfillment of Zionist aspiration, all which conspired to render assimilation easier (notably the absorption of proper Jewish culture into general culture) was culpable. However, with the establishment of a new Jewish state the existence of Jewish science as an agency of assimilation comes to the aid of Zionist ideology, for it assists the argument of which Zionist ideologues are fond: namely, the palpable impossibility of authentic Jewish culture in the Diaspora.

reactionaries, is an indication that its political ideology and expectation were hopelessly unrealistic.[12]

The Jewish scholars of the nineteenth century were either religious leaders engaged in the reformation and "modernization" of Jewish religious institutions or else lonely and disengaged students, raising up few disciples, communicating among themselves, despairing and even occasionally contemptuous of the ill-informed masses on whose behalf their researches were ostensibly pursued. The scientific study of Judaism never entered the life-stream of Jewry. The heart of its failure was that it was but marginally related to Jewish belief. Scholarship functioned without an anchor in ideology. This is not to say that ideology was not employed by reformers to justify the introduction of radical innovation or by conservatives to cut a middle way between orthodoxy and reform. Rather it was that Jewish science—with the notable exception of Krochmal—did not number the history and interpretation of Jewish doctrine among its proper subject matters. With all its modernity it was still trapped by the Mendelssohnian assumption that Judaism was a religion without doctrine, or, as a traditionalist opponent of Jewish science would put it—with equally narrow but in his view sounder passion—that Judaism is a religion "which enjoins six hundred and thirteen duties, but knows no dogmas." [13] With such a perspective it was obviously impossible for scholarship to be in any

[12] One has but to read the passionate statements of Zunz regarding Jewish emancipation from Prussian reaction (cf. Wallach, *Liberty and Letters*, pp. 46–70; Nahum N. Glatzer, ed., *Leopold and Adelheid Zunz: An Account in Letters* [London, Leo Baeck Institute, East and West Library, 1958], pp. xxiii–xxvi; Chap. 5, "For the Sake of Liberty," pp. 197–227) or Jewish replies to the novel and challenging anti-Semitic mythology of Bruno Bauer (Nathan Rotenstreich, "For and Against Emancipation: The Bruno Bauer Controversy," *Year Book IV*, Leo Baeck Institute [London, East and West Library, 1959], pp. 3–36) to see how ill equipped and trusting was Jewish apologetics in this period.

[13] Samson Raphael Hirsch, *The Nineteen Letters of Ben Uziel*, trans. by Bernard Drachman (New York, Bloch Publishing Co., Inc., 1942), p. 146.

way effectively tied to the task of theology. The historical "whole" which Zunz sought to make the object of science was but an arid phenomenalism organized by a system of abstract nomenclatures. The remarkable achievements of Jewish science were achievements wholly independent of the theoretical ideals of science. Judaism was not encompassed as a whole; the history of Judaism was not developed systematically; the interaction of ideas and history was not unfolded; the Jewish entelechy was not exposed, its life force not defined, its impulsion to persevere not clarified. Though Graetz's reading of Jewish history as the struggle to perpetuate the idea of God is, to be sure, more than Zunz had offered, Graetz succumbed to a kind of romanticism which took the place of an historical viewpoint. At the same time that he sought to write history "as it actually happened" [14] and criticized prevailing Hegelian interpretations of history as arrant theorizing, he did not write history without theory. He merely wrote it on a smaller budget of ideas than he would have employed had he recognized the value of theory in the writing of history. Jewish science could not help but earn the charge of antiquarianism. Investigation without principles can accumulate sources, classify literature, identify events and persons, but it cannot produce history.

V. SAMSON RAPHAEL HIRSCH (1808–1888)

The sharpest nineteenth-century attack against *Jüdische Wissenschaft* came from its foremost traditionalist

[14] Ranke's influence on Graetz is well acknowledged. Cf. Heinrich Graetz, *Die Konstruktion der Jüdischen Geschichte;* Ludwig Feuchtwanger, "Zur Geschichtstheorie des jungen Graetz von 1846," pp. 99–101; Hans Liebeschutz, "Jewish Thought and Its German Background," *Year Book I*, Leo Baeck Institute (London, East and West Library, 1956), pp. 217–21.

apologete, Samson Raphael Hirsch. With a directness and passion untempered by objectivity, Hirsch scorned Jewish science as but another manifestation of the complot by which the party of modernizers sought to destroy traditional Judaism. Jewish science had, according to Hirsch, no independent status; moreover, as it defined itself, it had no claim at all to being proper science. Indeed, it was at best but the occasion to exercise a perverse talent for arbitrary construction and pedantic preoccupation with the inessentials of Jewish faith; at worst, it was a dangerous attempt to relativize Judaism by submitting its certitudes to the arbitration of history. Fair and unfair argument, sound and hollow rhetoric abound throughout Hirsch's attack: one moment he will trounce *Wissenschaft* by accusing it of having substituted pretentious learning for the time-honored tradition of *lernen* (a grossly false charge); of having toppled *talmud torah* from its position of pre-eminence by weakening the classic link of Jewish learning with Jewish life (a true statement, but not a relevant charge); of having produced "not a physiology of living Judaism, but a pathological anatomy of a Judaism which according to their idea is already dead" (a rhetorical thrust at Zunz which is near to truth); and lastly, of having failed to accomplish what was most important and needed, namely, "a science of Jewish ideas of nature and history, and, in the light of these truths which have been handed down by Judaism, to judge from the Jewish standpoint the events of the present, and the struggles and expectations of the peoples, along with the principles and views which guide them." [1]

This last charge—to our view completely correct—could never have been met by Jewish science in such a way as to have satisfied Hirsch. Hirsch would have tolerated nothing less than a complete vindication of traditional Judaism. How could a science of Jewish ideas of

[1] Samson Raphael Hirsch, *Judaism Eternal,* Vol. II, trans. by I. Grunfeld (London, The Soncino Press, 1956), p. 285.

nature and history be constructed? In order to fulfill Hirsch's requirements, it would have had to commence from a dogmatic assumption which renders meaningful history self-contradictory, if not impossible: All temporal and historical truth proceeds from a single source which is outside of time and history. Since the origins of truth are beyond history, the action of history cannot affect it. History becomes irrelevant. It is meaningful only as the history of externals—of the actions of non-Jewish nations and cultures impinging upon the history of Israel.[2] The internal life of Israel is properly speaking not history at all, since it does not live in and through the medium of time and is not altered by its action nor deflected from its predestined unfolding toward messianic fulfillment. Judaism is, as Hirsch's disciple Isaac Breuer argued, a metahistorical community.

Hirsch's most profound criticism of Jewish science is rendered captious and impossible by his own assumptions. And yet it is his own assumptions—precisely those which make his criticism self-contradictory—which make his thought so interesting and relevant. The covenanted relations between the Jew and God, the binding of Israel to a body of undifferentiated and irreducible obligations, the unfolding of a life of sequestration and separateness: all this is the divine community of Israel. Any science having such a community as its subject matter would be indistinguishable from theology. The proper history of the Jewish idea is its theological exposition, for only the discipline of theology can introduce historical events into its argument without having to take account of their temporal dimensions. Such theology makes of time the a priori medium of revelation.

The theology of Hirsch, precisely because of its classic strength, was painfully ill equipped to speak to the moment which it sought to address. It had to have the consequence, as it did have, of hardening opposition, closing

[2] This is particularly evident in Hirsch's essay, "Hellenism, Judaism and Rome," in *Judaism Eternal*, pp. 187–209.

all lines of *rapprochement,* sealing tradition into isolation from and opposition to general culture and nontraditional Jewish culture. Although Hirsch courageously supported emancipation, struggled for the improvement of religious education, advocated the use of the German language, and encouraged the Jewish acquisition of general culture, he did so viewing all these phenomena as external to the life of Judaism. They could be supported precisely because they did not really affect Judaism—indeed, as Hirsch often informed Benjamin, the fictional correspondent of his youthful but fundamental work, *The Nineteen Letters,* general culture and Jewish culture are not in conflict; moreover, the faithful, unqualified observance of the Law would only earn the praise and admiration of general culture without compromising one's right to enjoy its benefits.

Where Hirsch's theology breaks down, where—to our view—all such orthodox theologies break down, is that in one crucial phase of doctrine they fail to integrally relate Jewish and general culture. To be sure, Jewish and general culture will achieve this interpenetration, if only through the revolutionary action of God; but when such action comes, Judaism will be placed at the *center* of, not *outside,* time and history. This will be the moment of the messianic consummation. At that moment Judaism will be forced—no longer as witness or through passive attestation—to upset the nations and to reform them, not simply in their historical life but in their true being. And it is here, precisely at this point, that Hirsch's forthright clarity breaks down utterly. For Judaism believes that a point will—indeed, must—come when its supernatural vocation will articulate the significance of its natural involvement in time and history. At that moment general and Jewish culture will be authentically joined and the Jew will come before the nations with more than passive testimony. He must be as ripe as God's time will be ripe. He can no longer be a providentially ordained abstainer from history. He must either be prepared to demonstrate the role which Israel plays *directly* in the culture of the nations, or he must be prepared, as was Franz Rosenzweig, to interpret the role of Christianity as an indirect medium of enacting the consequences of those principles which Israel had conserved for it. In all events the Jew cannot do what Hirsch did: make of secular history the dominion of secondary and unexceptionable principles of toleration, national self-expression, and the realization of those classic virtues (which Judaism believed itself to have transcended) of beauty, balance, and form. Such a neo-orthodoxy, separating as it does life ruled by revelation from life ruled by history, has a number of disastrous results. First, the religious cannot help but become monumentally arrogant and contemptuous, certain as they are of the purity of their world and the bankruptcy of all others; second, their doctrine permits them to judge the crises and alarums of history with a passive self-righteousness which is as useless as it is self-delusive; and last, having no *real* view of history (such neo-orthodoxy always has a spurious and putative doctrine of history) their doctrine is wholly vulnerable to its ravages.

Samson Raphael Hirsch had argued well; indeed, his argument proved profoundly influential; but it did not succeed, as he had hoped, in transforming European Judaism. His failure to penetrate the psyche and conscience of the lapsed Jew, the enlightened Jew, the reformed Jew—indeed, the failure of Judaism then and now to meaningfully contact the disengaged Jew—may be traced to Judaism's conditioned reluctance to understand the eschatological [3] nexus of Jewish and general

[3] By the use of the term "eschatological" it is not suggested that the relation of Jewish and general culture is limited by the concept of the end of history. It is used rather to enforce the idea that, at least from the perspective of the end of days, the relation of Jewish and general history is dogmatically *necessary*. There is no choice. If Judaism and general culture are not integrally related from the perspective of the "end," then Judaism is what its opponents say it is: a narrow, exclusivist, closed community. We should also add that

culture. Its refusal to press the development of a doctrine of the integral unity of Jewish and general culture was undoubtedly motivated by a justifiable terror of its political consequences; however, having granted the excuse of historical exigency, it is enough to say that it is an insubstantial excuse. Hirsch failed to convince the enlightened—leaving aside the inflexible right-wing traditionalists against whose desiccation of tradition he preached quite as ardently—because it was not enough to argue that the truth of Judaism need not be sacrificed in order to enjoy the benefits of secular learning and emancipation. By arguing in this fashion he accepted implicitly the common assumption of the enlightened that there was an intrinsic opposition between them. Their compatibility could not be demonstrated merely by arguing that the duties of Torah can be fulfilled without forgoing the opportunities of secular society. The rationalization of both worlds could not be lasting if it depended upon their rigid differentiation and the subordination of the latter to the former. This accomplished nothing but an invigoration of J. L. Gordon's disastrous formula of Judaism at home and *menschlichkeit* abroad. The real challenge was to demonstrate that secular history was the proper terrain upon which Judaism was obligated to work, that indeed the culture of the nations bore within it the seed of redemption whose growth and nurture was the task of Israel.

VI. MOSES HESS (1812–1875)

As Samson Raphael Hirsch wished to insulate the supernatural community of Israel from its natural involvement with history, Moses Hess—that remarkable intel-

---

if it is narrow, exclusivist, and closed, it is probably a false community as well. We cannot imagine that God should have spoken at Sinai that only Israel, then and forevermore, should hear him.

lectual vagabond, romantic socialist, and colleague of Marx and Engels—was to urge the regeneration of the national community of Israel as a natural outcome of what he judged to be the completely historical character of its God.

The thought of Moses Hess has played a generative role in the history of Zionism. Although it is common at present to consider Zionism a political movement and the State of Israel the outcome of political pressure and agitation, it is well to remember that modern Zionism arose as an inescapable ideological response to the worsening cultural climate of Judaism in the European Diaspora. Not the hope of Israel but the despair of assimilation was the initial impulse to the national solution of what was then—and even now is—"the Jewish problem." Moses Hess, himself an example of that problem, proved fully equipped to diagnose and prescribe for it.

Undoubtedly the Jewish substance of Hess's later thought was profoundly shaped by the socialist ideology with which he had been so long involved. Although these influences cannot concern us here,[1] they were remarkable in several respects. Hess's thought is dominated by a conviction regarding the destiny of nations; but such destinies—however shaped and formed by their historical experience—are in no way inexorable. The achievement of social revolution, the transformation of man's goals from acquisitiveness to sacrifice and service, rested finally upon good will. Unlike Marx, with whom he was often to quarrel, Hess believed history to be subject, not to a law of economic determinism, but to the actions of free moral agents. The specific nostrums for social disorder—the abolition of private property, the reform of social institutions, the education of the working class—Hess shared with his more dogmatic colleagues, but where they were willing to turn their aspiration into the in-

[1] E. Silberner, "Moses Hess," *Historia Judaica,* Vol. XIII (April, 1951); Isaiah Berlin, *The Life and Opinions of Moses Hess* (Cambridge, W. Heffer and Sons, Ltd., 1959).

evitability of law, Hess was unswerving in his conviction that only where the will had been changed and the conscience instructed would the social revolution be effective. Men betray revolutions even when they are thought to fulfill the laws of history; it is mankind, not only social systems, that must be revolutionized.

The humanism of Hess's socialism is the source of his Zionism. It will be recalled that one of the primary impulses to Jewish enlightenment was the identification of large sectors of Western European Jewry with the broader interests of humanity. All men, not merely the Jew among men, were to be redeemed from the isolation and insularity to which confessional differences consigned them. By Hess's day such particularist parochialism had been defeated—no "enlightened" Jew imagined that Judaism rendered his interests different from those of all men. Even the apologists of neo-orthodoxy, shifting ground, were to claim that Jews would be better citizens, indeed better men, by being better Jews. Henceforth Judaism would first demonstrate its serviceability to Western civilization before being permitted to advance its special claims. Relying upon this cultural ambience, Hess was to reverse the argument, indeed to reverse it with such anger, irony, and passion that his single Jewish work, *Rome and Jerusalem,* would remain not only a tract for those times but a tract for these as well.

Hess had come the way of the Enlightenment and Emancipation; but unlike Heine and Börne, who had taken the route of literature and conventional political journalism, Hess had—to the lasting good fortune of the Jewish people—entered the socialist movement. Unlike Marx, with whom Hess later became intimate and by whom he was contemptuously regarded, Hess had received a remarkably effective, if not profound, Jewish education. Left by his father in the care of his maternal grandfather when the family moved to Cologne in 1817, Hess received a formidable introduction into Biblical and rabbinic literature. Later, after a university education at Bonn, he broke with his father and traveled throughout Western Europe, gradually identifying himself with the radical movements then being shaped in Paris by Saint-Simon, Fourier, and the followers of that romantic communist Babeuf.

Rome and Jerusalem [2] is a disorganized work, incoherent, occasionally tortured, unreliable in details, but throughout a relentless, profound, and complete description of Jewish neurosis and its therapy. The subject of the preface, twelve letters, discursive epilogue, and expatiatory notes which form the text of *Rome and Jerusalem* is the present condition, the past glory, and the future rejuvenation of the Jewish nation.

Basing himself upon the example of European history (the Italians were at the moment of his writing seeking to wrest Rome from the control of the papal government and to incorporate it in a new and united Italy—hence Hess's title, *Rome and Jerusalem*) which exhibits the constant and undying desire of peoples to form themselves into free and independent nations, Hess argues that the nation is the natural unit of historical development. The people who would deny their nationality do more than falsify history; they betray their own nature. The natural nations—those who enjoy a common past, a language and literature, a living culture—are destined, if they are to fulfill their natures, to become self-determining. How much more so with the Jew; for the Jew, unlike the natural nations, has more than normal endowments with which to express himself. More than they, the Jew gave to mankind the religious knowledge by which it

[2] Being frankly unconcerned with *Rome and Jerusalem* as an example of the development of the Zionist idea, we cannot share Yehezkel Kaufmann's mixed attitude toward Hess's nationalist theory. Undoubtedly Hess had a confused theology, if it may even be called theology; moreover, his theory of the coming birth of the Jewish nation was naïve, romantic, and simplistic; but his diagnosis of the Jewish predicament in *galut* is unfailingly to the mark and well in advance of those other more disciplined diagnosticians, Simon Dubnow and Ahad Ha-Am. Yehezkel Kaufmann, *Golah v'Nechar* (Tel Aviv, Dvir, 1930), pp. 282–86.

might be perfected. It is corrupt for the Jew to deny his paternity when all which aspires to the ennoblement and education of man has its origins in Judaism.[3] It is not only corrupt, but self-contradictory as well.[4] Jewish reformers cannot propose that the Jew enlighten himself out of existence while at the same time insisting that he has a mission to humanize the nations; the orthodox cannot retreat from history into the unapproachable fortress of a world-denying supernaturalism.[5] The Jewish nation—that unity of purpose "becoming" toward perfection—cannot be resisted, least of all by Jews.[6] The historical world-view of Judaism, which Hess conceives to be mediate between the denial of nature implicit in Oriental tradition and the surrender to supernaturalism which characterizes Christianity, can complete the unfolding of human history. This unfolding is no condescension to the laws of history, to the inexorable logos completing itself; it is the free action of mankind striving to reconcile itself to its nature.

Unconfined by the knowledge of the absolute, untouched by the demands of revelation, unmoved by the theological claim of a God who spoke once and never more, Hess was not trapped by a simple supernaturalism. To be sure, he shows less comprehension of theology than of any other intellectual discipline, but his instincts were sure. He defined the theological problem without theology, for as he put it, the specific Jewish genius lay in its having "incorporated a partial negation of the natural world, without at the same time minimizing the value of the creative factor in history."[7] Although he expressed his willingness to become orthodox in practice, clearly such orthodoxy was for him a form of penance and

[3] Moses Hess, *Rome and Jerusalem*, trans. by Meyer Waxman (New York, Bloch Publishing Co., Inc., 1918), pp. 46–49.
[4] *Ibid.*, p. 117.
[5] *Ibid.*, pp. 112–17.
[6] Cf. *ibid.*, "The Genetic View of the World," pp. 211–16; "Note II" (on Jewish messianism), pp. 237–40; "Note VI" (contrasting Greece, Judaism, and Christianity), pp. 249–50.
[7] *Ibid.*, p. 238.

espousal. Orthodox practice was clearly unimportant unless it defined the normal expression of national life. The natural community—that is, the community defined by "sacred space" (one's own land)—was to be transformed into the historical community which mediates between God and nature, realizing the potential of the one to serve the other. The historical community and the historical nation are the juncture of a people and a decisive idea. Hess, one of the unique figures of nineteenth-century Jewish history, defined the national redemption of the Jew, but he defined it with a logic that could well serve to explain the continuing life of Jewry amid the nations. The Zionist therapy will cure the malignancies of the natural Jew only in separation from his natural life. Notwithstanding the grandeur and heroism of the Zionist achievement, it is questionable whether the Zionist solution—to normalize the Jew by integrating Jewish destiny with the dubious destiny of the national state—effects that reunion of nature and supernature which is the historicity of *Jewish* existence.

The history of Judaism in Western Europe in the nineteenth century is, on the whole, a dispiriting display of confusion, self-hatred, and neurasthenia. This is not to suggest that its malady was without cause. Indeed, Western European Jews had considerable provocation for their emotional disorder; however, it cannot be denied that it was disorder nor that its fundamental character was emotional. What Mendelssohn had sought to preserve, that pure distinction between the operation of the rational intellect and conscientious attachment to traditional Judaism, was destined to collapse. It was an artificial distinction at best; less reverential and committed followers would judge it to be artificial and ignore it. Why, they would argue, should reason be employed in the public domain but rendered inapplicable and irrelevant to the refinement of actions performed in the service of God? The Mendelssohnian logic—a logic with considerable tradition and precedent—could be jettisoned. It served well in an age where religious and secular culture were all but indistinguishable, where the logic of the intellect and the duties of the heart were not separated from one another by the formidable barriers of civic disqualification and social inferiority. If the Jew would not convert, the medieval Moslem or Christian was content that he remain a Jew, albeit a religious Jew. There was no advantage in those days for the Jew in abjuring his fealty to Judaism unless at the same time he became a Moslem or a Christian. The Middle Ages believed that every man must, by nature, have a religion. To cease to believe in one's natal faith without adopting another was to be not only *unbelieving* but *against nature*. The Middle Ages could tolerate the heterodoxy of the Jew but took a rather more strenuous and uncharitable view of his atheism.

All this had changed by the nineteenth century. The complex pursuit of social and political emancipation in Western Christendom, the rise of liberal religion within Christianity, the emergence of a capitalist ethos, the increasing complication of social life, and the crystallization of nationalism: all these influenced Judaism. The Jew was, as we have indicated, invited to become a Western man—it being assumed that to remain a Jew and become a Western man was a virtual self-contradiction. Therefore it could not be helped that many ideologues of Jewish enlightenment and emancipation, not wishing to abandon Judaism, should wish to transform it. The internal logic of Judaism, the theological imperatives which support, however inarticulately, the logic of its observances, were ridiculed or ignored and a new Judaism, a Judaism coherent with inexpungeable nostalgias, vestigal pride, and atavistic neurosis, was painfully created.

Whatever Reform Judaism has come to achieve in the present day, whatever the virtues it possesses, the values it conserves, the traditions it sustains, its origins and paternity were inauspicious. One can only imagine with disgust—and it is with disgust that we look upon the social antics of Jewish assimilationists—the early days of the Hamburg Temple, the vituperative and intemperate polemics of early German Jewish Reform apologists, their liturgical innovations which were little more than a Protestantism without Protestantism's political self-assuredness. Similarly, one cannot savor the bans and excommunications which a rigidified Orthodoxy hurled at the Reformers, their imprecations and uncompromising inflexibility, their refusal to recognize that the substance of Judaism did not require the forms of isolation and self-enclosure.

What is worthy of note in this era of decomposition is that both the Reformers and the Orthodox continued to acknowledge that they were Jews. The Reformers might disqualify the Orthodox from eligibility to the club of the enlightened and the Orthodox might charge the Reformers with betrayal and desertion, but the very tone of their mutual reproofs signalized the recognition that at worst they needed each other, and that at best they belonged equally to a community which sustained them both.

The natural community of Israel—small in numbers, beset by the hostility of anti-Semites, joined by a history of shared experience—preserved its collectivity. This fact, perhaps more than all others, explains why Reform could never develop—in its own tradition—as solid a theological doctrine as Protestantism and why Orthodoxy could not genuinely sever itself from Reform. Whereas Protestantism considered the Catholic Church to be a perversion of authentic Christianity and Catholicism considered Protestantism a diseased member of the Body of Christ—each in effect anathematizing the other—the Judaisms of Reform and Orthodoxy could not so view each other. Protestants and Catholics might well regard each other as Christians, and Reform and Orthodox might well regard each other as Jews; the latter might condemn and proselytize each other as did the former; but never could Jews slay Jews in the interests of doctrine. It may be countered, to be sure, that Jews never had the opportunity to kill each other, and to conclude that they would not (given the occasion) is unjustified. But it may be suggested with equal conviction that the Jew, not enjoying that mixed history of national and ecclesiastical attachment which froze nation and faith into political unity, nor having—as have Moslems and Christians—placed excessive value on the surrender of one's life for God and his eternal reward, were denied the political and theological advantages of fratricide. But negative reasons aside, the Jews are a people sharing the requisites of community in spite of their dispersion, bound by a common history, tradition, language, and literature. To kill another Jew is a form of suicide, and however paranoid Jews may be, they are not suicidal.

It is against such a background that the mature *haskalah* unfolded—the *haskalah* which embraced the scientific study of Judaism, the defensive apologetics of Samson Raphael Hirsch, the definition of Zecharia Frankel's historical Judaism, the rediscovery of the natural community of Jews which sparked the return of Moses Hess to Jewish life, the definition of Eastern European literary, cultural, and intellectual renascence, and the emergence toward the end of the nineteenth century of those combatant theoreticians of the Diaspora and Zionism, Ahad Ha-Am and Simon Dubnow.

VII. AHAD HA-AM (1856–1927), SIMON DUBNOW (1860–1941), AND CHAIM NACHMAN BIALIK (1873–1934)

It is finally the question of the proper relationship between physical peace and spiritual vocation which underlies both the agreements and disagreements of those two precise, serious, and unpretentious thinkers of late nineteenth-century Eastern European Jewry, Simon Dubnow and Ahad Ha-Am.

Unlike the typical Jew of Western Europe, the Eastern European Jew regarded enlightenment and culture, not as a means of negating Judaism and the Jewish people, but rather as a means of serving the Jewish people other than by traditional study and observance. New virtues—intellectual honesty, realism, revolt against sentimentalism, the quest for cultural parity and the manifestation of the indigenous strengths of Jewish history and culture—became motivations for a whole generation of Eastern European Jews. The dedication and incorruptible integrity of Ahad Ha-Am as editor of his monthly *HaShiloach* and Dubnow's histories and monographs supplied the occasion of a renascence of intellectual pride in Eastern European Jewry. However, it is not their specific achievements—Dubnow's masterful studies of the Jewish communities of Poland and Russia, his history of Hasidism, his comprehensive history of the Jewish people, or Ahad Ha-Am's formal, impeccably logical essays—that concern us, but rather that profound and abiding conflict which makes their work so painfully contemporaneous. One realizes, reading Dubnow's *Letters on Old and New Judaism* or Ahad Ha-Am's essays on Nietzsche, Maimonides, or Montefiore's *The Synoptic Gospels,* that nothing has really changed; that with six million Jews dead and the State of Israel born, Jews continue to wonder—in almost the same terms as did Dubnow and Ahad Ha-Am—about the proper relations between Zion and the Diaspora, about the pre-eminence or subordination of the spirit and the moral law in Jewish life, about the waning resources and spiritual flaccidity of Judaism in the Exile and the hopes that Zion might become a center of illumination to the Dispersion. The arguments of Dubnow and Ahad Ha-Am resolve themselves finally into cavils of emphasis; into disagreements regarding the logistics of numbers and influence which Jews in

Israel (primarily from Eastern Europe, at that time) would have on the communities of Eastern Europe; into the difference in quality between Ahad Ha-Am's view of Israel as "the spiritual center" (with emphasis, as Ahad Ha-Am was at pains to point out, on "the" and "center" —"spiritual" going without saying) and Dubnow's concept of Diaspora centers of Jewry which would be autonomous, self-contained, articulate, and culturally productive, relying upon Palestine only for the example of the fulfilled national reality.

Dubnow's complaint—and it was one which Ahad Ha-Am understood—was that the latter's formulation made the communities of the Dispersion nothing but automated appendages, receiving their charge and impulse from the living Jewry of Palestine. The Diaspora, however, could not live on the borrowed life of Zion. It had to define its internal character, its own cultural ambience. It had to be European and it had to be Jewish. It could not suspend its vitality in preparation for a miraculous resurrection on the soil of Israel; it had to recognize that many Jews would not abandon the *galut;* it had, furthermore, to reckon with that bizarre phenomenon of Jewish life, masochistic self-immolation— the persistent Jewish tropism toward discomfort and alienage. Ahad Ha-Am, on the other hand, granting Dubnow's discerning phenomenology of life in the Diaspora, had still to insist that Zion must be preeminent, that there could be no focus or direction to the life of the Dispersion were there not the meaningful counterpoise of Zion. Jewish life in Israel was to be the concrete display of meaningful, integrated, significant Jewish life—life uncompromised by abnormality.

In a profound and simple essay,[1] Chaim Nachman Bialik—the modern Hebrew poet of the Exile—was to describe the dualism of the Jewish personality. On the one hand, Bialik suggests (adopting the formulation of

[1] Chaim Nachman Bialik, "Jewish Dualism," trans. by Maurice M. Shudofsky, *The Jewish Frontier*, July, 1961, pp. 19–22.

the Russian religious thinker Vladimir Soloviev), the Jewish person (that natural-supernatural mutant of which we have spoken) doggedly and unceremoniously presses forward to great achievement, to the triumph over circumstance, ignoring with supernal indifference the obduracy of his environment, and on the other hand he affirms—in liturgy and doctrine—a disclaiming humility and insufficiency to the task which his God has laid upon him. Bialik documents from Jewish history the dual pressure to expand and overwhelm and to contract and retire.

Bialik describes a dialectic which Dubnow and Ahad Ha-Am, constrained by the press of events, did not envisage. Where Dubnow was to dissect the national sentiment in the Diaspora, defining the Jewish people as the Jewish nation—that rare and pure nation which wishes nothing from the aggrandizing nations of the West other than to live and create in their midst—and Ahad Ha-Am was to spurn the unnatural nationality of a people without a land and espouse the national contraction—the national center on the soil of historical longing and association—Bialik could poetize. He could say nothing to either except that both were right and both wrong. Indeed, the pathos of the conflict between Dubnow and his older contemporary Ahad Ha-Am concerning the relation between Diaspora and Zion-centered Jewry is that each was right to precisely the extent that the other was wrong. Jewish nationalism in the Diaspora is nearly dead (except to the extent that it lives on the distant oxygen of Zion) and the "spiritual center" in Zion, which would pace the life of the Diaspora, is more than ever cut off from the blood-stream of those exiled Jewish communities that remain. Dubnow did not know that his world would be utterly destroyed, and Ahad Ha-Am did not envisage that what he conceived as a spiritual—indeed symbolic—center would become an assertive nation of more than two million Jews.

Bialik intuited perhaps more accurately than either

the historian or the essayist because he was willing to take his own ambiguous relation to the Jewish religion as an index of the natural life of the nation. Where both Dubnow and Ahad Ha-Am were consciously distant from the putative myths of the divinely instructed and elected nation, Bialik seems to say that these myths (who calls them myths other than he for whom other myths are more true and impelling?) cannot be foreclosed, that they have supplied the impetus to a history which has always been both exile and estrangement, national contraction and concentration. Indeed in the present moment—in every man's present moment—one addresses the present, one determines one's own destiny (exile or ingathering) and settles for one pole of the duality. But the poet who could be more humble than the humble in his early verse and bitterly contemptuous and full of loathing toward humility in his middle verse, and utterly silent and withdrawn in his twilight years, can bring together in himself, as men of program and action can rarely do, the many frayed and contradictory strands that form the whole pattern. It is not surprising, therefore, that Bialik closes his essay on Jewish dualism by suggesting that the Jewish people after some centuries of containment and concentration in the reborn Israel "will be emboldened to make another exodus which will lead to the spreading of our spirit over the world and an assiduous striving toward glory." [2]

Bialik always keeps the daemon of the divine presence uppermost: not simply a good and charitable God and not simply an angry and avenging God, but a God *who is impulsion,* who motivates the disconsolateness and unease of the Jewish people, who is all pressure and weight and the moving agent of the Jewish conscience. And perhaps all that can finally be said is that this God is our daemon and that we come to rest nowhere but in the midst of his agitation.

[2] *Ibid.,* p. 22.

VII. Ha-Am, Dubnow, and Bialik

Undoubtedly the acceleration of the Zionist movement in the early twentieth century absorbed the geniuses of Polish and Russian Jewry in the work of national reconstruction, leaving behind in the centers of Eastern Europe sequestered intelligences working out the day-to-day problems of Jewish religion, Jewish literature, and Jewish community. The Jewry of the West, however, had not acceded to the wishes of Odessa and Warsaw. Their Zionism was neither cultural nor spiritual in orientation, but political. Although by the twenties of this century Ahad Ha-Am had made converts in the West, the problem of Western Jewry was sharper, more bitter, and divisive. Zionism afforded political egress for those who could neither assimilate nor be religious. As such, Zionism did not become really important until the critical days of the late twenties and early thirties, when Jewish life became more and more questionable on the soil of Western Europe. Before those disastrous days of post-World War I economic collapse and the rise of totalitarianism, Western Jewry attempted some novel intellectual experiments, experiments designed to interpret and interlineate the culture of Europe with Jewish marginalia, to introduce into the religious life of Jewry the parallel and coeval impulses of Western tradition.

2

The German Jewish Renaissance

I. REFLECTIONS ON A PSYCHOLOGICAL ABERRATION

One cannot help but regard the tragic destruction of German Jewry in this century as incomparably ironic, for of all the Jews of Western Europe none had so passionately embraced the opportunities of enlightenment and the responsibilities of emancipation and none had anguished so bitterly over the preservation of the Jewish community and faith as had German Jews.

French Jewry, whose blood was thinned by more than a century of relatively undisturbed emancipation, has not conserved more than a polite Judaism, neither ardently Reform nor strenuously Orthodox. Italian Jewry, long identified with the secular causes of liberal national revolution, worked out an adjustment to the temperament of Italy: it was congenially Orthodox—as all Italy was orthodox—but it had no need to take its religion more seriously than the average bourgeois Italian took his Catholicism. English Jewry, gradually relieved of disabilities during the nineteenth century, was confident that the formidable glacier of English decency and good will would erode the rough and eccentric exterior of Jewish cult and manners. The Jews of France, Italy, and England were not notably creative in the early phases of the Emancipation; they are not now. At the same time, it should be noted that the ethos of these nations did not lend itself to more than social and political anti-Semitism in the nineteenth and early twentieth centuries. The Jews of France, Italy, and England were in no wise as victimized by the totalitarianisms of the twentieth century as was that other great center of Western Jewry, Germany.

The definition and interpretation of the German character—of what makes the German stolidly serious and yet spectacularly romantic, law-abiding and slavish before authority and yet capable of monumental excess and cruelty, incomparably regional and yet frighteningly nationalistic, arrogant and proud, meticulously middle-class and yet creative in all the disciplines of the mind and the imagination—should not occupy us except insofar as we are obliged to understand how it was that the Jew and the German lived with one another at the same moment so brilliantly and so tragically. We have but one suggestion, which we put forth fully conscious of its precariousness: the Jew and the German had much in common but expressed their community of character in vastly different ways. The Jew was no less proud, arrogant, respectful of law and authority, sentimental, bourgeois, and talented than was the German. In these qualities (and in others that one might cite if one pretended to an exhaustive descriptive psychology) they were deeply alike. Yet when the honor of a Jew was offended, he might torture himself with self-criticism instead of demanding satisfaction; when his genius was celebrated, he might view it with irony instead of accepting it as his due; when his middle-class conduct was chided, he might disclaim responsibility for having created the middle class instead of seeking to universalize its pretensions into the bulwark of European society; his nostalgias and sentiments were shot through with humor and the need for folk identity, instead of being elevated into a communion of race and nation. The Jew, conditioned as he was to look upon his characteristic strengths and defects as the product of his past, could ensure a realistic awareness of his times and his condition by maintaining a ballast of showmanship, irony, humor, and self-deprecation. He could not afford to take himself too seriously, because he was acclimated to the experience of sudden reversals of fortune. Whereas the Jews of France, Italy, and England progressed gradually and steadily toward complete equality throughout the nineteenth century, the German Jew knew but a continuous alternation of encouragement and despair, progress and reversal, the giving of freedoms and the curtailment of freedoms.

The Jew of Germany, sharing much with the German character, could not help but look upon the German and, more importantly, German culture and institutions with admiration and longing. It is no wonder that the Jew should seek to enter the German mind, to become like it, to be suffused and shaped by it. He felt so near to the German spirit, so complementary, so compatible with it, that it was only natural for him to attempt to bridge the narrow abyss which separated them. It is our view that the Jew did not merely seek to become the equal of the German, to enjoy his rights, to share his society, to be afforded his opportunities. The Jew of Germany was tempted by his historic alienation and his intuited apprehension of similitude to risk all upon the possibility that he could become the creative leader of German culture—to attempt to prove to the German that he was both the source and the flower of German cultural, religious, and intellectual genius. He almost succeeded. In attempting to bring likeness and compatibility to identity, he was destroyed.

The foregoing description of the Jew of Germany is

both synthetic and psychological. It makes no pretense at precise historical analysis. It is an effort to interpret a perhaps inexplicable phenomenon: why, indeed, did Jews so monumentally miscalculate the nature of the culture and the people under whom they had so long suffered and been betrayed? This is no longer an historical problem, pure and simple, for we cannot isolate all of the tributary causes and events which would explain such massive self-deception. We feel obliged to conclude that it is a psychological phenomenon.

If the Jew is both a natural and a supernatural creature, the historical relevance of this unity can be felt and interpreted only psychologically. The amalgam may enjoy metaphysical status when isolated from history and examined by the religious thinker; it may enjoy a symbolic relevance to history when interpreted by the eschatologist as the bearer of meaning in history; but it becomes, in its own right, an historical phenomenon only when it is considered as a psychological aberration.

The natural Jew sustains his connection with his appointed destiny, drawing out of nature all that is open to sanctification, preparing nature for redemption. He does this through simple acts of love and compassion; he does this symbolically by placing time and nature under the unifying regiment of the festivals and the commandments. The supernatural Jew sustains his connection with the fatality of his past by sinking into nature the anchor of eternity, by breaking up the constellations of determination and fixity which give men the illusion of security and endurance. The natural and the supernatural Jew are never disjunct: they are one and indissoluble in the authentic Jew; inseparable in fact, separable only in the mind. There are, however, delusions which enable the Jew to imagine on occasion that all nature has been raised up to eternity even though he continues to live amid time and move within history. At such moments he convinces himself that he is already redeemed, that he has been united with eternity, that he has passed over and beyond nature. Such moments are demonic assertions of man's desire to rush God, to redeem himself in the absence of God, to behave toward the world as though he were even empowered to take God's place. These demonic assertions, though they have rarely become specific movements in Jewish history, are ever present in the temptation of the single believer to pass judgment upon the whole community, to absent himself from its imperfect efforts to serve God.

The opposite perversion of the unity of nature and the supernatural vocation is to be found in the effort to naturalize eternity, to identify the supernatural task with the correction and improvement of society and culture, to dissolve the Jew's skeptical alienage from the centers of power and influence in an identification with a particular institutionalization of such criticism, whether it be socialist reform, the extension of political liberty, or the renascence of nationalist culture. The Jew cannot succumb to either alternative, whether it be the evaporation of the natural or the dissolution of the supernatural. He must maintain himself in limbo. When he maintains the limbo of the "between" he sustains the unity of his nature.

By the late nineteenth century it was already clear to many of the most perceptive thinkers of German Jewry that one perversion of the Jewish vocation was common, indeed prevailing. The Jew had come to believe that his interests and those of the German nation were, in all respects, one and the same—that German culture, German nationality, the German past and future were his own. The Jew had come to believe that what was best, most meaningful, most congenial in his own tradition also expressed what was best, most meaningful, and most congenial in the traditions of the German people. It is no wonder then that the tension and conflict which surrounded the German Jewish religious renaissance of that era should have as its defining environment the relation of Jewish and German culture; nor is it any wonder that in the greatest moments of that renaissance—in the work of Hermann Cohen, Leo Baeck, Franz Rosenzweig, and Martin Buber—instructive achievements and failures should emerge as both explicit and unconscious commentaries upon what their authors believed to be historical connection and interpenetration of the Jewish and the German spirit.

The discussion of Cohen, Baeck, Rosenzweig, and Buber which follows has the intention of unfolding the manner in which they saw the grand problem of Jewish destiny: the balanced unity or the demonic imbalance of the Jewish nature.

II. HERMANN COHEN (1842–1918)

It was not remarkable, given the ambiguous status of Jews in post-Emancipation Europe, for Hermann Cohen to have written a patriotic essay in 1915. This essay, distinguished not only for its exaggerated approbation of German national tradition, affords considerable insight into the atmosphere and rhetoric of Cohen's thought. "The Spirit of Germany and the Spirit of Judaism" [1] is really a polemical history of philosophic idealism. The polemic consists, most obviously, in the impassioned conviction that what is most noble in the German spirit—a philosophic idealism vivified by ethical humanism and pure religion—was anticipated, projected, and defined throughout the long history of Judaism. There can be, in

[1] It is quite difficult to be precise in the translation of such terms as *Deutschtum* and *Judentum.* Clearly Cohen is not concerned with German or Jewish nationality or national characteristics but with qualities of mind which characterize the unfolding of both traditions. It is proper, we think, to translate both terms as we have done. "Deutschtum und Judentum," *Jüdische Schriften,* ed. by Bruno Strauss, intro. by Franz Rosenzweig, Vol. II (Berlin, C. A. Schwetschke & Sohn, 1924), pp. 237–301.

effect, no polarity between the German and the Jewish spirit, for both derive their motive power from the same sources. The tension, long nourished in the German intellectual world, between German national ideals and the presumably alien civilization of the Jews, is resolutely denied. Germany thrives, in fact, Cohen argues, on Jewish ideals. The Protestant Reformation, moreover, marked the end of the "old man" of classic and Catholic tradition. The new man of the modern world—Protestant in Christianity and liberal in Judaism—depended upon the renewal of ideals and passions which Biblical Judaism had defined.[2]

It is clear, however, if one examines carefully the argument which Cohen advances, that something more subtle and insistent underlies the German Jewish spiritual identity. What establishes the community of the German and Jewish enterprise is not the mere sharing of historical sources, the approval of Reformation criticism of Catholic sacerdotalism, nor the sympathetic appreciation of an intellectual tradition that draws its strength from the Hebrew Bible. More than this is the conviction of Cohen that the German spirit and the Jewish spirit join in the elevation of ethical idealism; that religion becomes the instrument, not the opponent, of human perfection; that, in opposition to the attitude of the French Enlightenment,[3] religion is able to become a genuine bearer of truth.

For Hermann Cohen, son of the cantor of Coswig, student of the Talmud, and candidate for ordination at the rabbinical seminary at Breslau, to project a vision of the common destiny of the German spirit and Jewish religion must seem, at this later moment of history,

[2] *Ibid.*, p. 242. "Mit der Reformation tritt der deutsche Geist in den Mittelpunkt der Weltgeschichte." Cohen goes on to indicate the Biblical sources of those attributes of Reformation faith which express its uniqueness. Pp. 242 *passim.*

[3] *Ibid.*, p. 243, ". . . die deutsche Aufklärung gegen das Zeitalter Voltaires und der Enzyklopädisten bildet. Die religion ist nicht die Infamie. . . ."

bizarre. Two generations after his death his views appear tragically imprecise, for nothing could seem farther apart than Germany and Judaism. And yet, on closer scrutiny, such a judgment would be precipitous. Though Cohen's conception of German tradition was in part romantic and unrealistic, it described quite accurately a profound dimension of the German mind. Whatever its partiality and incompleteness, whatever its stubborn conviction that error and venality could not survive rational challenge, Cohen had succeeded in appropriating that valid tradition of German intellectual genius which commences with Lessing, Goethe, and Kant.[4]

Hermann Cohen was a German, but a specific kind of German—that kind of German whose patriotism was sustained by other figures of destiny than Bismarck and Von Hindenburg. The patriotism of Lessing and Goethe, no less than the patriotism of Moses Mendelssohn and Hermann Cohen, centered about the education of the German spirit, the definition of its national genius, the location of its specific capacity and talent. Such concern is nothing more than the expression of historical consciousness, the insistence that a nation must play a unique role in history or be satisfied with pedestrian achievement and eventual disappearance. As a Jew, as well as a German, Hermann Cohen was doubly beset. To him fell the task, as to no other of his generation, to be the spokesman of Judaism to the Germans, for he, perhaps alone, had succeeded in making a German his specialty, reviving his name and restoring the power of his genius. Cohen could address Germany as a Jew, since

[4] This view is manifest in Cohen's response to the anti-Semitic fulminations of the German historian Trietschke, who had sought to put anti-Semitism and what had become known as *die Judenfrage* upon a sound, scientific basis. Cohen's response—which years later he dated as the beginning of his return to Judaism—"Ein Bekenntnis in der Judenfrage" (1880) is shot through with an optimistic reading of German culture (*Jüdische Schriften*, Vol. II, pp. 73–94). See also the comment of Franz Rosenzweig in his introduction to the *Jüdische Schriften*, Vol. I, p. xxvi.

Cohen had, in the waning days of Hegelian absolute idealism, returned Immanuel Kant (like Goethe, a German national saint) to prominence.

Philosophic idealism, Kantian or otherwise, had long fascinated and instructed Judaism. Construed most broadly, it represented the effort to embrace and interpret the entire universe of experience by a few comprehensive rational principles. All experiences were held to be related and therefore susceptible, regardless of their apparent differences of content and form, to the unity which single, all-embracing principles can educe. Though sciences and arts may be differentiated, their rationality and truth derive (whether actually or by analogy) from the identity of principles which serve to define and govern their operation. Whether one caps the universe with a Platonic form, a Philonic Logos, an Augustinian Godhead, a Leibnitzian monad, or a Kantian schema of pure reason, the intention is clear—to bring the diversity of human experience under the governance of a single intuition, to draw the multiplicity of perceptions and events under the dominion of a single directive, constitutive, and real idea. The principle of interpretation cannot be a chimera, a mere device of investigation. It must do more than interpret the universe to the mind; it must itself have reality for the mind. Inescapably, however, such monumental principles of interpretation, by their very lucidity and comprehensiveness, will often, rather than assist the man of faith to persevere, tempt him to abandon faith. To be sure, philosophy does not win its converts so simply. Truth, unmixed with personal disposition and passion, does not shine forth with such commanding radiance. The man of faith who is won to philosophy and surrenders faith is—whatever the reasons—already lost to faith. Philosophy comes to supplant faith, to transform the delusions and deceptions of faith into the hard and clear truths of reason. Philosophy and faith nevertheless are not so unmixed as to allow one to speak of the pure philosopher, who accepts nothing but what reason has commanded him, or of the pure man of faith who believes all without need of rational scrutiny and discrimination. Although Franz Rosenzweig intended something different when he observed that "a healthy man needs both faith and philosophy,"[5] it is perhaps not untrue to argue that every man who pretends to think has both faith and philosophy. It is unjust therefore to exaggerate more than is necessary the tension between philosophy and faith. The tension, in fact, is not between philosophy and faith so stated, but between faith and those philosophies which deny legitimacy to the preoccupations of faith. It is one thing for a philosophic system to legitimate the problem of God; it is quite another for it to conceive the universe in such fashion as to dispense with God or so to order the relation of man to the universe as to allow God to play but a limited and coincidental role. Ultimately the man of faith is concerned that the God he conceives be not only real but personal, not only a metaphysical requirement but a God before whom he might stand.

Kant's *Critique of Practical Reason* endorsed not merely the metaphysical but the moral utility of the divine. God, Kant argued, is the one concept which can serve to impel common acceptance of and submission to the sway of the moral law. God guarantees the moral law, not only by force of his person (for as person, philosophy can properly say little) but by promise of immortality. Both the activity of God and the putative nature of immortality exceed the competence of critical philosophy. They represent, for Kant, a valid deduction from the moral law. The moral law requires both the authority of God and the rewards which only he can bestow. Philosophic idealism brings to religion, therefore, a confirmation of its ethical passion. Where eighteenth-century

[5] "Ein gesunder mensch braucht beides glauben und denken." Franz Rosenzweig, introduction to Cohen, *Jüdische Schriften,* Vol. I, p. xxv.

French philosophy might find the clarity of reason compromised by the introduction of religious considerations, religious principles were for Kantian philosophy indispensable. Only God proved able to unify the worlds of knowledge and action, to supply the principles which allow nature and morals to be joined.

It was to be expected that the idealism of Kant, and more specifically the absolute idealism of Hegel, would have a prodigious influence upon Jewish philosophy. It seemed to such diverse Jewish thinkers as Naḥman Krochmal, Abraham Geiger, Samson Raphael Hirsch, and Solomon Formstecher that the confluence of reason and history afforded mankind an instrument wherewith to interpret the nature and destiny of Judaism and the Jewish people.[6] Indeed, the compelling preoccupation of nineteenth-century Jewish rationalism was to accommodate the idiosyncratic history of Judaism to the monumental unraveling and consummation of the Absolute. Hegel had found it conclusive to consider the national destiny of Germany to be the synthetic fulfillment of the Absolute.[7] All the lines of Greek and Christian tradition

[6] Naḥman Krochmal we have already treated earlier (pp. 29–39). Abraham Geiger (1810–1870) was an impassioned and often profound interpreter of an evolutionary view of Jewish religious thought and tradition whose indebtedness to idealist categories is apparent. Samson Raphael Hirsch was afforded, by Hegel's method of entering into a reality in order to understand it, a most useful device with which to reinterpret Jewish religion (cf. the illuminating discussion of Noah H. Rosenbloom, "The 'Nineteen Letters of Ben Uziel,'" *Historia Judaica,* April, 1960, pp. 23–60). Solomon Formstecher (1808–1889), a German rabbi, sought to harmonize the religious life of the Jews with the general requirements of modern civilization. In Formstecher's major work, *Religion des Geistes* (1841), he undertook, anticipating many attitudes of Reform Judaism, to show that Judaism inevitably moves in the direction of a universal religion. The idealist tradition, viewing history as a unity which contains the goals toward which men progressively strive, gave impetus to an ethical interpretation of Judaism.

[7] "The German Spirit is the Spirit of the New World. Its aim is the realization of absolute Truth as the unlimited self-determination of Freedom. . . ." Hegel continues with comparable passion and vigor for the remainder of *The Philosophy of History.* G. W. F. Hegel,

converged in the formation of German culture. Since German culture appeared in many Jewish eyes to be the epitome of rational order and intellectual sophistication, it became necessary to introduce Judaism into the mechanics of Hegelian idealism. Though there were opponents, even Jewish opponents, of Hegelian idealism,[8] it was not until Hermann Cohen that its influence on Judaism was checked. It was checked, however, not by the projection of a superior and more comprehensive system, for Cohen was not a successful builder of systems. It was rather that Cohen reflected the summation of idealism and the final statement which it could make on Judaism.

Hermann Cohen was the last and the first. He ended the contribution of philosophical idealism to Judaism and he defined a new beginning for Jewish religious thinking. What constitutes the new beginning is that he brought reason to the limits of reason, pressing it to perform agonizing yet unconvincing feats of daring. In the effort to fix Judaism within the precincts of reason, the philosophic passion drove him to the statement of an almost painful dialectic—for the more reason commands, the more faith protests; the German idealist asserts and the Jew responds. The result, it will be observed, is that though philosophy achieves the formal triumph of defini-

---

The Philosophy of History, trans. by J. Sibree (New York, Willey Book Company, 1944), p. 341.

[8] Both Heymann Steinthal (1823–1899) and Moritz Lazarus (1824–1903) sought to found ethics, particularly Jewish ethics, upon the individual foundations of Kant rather than upon the world-historical identities which Hegel had defined. Although Cohen bitterly attacked Lazarus for presumably ignoring the historical maturation of Jewish ethics, it is the opinion of other students that the former's critique, *Das Problem der jüdischen Sittenlehre. Eine Kritik von Lazarus's Ethik des Judentums* (The Problem of the Jewish Doctrine of Ethics. An Examination of Lazarus' Ethics of Judaism) was both an unjust attack and inferior (Cohen, *Jüdische Schriften*, Vol. XIII, pp. 1–35). Cf. the discussion of David Baumgardt, "The Ethics of Lazarus and Steinthal," *Yearbook II*, Leo Baeck Institute (London, East and West Library, 1957), pp. 205–17.

tion and Judaism is embraced as a religion of reason, there breaks through a series of intuitions and judgments which render faith finally independent from reason and establish a fresh direction for the formation of Jewish theology. Though one begins with the God who is only idea, one ends with the recognition that behind the shadows of reason there may be discerned the living God.

In 1914, shortly before his visit to Russia, Hermann Cohen was tendered a banquet in Berlin. One of the speakers, no doubt intending a compliment, referred to the aged philosopher (then seventy-one years old) as a recent *baal Teshuvah*. Angered less by the description than by its dating, Cohen interjected: "I became a *baal Teshuvah* thirty-four years ago." [9] Presumably, as Rosenzweig surmises,[10] Cohen dated his return to Judaism from 1880 when he wrote his first major essay on contemporary Judaism. This essay, "A Confession on the Jewish Question," was composed in response to the Prussian historian Treitschke, who had earlier written a series of essays designed successfully to dignify the popular forms of anti-Semitic racism with the jargon of nationalist historiography.[11] To Treitschke's claim that the Jews constituted an alien, unassimilable national community in the midst of Germany, Cohen's reply was directed. It was, to say the least, an unconvincing document of rebuttal—unconvincing because it was overly defensive and needlessly ironic. Whatever importance Cohen's "Confession" possesses derives from the fact that it suggests the lines of argument which he was subsequently to develop and deepen. Cohen's conviction, the conviction which led him in 1880 to defend an almost

[9] Franz Rosenzweig, introduction to *Jüdische Schriften,* Vol. I, p. xxi. Rosenzweig says that his source for this story was an oral description of Boris Pines (note to p. xxi, p. 331).

[10] Rosenzweig interprets Cohen's banquet affirmation to mean that his return to Judaism was signalized by his apologetic reply to Treitschke. *Ibid.*, p. xxi.

[11] See footnote 12, p. 81.

assimilationist program for Jewish life, was that Germany was "the nation of Kant." [12] To be the nation of Kant meant more than to have been the birthplace of Kant. To be sure, this is Cohen's fundamental error. To assume that national histories enjoy more than the fortuitous conjunction of natural and historical circumstance, that one can conclude from the appearance of intellectual genius some popular tendency to high culture and morals, is deceptive. Such deception was, however, common in the days of Cohen and Treitschke—both philosophic argument and political statecraft were founded upon the presumption of German intellectual superiority. Cohen could confidently point to two concepts, ethical autonomy and the uniqueness and transcendence of God, and argue that they reflected the continuing and enduring community of German and Jewish tradition. The former concept, matured in the centuries between Luther and Kant, was commonly accepted by the liberal Judaism to which Cohen adhered as the religion of modern Jews. The latter concept, given to the world by classic Judaism, was the patrimony of German Protestantism. In either case, Cohen concluded, the racial exclusiveness and separatism with which Treitschke had belabored the Jews were unfounded. Judaism possessed the same ethical intensity and religious universalism which Germany had projected as its own.

How is it possible that in a period of thirty-six years—from 1880, when he wrote "A Confession on the Jewish Question," to 1916, when he wrote "The Spirit of Judaism and the Spirit of Germany"—Cohen's philosophic position, however developed and sophisticated, had not achieved a more profound understanding of history? Cohen was as little realistic in his judgment of history at the beginning of his reflections upon Judaism as he was at the end. Substantially his position remained the same.

The answer lies in the fact that history as such was

[12] "Ein Bekenntnis in der Judenfrage," *Jüdische Schriften,* Vol. II, p. 73.

always a concept, never a reality. Cohen could speak of the suffering and martyrdom of Jewish history, could comment at length upon the Dreyfus affair, or upon the history of the Jews of Poland, but the understanding of isolated historical events and the consciousness of "history-in-general" never brought him to reflect upon the *movement* of history. History was either the source of citation and evidence or a moment in the unfolding of the spirit.

It could not be otherwise for Hermann Cohen. History could afford but final confirmation to the spirit. It could never be its source of power. Spirit preceded history and reason ordered the spirit. The effort to comprehend the totality of human experience, to interpret the breadth of the phenomenal world, was an intellectual obligation which the philosophic vocation had imposed long before the problem of religion, much less Jewish religion, had asserted itself in Cohen's life.

As for Kant, the problem of philosophy commences for Cohen with the effort to interpret reality according to the laws of thought. Reality cannot be defined in itself. The human mind cannot push beyond its own laws to an assertion of what reality is independently of thought. The forms of thought limit and circumscribe reality. Philosophy can be no other, therefore, than a critique of reason, for the categories of reason fashion the molds in which reality is inescapably cast. Reality in itself (the notorious Kantian *ding an sich*) remains unavailable to rational apprehension. The only ray of light which penetrates the phenomenal world derives from the laws of ethics. Otherwise a dualism remains, consisting of the matter of experience and the form of rational intuition. Hegel, seeking to overcome this dualism, developed the concept of the Absolute which purportedly accounted for all the experiences of the phenomenal world, whether they were those of the physical world, ethics, or art.[13]

[13] Cohen, unlike Hegel, sought to overcome the Kantian dualism, not by developing a comprehensive methodology, but by locating the

II. Hermann Cohen (1842–1918)

If there is one process for which Cohen will claim utter and unqualified objectivity, it is the process of thought. Thought is a general, real, and objective process regardless of how human beings may exhibit its characteristics.[14] It is, however, but one among three processes by which man comes to a complete expression of his drive to achieve

---

primary source of thought beyond which investigative speculation could not go. This source, for Cohen, was mathematics. In the development of thought, logic—the science of thought—can assume nothing other than itself to be its proper subject matter. Logic, being mathematics, consists neither in the projection of particular and general conclusions, such as classic syllogistic logic would suggest, nor in "the tracings of general lines of connection between comparable bodies of experience." (Cf. Hermann Cohen, *Logik der Reinen Erkenntniss* [Berlin, Bruno Cassirer, 1902], pp. 1–58 *passim;* in Part 1, *Einleitung und Disposition,* Cohen undertakes a criticism of both historical traditions of logic and displays their shortcomings in the light of his own system.) Logic is fundamentally the abstract schema of mathematics. To the extent, however, to which mathematics continues to unfold and develop, logic, by analogy, must be defined as a continuous process. For thought to commence, for the stream of mathematical continuity to be interrupted at some point, a symbol, expressive of the endless process of logic, is needed. By a complicated argument (*Ibid.,* pp. 218–66) Cohen defines the mathematical derivative to be the Idea. The Idea, Cohen's alternative to Kant's noumenon, is not, however, an independent, self-subsisting metaphysical entity like the *ding an sich.* The Idea, that fundamental derivative from the infinite mathematical continuum, is capable, Cohen believed, of producing its own world. Whereas Kant insisted that concepts require the confirmation of perception, Cohen considered such a use of the phenomenal world to be the beginning, but not the end, of the noetic process. Ultimately he felt that pure knowledge would be achieved by the systematic pursuit of mathematical reasoning. (See Jacob Agus, *Modern Philosophies of Judaism* [New York, Behrman House, Inc., 1941], pp. 61–72, for an excellent discussion of Cohen's basic philosophic position; particularly an interpretation of the "mathematical derivative.") Such pure knowledge would consist in the achievement of an embracing concept (*ein Begriff*) which would reduce the multiplicity and variety of perceived actualities to the quantitative terms of mathematics.

[14] It is difficult to imagine, although Cohen denied any such implication, how thought can be construed objectively and yet be indifferent to the behavior of the thinking man, unless the world is, in some sense, the thought of a being transcendent to it. (Cf. Agus, *Modern Philosophies of Judaism,* p. 71.) Such a metaphysical claim Cohen vigorously declined.

a comprehensive concept. *Thought,* the process of *logic; feeling,* the process of *aesthetics;* and *will,* the process of *ethics,* work out their destinies on an infinite continuum which stretches from their Source to their Object. This world—limited by its own inaccessible dimensions and determined by the categories of perception—is the stage of process and travail. Being is the goal, but becoming is all that can be known.

Logic is lawful. It projects order and systematic unfolding. All of the directions of the spirit must share in the lawfulness of thought. As such both aesthetics and ethics must be rational. It is clear, however, that ethics must enjoy autonomy unless it is to become but one phase in the unfolding of logic, subsumed under the laws of thought and reduced to but an ancilla of the behaviorist sciences of biology and psychology. The Idea of ethics is accorded autonomy, somewhat tautologically, because it is a moral obligation to assume its independence. As Cohen observed in his earlier study of *Kant's Theory of Experience,* "Whoever does not acknowledge this Ought, does not wish to have an ethics." In the same fashion as it is our duty to pursue the search for the mathematical realm of being, it is our moral duty to press for the realization of ethical being. The foundation of ethical certainty is therefore beyond the scope of logical certainty. It is the result of a human intuition—a conviction that ethics is necessary to distinguish man from the beast.

It would appear, however, that although ethics is to be considered a pure direction of the spirit, akin to logic, it is founded upon a fundamentally irrational intuition. To preserve the noetic quality of ethics it is necessary to discover a common ground which unites the enterprise of logic and ethics. This ground is what Cohen calls "the basic law of truth." [15] This fundamental law states that however ethics and logic may differ in their content their

[15] Hermann Cohen, *Ethik des Reinen Willens* (Berlin, Bruno Cassirer, 1904), "Das Grundgesetz der Wahrheit," pp. 79–103.

method of operation is the same. In effect, truth is independent of both logic and ethics, but joins them together in common enterprise. The feeling of truth is thus the final source of certainty, the criterion of authentication to both thought and will.

Ethics does not have as its primary intention the amending of human conduct, the projection of maxims and injunctions for the direction of conscience. As the analogue of logic, ethics must project the concept of a complete order, a totality to which all tributary activities are directed. The mere alteration of behavior or reproof of conscience would compromise the intellectual structure of ethics. The goal and content of ethics is not simply individual right conduct, but nothing less than the achievement of the ideal human society. The individual ethical conscience ought not be concerned with its own perfection except insofar as that perfection bears upon the realization of the unity and perfection of mankind. A self-conscious pursuit of sanctity would be a sin against perfection, sundering, as it would, the connection which binds the individual to the whole of mankind. An ethical conception of man consists therefore in a view of humanity as the development and unfolding of the self-perfecting individual.

There is to be found in Kant's notes and journals the following entry: "God is not an entity outside me, but merely a thought within me." At the same time as Kant observes the insufficiency of this God, acknowledging that the God of thought is, however, the only God he feels justified in affirming, Kant elsewhere observes that it is inadequate to believe "in an entity which is only an idol and not a personality."

The God of Immanuel Kant performed an indispensable role in his metaphysical system: He guaranteed to thought the validity of its ethical maxims. At the same time as the idea of God functioned constructively in

Kant's system of ethics, Kant was aware of the abyss which separates the God of philosophy from the God of faith.

The God of Hermann Cohen was also an indispensable idea. However much Cohen sought to enhance God's significance by identifying Him with truth, with eternity, with the perseverance of the universe, He remained, finally, an idea. In the same fashion as Kant had found God indispensable for the operation of practical reason, the device of shoring up the conscience of man against the erosions of temptation and injustice, Cohen required God in order to validate his ethical doctrine.

The ethical impetus of man is directed toward the achievement of a concept, the perfection and unity of human society. At any moment a man may choose to perform a moral act. In its performance he is liable to all the temptations of expediency and compromise. What compels him to the fulfillment of his obligation is the anticipation that, in the moment of its performance, the deed is an irreplaceable link in the unfolding of perfection. Amid the passage and uncertainty of time the ethical man comprehends the eternity of performance. The straining toward infinite achievement, the awareness of unlimited striving and moral advance impel man to completion. Eternity becomes therefore the "time" in which the ethical act is consummated. The awareness that the ethical act is not lost in the moment, but is rather sustained in the continuum of man's becoming toward the goal, ratifies the intentions of the ethical will.

But what prevents the universe from running down, from dying out before the ethical ideal is accomplished? Surely the foreknowledge of its end would appear, Cohen believed, to deprive the ethical enterprise of its vitality and hope. Were the law of entropy to reduce all life and becoming to inertia and equilibrium, enthusiasm for the ethical ideal would be deflated and ethics would collapse. What is needed is some concept which can authenticate the reality of eternity, which will ensure that nature will always exist as the background against which the ethical ideal may be pursued.

It is at this point that Cohen discovers the idea of God. The history of religious belief, Cohen argues, has always evidenced the recognition that the gods sustain nature for man, that the universe endures because the gods will it. It is a legitimate philosophic use of mythological conception to employ the term "God" to signify that the physical world is sustained for the sake of the eternity of the ethical task. God establishes the relation between nature and morals, between logic and ethics. It is not necessary to take this God on faith, for the system has already made provision for his authentication. As logic and ethics share their dependence upon the "basic law of truth," it would appear justified to argue that God is but a valid deduction from the law of truth.[16] "It is not that man demands God for his subjective support but He is demanded by the need for the objective grounding of ethics." [17]

God is an idea demanded not by the sentimentality of man but by the requirements of the ethical enterprise. It could not have been otherwise. The rational system always demands that God perform a stabilizing function, guaranteeing the structure of knowledge, defining the emergence of the natural world, authorizing the moral law and compelling its obedience. In the history of Western philosophy God has been more resolutely described at some times than at others. The Christian tradition conceived the role of philosophy to be that of organizing and defending by reason what revelation had already disclosed. Jewish philosophy was similarly unembarrassed by the effort to construe with reason the axioms of belief. Reason might clarify what faith merely stated without embellishment. Reason, in effect, did not reconstitute the content of faith, but surely opened it to more lucid state-

[16] Agus' criticism of Cohen's deduction of God from the basic law of truth seems valid to us. *Modern Philosophies of Judaism*, pp. 88–93.

[17] Cohen, *Ethik des Reinen Willens*, p. 55.

ment and understanding. To begin the philosophic inquiry without the obligation of faith was to reverse the procedures of religious speculation.

At the end of his career, having already used the idea of God in his *Critique of Practical Reason,* Kant could still write: "The function of transcendental philosophy is still unresolved. Is there a God?" To effect the transition from philosophic vocabulary to existence, to demonstrate to reason what only reason, in its limitations, can accept, is obviously insufficient. Kant posed to himself the question of faith and it remained unanswered.

Reason can never answer the question of God. Faith can never satisfy reason. It is only the reason which defines its task in such a way as to permit the possibility of God's existence which will believe in his existence. Reason—never an unqualified and general instrument of understanding—is defined anew by each man; granted some powers and denied others; afforded scope of comprehension and hedged by limitations. Reason can accomplish only what it is permitted. As such it is foolish to invest demonstrations of God's existence with more seriousness than they deserve. They may serve to make faith conscious of its own unarticulated presuppositions. They may enable the philosopher to make comprehensible and clear aspects of his speculation which otherwise remain opaque. In all events the God which faith demonstrates by reason is but the shadow of Him whom faith believes; and the God which philosophy demonstrates is but a function of the System, remote to feeling and useless to faith.

It might be imagined that Cohen was impervious to the historic contrast of faith and reason. Nowhere in his writings does this contrast receive specific consideration. The explanation (if there is one as such) is that the God of faith and the God of reason were conceived by him to be the same. There cannot be two Gods—one defined by reason and the other by faith, one performing the role described by scientific ethics, the other answering the entreaties of prayer. There is but one God—an idea, for an idea is all that reason can properly compass. God is, for Cohen, no less real for being only an idea, because the function he performs for ethics is indispensable for the sustenance of the universe. God is universal and unique—these are the proper attributes of *the* Idea. Having located the function of God and qualified the sense in which he is to be understood it is necessary to transform him from the structural underpinning of the System into an agent of the ethical enterprise. It would be an obvious misuse of God to retain him merely as an intellectual device. The System is never *only* a construction of the mind. It is improper and unjust to consider the philosopher a cavalier, a highwayman of the mind, who sallies forth for pleasure and vanity and returns to his remote and formidable castle for protection from reprisal. The employment of the intellect is never an excursion for an authentic philosopher. When Cohen deduces the idea of God from the fundamental law of truth he does so because he believes the idea, the deduction, and the law to be valid instruments of achieving accurate knowledge of the real world. Since the goal of ethics is a real goal no effort must be spared to turn man toward its fulfillment.

Religion, that historic and well-enforced sanction of the conscience, exists to compel man to the fulfillment of the divine will. Religion, properly refined and understood, can become the instrument with which man directs himself to the ethical task. This is possible only if religion is molded to ethical self-consciousness. Religion cannot properly be concerned, Cohen argues, with problems of cosmology and metaphysics, much less with eschatology. Such concerns trespass upon religion and are not resolved by it. Religion can say nothing about being as such, about time or space as such, about the actual structure of reality, even about the nature of God. To turn it to such questions is to compel religion to assume improper functions—functions, moreover, which it cannot discharge. Scientific knowledge, the knowledge which only logic can provide, is the basis of all truth, religious or otherwise.

Questions of metaphysics are ruled out as being beyond the competence of scientific philosophy. Religion is the concrete exploration of the ethical will. As such, it too is a province of ethics.

However, if religion is but the historical agency of ethics, what is its independent content? From where does its autonomy derive? This problem, which Cohen recognized early in his discussion of religion, is never satisfactorily resolved. By the time of his magnum opus, *Religion of Reason,*[18] it is clear that the only autonomous content of religion lies in the achievement of the relation between God and the "individuum *quand même.*" Yet even this relation, unique though it may be, is disqualified from serious philosophic attention because the relation of the individual to God is without cognitive value—it cannot serve to relate the individual to his fellow man or to the whole of humanity. Its value is paradigmatic, a mere analogy to proper religious concerns.

It is to the cognitive definition of religion that Cohen's brilliant essay *Religion and Ethics*[19] was directed. In its opening pages Cohen sets forth the conclusions of his earlier work, *The Ethics of the Pure Will:* Ethics is to the will what logic is to thought; they are related by analogy; there is no fundamental opposition between ethics and science; both are indispensable to the achievement of a complete concept of nature and man.[20] Any theory, such

[18] Cohen commenced formal preparation of *Religion der Vernunft* in the years 1917–1918. He died on April 14, 1918, and the work was published posthumously in 1919, a second revised edition appearing in 1929: *Religion der Vernunft aus dem Quellen des Judentums,* 2nd ed., supervised by Bruno Strauss (Frankfurt am Main, J. Kauffmann Verlag, 1929).

[19] Hermann Cohen, *Religion und Sittlichkeit: Eine Betrachtung zur Grundlegung der Religionsphilosophie* (Religion and Ethics: A Consideration of the Foundations of the Philosophy of Religion), (Berlin, Verlag von M. Poppelauer, 1907); reprinted in *Jüdische Schriften,* Vol. III, pp. 98–168. All citations will be from the edition which appears in the *Jüdische Schriften.*

[20] *Ibid.,* p. 105. "Wie die Logik das Zentrum der auf Mathematik begründeten Naturwissenschaft ist, so ist die Ethik das Zentrum

as the materialism of Hobbes, which postulates a war of all against all, betrays the essential meaning of humanity.[21] Such materialism makes impossible any effort to construct an adequate theory of humanity because man is disjoined from nature. Only if the coherence of man and nature can be maintained is it possible to found both upon a common theory of knowledge; and only if there is a single theory of knowledge is ethical idealism possible. This may be a somewhat tortured means of establishing a principle, and yet it exhibits Cohen's own passion, which is quite capable of accelerating the methodical push of reason in order to gain the objective quickly, even if not quite convincingly. What is essential is that Cohen locates that form of religion which validates his idea of God, which transforms God from an element of the System into an instrument for achieving human perfection.

It is remarkable to observe the development of Cohen's theory of religion. It is distinguished, in contrast to his theories of nature, aesthetics, and ethics, by constant and uncharacteristic reference to history. Unlike his theory of knowledge, which exhibits little or no concern for the history of philosophic theory—much less for the natural history of knowledge so characteristic of empiricist philosophers—his theory of religion begins with an assessment of religious history. One might wonder what possible value history might have for knowledge. History is, at best, opinion. It can disclose what men have thought and done, but it cannot reveal truth. It cannot reveal truth unless, to be sure, one has decided that the truth *has been* revealed; that there is an essential conformance between some domain of history and some construction of theory. This would be to say that history is not merely the record of opinion, but itself registers unquestionable sources of truth; that history has, in spite of the prejudices of idealist philosophy, some contribution to make to scientific

der Geschichtswissenschaft." Cf. particularly on recapitulation of the position of *Ethik des Reinen Willens*, pp. 100–13.

[21] *Ibid.*, pp. 108, 109.

knowledge. It will be recalled that Cohen would not countenance the attention of logic to the evidence of perception. Perception can yield, at best, relative confirmation. It cannot be a fully reliable medium of truth. Its information is contingent, irresponsible, variable. How can history, being but the record of events (coagulated perceptions), be accredited? How can Cohen arrive, as he does in *Religion and Ethics* and later in *The Concept of Religion* [22] and *Religion of Reason,* at the conviction that Jewish monotheism is true religion? He can do so only on one of two assumptions: either that his fidelity to the system wavered before the pull of ancestral obligations or that religion is ultimately—at best—the source of useful but unreliable knowledge.

There is convincing evidence that Cohen was intensely ambiguous in his views of religion, particularly of Jewish religion. On the one hand his ethical passion was incomparable—it was a matter of considerable urgency to save God and ethics from the curse of mere theory. The good life and the perfection of man could not be allowed to weather in the corrosive atmosphere of theory. Cohen was acutely sensitive to the fate of the poor, to social injustice, to the tyrannies of nations and societies.[23] It was

[22] Hermann Cohen, *Der Begriff der Religion im System der Philosophie* (The Concept of Religion Within the Philosophic System), (Giessen, Verlag Von Alfred Töpelmann, 1915).

[23] The socialism of Hermann Cohen, stemming from liberal exultation with the French Revolution and the later Revolution of 1848, was purged by him of its materialist preoccupations. Socialism was not restricted to issues of economic and material progress, but centered upon the regeneration and liberation of man's spiritual capacities. This socialism was essentially ethical in character. (Cf. *Religion und Sittlichkeit,* p. 109, "Der Materialismus . . . ist der schroffste Widerspruch zu dem ethischen Idealismus, in welchem der Sozialismus . . . seine Wurzel hat.") Steven S. Schwarzschild's comprehensive and suggestive analysis of Cohen's socialism, "The Democratic Socialism of Hermann Cohen," *Hebrew Union College Annual,* Vol. XXVII (1956), pp. 417–38, makes the valuable point that Cohen's programmatic socialism, however moving and laudable, was naïve and hopelessly unrealistic. We would object, however, that Schwarzschild's stricture that "the concept of God as an idea and ideal" is equally a phenomenon of a moribund nineteenth-century

crucial that man be set on the path to his real perfection. On the other hand, Cohen's philosophic obligations were equally exacting. No theory could be validated which did not survive the scrutiny of investigation. One could not sacrifice the labors of a half century merely to accomplish the dubious end of concretizing one's ethical passion. Ethics had to be correlated with logic. Ethics could not be pressed to affirm more than its principles allowed. In effect, a polarity existed between Cohen the reformer and Cohen the thinker.

This polarity is strengthened when it becomes clear that ultimately religion is to be split off from ethics. It is not imagined that this thesis will meet with ready acceptance. If anything, the effort has been to argue that Cohen's *Religion of Reason* is the natural culmination of his philosophic deliberations, that Judaism is the capstone of his system. There are reasons—all too impressive reasons—to think otherwise. There can be no question but that Cohen was a warm, intense, and loyal Jew. But this is only to say that he was a generous, passionate, and dedicated human being, who could betray no obligation, shirk no duty, reject no responsibility. Jews were misunderstood and Cohen defended them. Jews possessed a great tradition and Cohen made himself master of it. All this is evidence of contingent loyalty and dedication. It makes one grateful that Hermann Cohen was a Jew. It does not certify that his thinking returned him to Judaism.

Assuredly it is not to be denied that Cohen believed that his philosophy of Judaism was Jewish. His disciple Franz Rosenzweig reports that when the manuscript of *Religion of Reason* was completed he had exclaimed in the language of Virgil, *"Cedite, gentiles, scriptores, cedite, no-*

liberal philosophy of history and is overstated. God the ideal is dead, though Jewish movements such as Reconstructionism would keep it alive. But God as "Idea" is a terribly real problem. We tend to confuse "idea" and "ideal," forgetting that God may be, in some sense, an idea—it merely depends whose idea He is and whether conception is intended as a substitute for or only as an index of reality.

stri! Nescioquid majus nascitur Maimonide," and Cohen had replied, delighted by the compliment, "Yes, the *Rambam* would be pleased." [24] Perhaps, indeed, the *Rambam* would have been pleased; however, the ingenuity of Hermann Cohen was neither as self-conscious nor as carefully contrived as that of Maimonides. The gap which exists between the religion which serves ethics and the religion of the believing Jew remains vast. Though Hermann Cohen believed it had been bridged, the abyss continued to yawn. It is well, however, to reflect upon his efforts to join philosophic religion and Judaism; because it is here, in Cohen's painful attempts to define their unity, that his greatest contribution to Jewish religious thought lies.

In *Religion and Ethics,* a transitional work bridging the career of the academic philosopher and the Jewish educator, Cohen distinguishes between polytheism and monotheism, between the religion of myth and the religion of ethics. Paganism demands that the gods submerge man, that man be rendered marginal and contingent before them. The sway of caprice and irrationality binds man in submission to the gods. There is no possible relation—other than that of obeisant piety and the projection of myth—to bind man and God. There is no relation between them because there is neither difference nor reciprocity. There is no difference because the universe, which contains both gods and man, is conceived univocally; it is a universe which is unpredictable, an emergence from chaos in which both gods and man are the progeny of an inexorable fatalism. The individualized gods and the individual man are both victims of the cosmos.[25] There is no reciprocity because there can be no common concern and meeting when gods and men compete to charm or vanquish each other. In monotheism,

[24] Rosenzweig, introduction to *Jüdische Schriften,* p. liii. *Rambam* is the Hebrew locution for *R*abbi *M*oses *b*en *M*aimon, referred to as Maimonides.

[25] *Religion und Sittlichkeit,* pp. 119–23; particularly p. 120.

however (which Cohen identifies with the religion of the prophets[26]) there is authentic relation. This relation is defined, however, not merely by the formal communication of man and God, but by the articulation of the reality of the "fellow man." [27] It is only in the search of man for man that man discovers the meaning of God. "Not from God backwards to man," Cohen emphasizes "but from man upwards to God." [28] Not satisfied with apostrophizing his insight with a metaphor, Cohen elaborates. The prophet Micah bespeaks Cohen's view in his assertion, "He has made known, O Man, what is good." [29] It is not that the prophet discloses something which God *has* done or which God *wishes* to do. He discloses rather what God wishes man to do. The revelation of God's essence consists, for Cohen, in the divine appeal to human obligation. God's action is his passivity. God's independence is his reliance upon man. As Cohen makes clear, it is Micah's emphatic "O Man" that moves him, for it is in this directional call that the relation of monotheism and ethics is defined. God is the source of the directive; but God is only the potential source of the good. The actual source is man.[30] To be sure, the Greeks speculated regarding the nature of the good, but speculation is unavailing to conduct. The concept of the good was always prominent in their philosophy, but life was given over nevertheless to good and ill, success or disaster.[31] The Delphic oracles did not disclose as did Micah. The Greek could but faintly perceive in the confusing interplay of nature and historical events the precarious relation of man and God. The

[26] *Ibid.*, p. 123.
[27] *Ibid.*, p. 124. "Sondern ein anderes, ein ganz anderes Verhältnis muss in die Blicklinie eintreten: das Verhältnis des Ich zum Mitmenschen."
[28] *Ibid.*, p. 124. [29] *Ibid.*, p. 124.
[30] "Bei dem Guten handelt es sich um den Menschen. Daher ist diese Apostrophe: 'O Mensch' hier so innerlich bedeutsam. Wo das Gut kundgetan wird, da wird der Mensch angesprochen. Und das allein erscheint jetzt als die Aufgabe Gottes: den Menschen anzusprechen, und was gut sei, ihm zu künden." *Ibid.*, p. 125.
[31] *Ibid.*, p. 125.

disjunction of speculation from the operative and energizing myths which instructed Greek conduct made the ethical imperative at best advisory and prudential. The prophetic conception of God rested, however, on the moral relations between man and man.

Cohen's fundamental conception of God as *He Who makes known man's obligation to man* is assuredly prophetic. It is assuredly Jewish. There can be no question but that Cohen's fundamental direction is Jewish—that his ethical passion, his conception of monotheism, his valuation of the prophetic tradition reflect authentic Jewish concerns. And yet there remains unexamined what is most distinctively and indispensably Jewish. It is that which is most central to any religious position: the autonomous person of God.

It took little effort, as Cohen's subsequent studies indicate, to rationalize the whole structure of Jewish religion—the concept of sin and atonement, the Law, messianism. All are interpreted to be instruments for forming the moral conscience. The whole corpus of Jewish belief is rationalized by its service to ethics. Only when God supplied the directive to ethical activity was religion true to ethics and serviceable to the human race. And all could be justified to liberal Judaism by the appeal to the ethical conscience. God vitalized ethics, religion vitalized God, and Judaism vitalized religion.

Judaism came last in the emergence of the System. It came last and it came first. That it came last is clear; that it came first is apparent only if one observes the unconscious break which separates the mystery of God from his function as the principal catalyst in the reformation of human conduct.

It is only to faith that God is first. Faith commences with the person of God and only later discovers the Being of God. Faith is inescapably predicated upon the priority of man's certainty of God's existence to all reflection regarding His nature and being. God's existence is the shock to human finitude. Essence is the rationalization of shock. Faith makes an existential discovery. This need not be the leap of Kierkegaard—unless one chooses to find God by forsaking reason. It is only where reason has defined the circumference of existence and God penetrates —how, we cannot hazard to surmise—that circumference, that reason is abandoned and faith embraced. But reason is never wholly abandoned nor is faith ever completely secure. The slow ascent of reason to faith, affirmed by pious naturalism, is not the only process nor is the God of naturalism the only God. It is therefore idle to attach to existence the onus of the self-abandoning leap—to assume that reason is betrayed when a man believes. Reason is only abandoned, the leap is only undertaken, when one was previously certain that all that he possessed was reason and all that he could know was rational. The leap becomes not merely a leap into the abyss but a leap of discovery. It is an existential leap because that which had been ruled out by reason is found.

The approaches to God are various; the abandonments and the discoveries, the lost and the found are inextricably blended. Hermann Cohen attached himself to the Idea of God. He went in search of history to confirm that Idea. He discovered, however, something which extended farther and probed deeper than the self-limiting Idea. He discovered, but he could never believe. He could affirm that "the essence of God is a great mystery," [32] but then it was only his essence which bespoke his mystery. The discovery of the person of God and the mystery of that person could never be apprehended as such. It could be inferred only from the equally profound mystery of man's relation to God. Here—only here—does Cohen approximate to faith. The mystery of man's dependence upon God is an object of wonder and incredulity. Reason will supply the ethical counterpart to the human-divine dependence, but that will not explain the dependence as such. It can rationalize the dependence, as Cohen does

[32] "Die Lyrik der Psalmen," *Jüdische Schriften,* Vol. I, p. 253.

when he speaks of monotheism as a "psychological *Mysterium,"* [33] but it cannot avoid the fact of that dependence.

It is in the effort to rationalize this acknowledged mystery that Cohen formulates his principle of correlation. Franz Rosenzweig was not incorrect in considering the principle of correlation to be a landmark, although less a landmark in the history of religious thought than a signal development in Cohen's own religious thinking.[34] The principle affirms quite simply that, in spite of the incommensurability of man and God, they are related. Man cannot be properly thought without God; God cannot be properly thought without man. Indeed, to the extent that they are internally related their experience of each other affects and defines both. Creation, revelation, and redemption, previously opaque conceptions, can now be defined. Correlation establishes the sense in which each movement of God is related to a movement of man. God creates; man is created. God reveals; man receives. God redeems; man is saved. The action is correlated to a response. Man—no longer the general concept of humanity—is at last before God. The principle of correlation, to be sure, has no metaphysical value, for it will not define what God or man is in himself; nor does it have noetic value, for it will not enable the pure direction of spirit—as scientific ethics requires—to achieve a fulfilled conception of humanity. Its only value lies in the fact that man and God are no longer functions of each other, ideas which serve to locate objective co-ordinates of the System. To correlate man and God is to hold that man and

[33] *Jüdische Schriften,* p. 239; introduction by Franz Rosenzweig, p. li.

[34] The principle is formally articulated in *Der Begriff der Religion,* pp. 47–61. Cohen explores the correlation of God and world, God and nature, God and man, God and the individual. Cf. *Jüdische Schriften,* introduction by Franz Rosenzweig, pp. xliv–l. Cf. the shortly to be published German essay by Alexander Altmann, "Hermann Cohens Begriff der Korrelation."

God—individual man and personal God—seek and address one another. One would not need correlation to define the ethical relations which Cohen had elaborated in *The Ethics of the Pure Will* or *Religion and Ethics.* The philosopher was able to confer truth upon Judaism up to the point where it became clear that Judaism possessed dimensions which philosophy could neither ignore nor incorporate. Although Cohen continued until the end of his life to recruit theological concepts to the cause of ethics, he was compelled to take account of the demand for individual religion and personal belief.

This demand is faced but once. In his attempt to make clear the meaning of the love of God, Cohen expresses the fullness of his existential discontent; for on the one hand he feels compelled to restrict the love of God to the knowledge of morality,[35] and on the other hand he is able to recognize that to love God is to surpass knowledge. The perplexity endures, for Cohen is unwilling finally to make the love of God the *mere* love of God. To love God is to love God's action, to love what God enables man to perform, to love the father of the poor, the redeemer of the sinner, the agent of man's perfection. It is not to love *the person* of God, but *the idea of his person.* Cohen never succeeds in moving beyond the Idea. Though he is able to identify the Idea with the historical destiny of Judaism and the Jewish people, to enlarge and texture the Idea with the heart-pangs and cries for justice to which the prophets and the Psalms testify, he is left at the end with the Idea.

At the same time as he will affirm that "the love of God shall surpass all, that nothing is left over in the consciousness of man when he loves God," [36] Cohen will interpret the Deuteronomic injunction as follows: "I cannot love God without devoting my whole heart (insofar as

[35] "Die Liebe zur Religion," *Jüdische Schriften,* Vol. II, pp. 142–61. Cf. p. 142, "Die Liebe zu Gott ist . . . die Erkenntnis der Sittlichkeit."

[36] *Jüdische Schriften,* introduction by Franz Rosenzweig, p. xlviii.

it beats for the sake of my fellow men), without devoting my entire soul (insofar as it is responsive to all currents of the spirit in the world around me), without devoting all my strength to this God (insofar as he has a correlation with man)." [37] The recognition that love transcends understanding, that it is beyond the rationale of uses and effects, is contradicted by the equally profound conviction that such love is ultimately unavailing. Cohen may create religion for the individual and salvage the person of God for faith; yet such allowance is to surrender to unreason.

Hermann Cohen was, alas, more modern than he knew. The God of the Middle Ages was known by his effects and verified by the regularity of his manifestation in nature and the human heart. He was known by his effects because it was believed that God existed and therefore could and would act. The solutions of the philosophic enlightenment were to withdraw nature from the provenance of God and interpose between God and the world a complex structure of intermediate agencies.[38] If there is idolatry in the world it is the idolatry of which the rabbis spoke: for the visible presence and evident power of sun and moon do indeed convince men that they, not their maker, should be worshipped. It is but one remove from the natural idolatry of the ancients to the sophisticated idolatry of the present world: what better than that man should worship only what his reason can allow? The idolatry of philosophy, the idolatry which confuses finitude with finality, is quite modern. Hermann Cohen struggled with this idolatry, perhaps knew it to be an idol, and yet could not destroy it. The idol and the true God were maintained in tension—avowed and repudiated, affirmed and yet qualified. It is true nevertheless, as Buber observed, that

[37] Rosenzweig quotes *Der Begriff der Religion,* introduction to *Jüdische Schriften,* p. xlviii.
[38] Arthur A. Cohen, "The Eclipse of God: Martin Buber" (review), *Judaism,* July, 1953, pp. 280–82.

in the effort to sustain the love of God as the love of an idea, the love itself testifies to the existence of the Beloved.[39]

The natural and the supernatural, much less the natural and the supernatural Jew, did not enter Cohen's philosophic perspective. These terms were essentially meaningless. Although they might enjoy a formal status independent of each other, they could not—ontological crystallizations which they were—be meaningful together. The natural and the supernatural operate as realities which correlate not only man and God at each moment of historical time, but the unity of those moments in their continuing occurrence from creation to redemption. The natural and the supernatural function both vertically between time and eternity and horizontally from the beginning to the end. Cohen could understand the past as reality which gave structure to the future, but the future—although he speaks of it continually—was somehow hazy and unclear. The future would see the victory of the Idea—the perfection of man and nature, but always a perfection which endured within time and was enclosed by it. God was at best the regulatory agency of the conscience, the pure ideal and the real goal. He was less over and against man, his opponent and counterfoil, than he was his rock and his support.

There is a pathos in Cohen's system of thought which is perhaps suggestive of the pathos of German Jewry: a passion to be individual and authentic (true to one's own nature and history) and a passion to be universal. The passion to be individual and authentic emerged in Cohen's proud recovery of his Judaism, but the passion to be universal was—in that particularly German syndrome—fated to be finally the desire to be the best German. As

[39] Martin Buber, "The Love of God and the Idea of Deity," trans. by I. M. Lask, *Israel and the World* (New York, Schocken Books, Inc., 1948), p. 65.

a result Cohen never succeeded in overcoming that particularist universalism which passes as German culture in favor of that universal particularism which is Judaism.

III. LEO BAECK (1874–1956)

It is not surprising that the late Rabbi Leo Baeck should have defined in 1954 the characteristics of his own theological understanding in an address on Moses Maimonides.[1] Maimonides, like Plato and Aristotle, serves to register the prevailing temper of Jewish thought. As he was a thinker of prodigious achievement and scope, each generation will find in him that which records and transmits the tendencies with which it is most concerned. What commends him to the attention of Jewish thought is that, above all, he was an intellectual—detached, patient, encompassing, and rational. Maimonides, like Thomas Aquinas, is the paradigm of belief informed by reason. As Thomas wept in supplication for the grace of wisdom before retiring to write, Maimonides trod the way of conventional observance and prayer while girding the universe with the bonds of reason. The intellectual is not encumbered by his faith; he surmounts its limitations by preparing for it the traps and cabals of reason. So Maimonides was to generations of Jewish intellectuals and believers who have used him as the justification for free and obedient reason.

The work of Maimonides is understood by Baeck to press forward from thought to life, from speculation to the historical act. "To the historical must be added the

[1] Leo Baeck, *Maimonides, der Mann, sein Werk und seine Wirkung* (Düsseldorf, Verlag Allgemeine Wochenzeitung der Juden in Deutschland, 1954). In English: "Unifying Philosophy, Science, and Prophecy: Moses Maimonides: The Man, His Work," trans. by Irving Pfefferblit, *Commentary Magazine*, April, 1955, pp. 346–55.

moral, for the historical is based on the moral." [2] The life of Maimonides is construed to exhibit an inner logic, a necessary unfolding from law to the principle of law, from the principle of law to the structure of the universe, from universe to God and then, by that rapid descent which Baeck believes indispensable to the great thinker, that plunge into concreteness in which the affairs of men unfold. The metaphysician becomes moralist because life compels thought to moral decision. It is not remarkable, therefore, that Baeck's view of Maimonides should coalesce with Baeck's view of the task of Judaism; for to his view, as to that of Maimonides, the pre-eminent concern of the Jew is moral action and the pre-eminent sources of moral action are the conscience and the intelligence. The significance of Maimonides to Baeck derives from the fact that life demands knowledge, and piety in knowledge is directed toward life.

The Maimonides of Leo Baeck emerges from that typically nineteenth-century liberal Jewish dilemma: How is it possible to relate the moral earnestness of prophetic Judaism, the imperative obligation of Kantian ethics, and an empirically objective and sound estimation of values and history (which Ernst Troeltsch and Wilhelm Dilthey, both Baeck's teachers, had so accurately described)? The dilemma of Leo Baeck is a real dilemma. It underlies his apologetic study, *The Essence of Judaism;* it defines the scope of his brilliant *tour de force,* "Romantic Religion"; it accents his marvelous recapitulation of the spirit of Judaism in *Dieses Volk.*[3] And yet, one is

[2] *Ibid.,* p. 355. "Maimonides became, wherever he was known and understood, a voice of conscience. He was like an admonition to that reverential thought which never loses itself, because it is concerned with the essential, with the idea; to that integrity of thought which does not make things easy for itself or play false with its task by superficiality or approximation; to that humility of thought which is always conscious of how much remains to be done; to that veracity of thought without which all knowledge and all sharpness of wit remain meaningless."

[3] Leo Baeck, *The Essence of Judaism,* trans. by Victor Grubenwieser and Leonard Pearl, rev. by Irving Howe (New York,

compelled to remark in Leo Baeck a strange unreality, a form of nineteenth-century eloquence and intensity, indignation, and hope which seem out of touch with the monstrous realities of the twentieth century. Were it not for the insistent presence of the man Leo Baeck—his moral heroism and his intellectual defiance of the conventions of his own liberalism—one might be tempted to brush him aside as but a cobweb of innocence which had been blown from the world of Kantian idealism and had come to rest—out of place—in this most uncongenial age.

Leo Baeck, however, cannot be dismissed. Though his thought may lack the abstract brilliance of that of his coworkers Cohen and Rosenzweig, it has an adamantine stubbornness and realism on which moral courage—never a virtue solely of the mind—is founded. Baeck, possibly more than any other thinker of the German Jewish renaissance, really believed unambiguously in his Judaism. That we cannot learn as much from his thought as from his life is not to denigrate his thought but to praise his life.

The life of Leo Baeck testifies to the moral power of his thought. But the problem of intellectual history is that not life but thought survives. Since life passes and a man's spirit returns to God, Judaism does not remember lives *as such*. It forgets the martyr, but remembers the martyrdom. It forgets the life, but recalls the deed. It dismisses the figure of the man, praising not him but what he affects and the influence he discharges. And not even the life, but history which confirms the life, demands the recollection of the Jew. We are compelled to consider the thought of Leo Baeck because of the heroism of Leo Baeck. It is the recollection of his life which makes his thought so exasperating and so painful, for our lives are

---

Schocken Books, Inc., 1948); "Romantic Religion," in *Judaism and Christianity*, trans. by Walter Kaufmann (Philadelphia, Jewish Publication Society of America, 1958); *Dieses Volk: Jüdische Existenz*, 2 vols. (Frankfurt am Main, Europäische Verlagsantstalt, 1955, 1957).

palpably unequal to his own, either in heroism or in the opportunity for heroism. To measure thought by the proof of life, to hold up the image of Jewish heroes to testify to the whole of Jewish history as though such can serve to strengthen our sense of obligation, is to mistake the modern world. It is surely to mistake the character of a world that survived the last war and approaches another. The energies of religious thought are no longer mobilized by the incentive of the "eternal task"; the ethical obligation fails to address us with commanding truth.

The life of Leo Baeck, to which his thought but testifies, is what remains to fortify thought. The conviction that life must vitalize intellectual truth, that only living in the midst of the world authenticates theology, underlies the whole of Leo Baeck's career as rabbi and thinker.

During 1899 and 1900 Adolf von Harnack, the influential interpreter of early Christianity and historian of the development of Christian dogma, delivered a series of sixteen lectures at the University of Berlin. These lectures were transcribed and published under the title *Das Wesen des Christentums*.[4] In the opening lecture, having debunked the late nineteenth-century (and a curiously mid-twentieth-century) penchant to cry up "religion as though it were a job-lot at a sale," Harnack observed: "The Christian religion is something simple and sublime; it means one thing and one thing only: Eternal life in the midst of time, by the strength and under the eyes of God. It is no ethical or social arcanum for the preservation or improvement of things generally." [5]

Leo Baeck, then rabbi of the Jewish community of Oppeln, reviewed Harnack's work. The review was penetrating and decisive. In 1905, without mentioning its predecessor, Leo Baeck wrote *Das Wesen des Judentums*

[4] Adolf Harnack, *What Is Christianity?*, trans. by Thomas Bailey Saunders (London, Williams and Norgate, Ltd., 1901).
[5] *Ibid.*, p. 8.

(The Essence of Judaism). This work, which defined Baeck's response to the religion of Adolf von Harnack, also defined the axes on which the belief of Leo Baeck was to rest: the tension of Judaism and Christianity; involvement in the uncompleted moral task of mankind and continuing trust in the unfulfilled promise of redemption. Where Christianity was to compromise, in Baeck's view, the meaning of creation in order to exalt a fulfilled redemption in Jesus Christ, Judaism was to insist upon the openness of creation and the absence of redemption.

Leo Baeck was the first contemporary Jewish thinker to see the problem of Judaism as existence before the face of Christendom. Hermann Cohen will insist, to be sure, upon the uniqueness and distinction of Judaism in a Christian world, but the distinction will be sharpened only by reference to the putative purity of Jewish "metaphysics"—its unequivocal assertion of the unity of God, its unqualified ethical direction, its insistence upon the inner perfection of creation. These concepts, tempered and joined in the optimistic forge of Kantian idealism, German socialism, and Jewish prophetism, will contrast with the passivity of late romantic religion. It will not, however, put the issue squarely: Judaism or Christianity?

With *The Essence of Judaism,* the contrast of Judaism and Christianity is stated and the case for Jewish faith and expectation defined. At the outset Baeck argues, hearing the echoes of Harnack's call to Christian commitment, that Judaism "has no dogmas and therefore no orthodoxy, as religious orthodoxy is usually understood." [6] Dogma, Baeck argues, is relevant only to a religion at whose heart "lies a mystical, consecrating act of faith—an act which alone can open the door to salvation." Such a religion requires, therefore, definite and historically

[6] Baeck, *The Essence of Judaism,* p. 12. See also the important historical and critical essay, "Hat das überlieferte Judentum Dogmen?" *Aus drei Jahrtausenden* (Tübingen, J. C. B. Mohr [Paul Siebeck], 1958), pp. 12–27.

transmissible conceptual images in order to accurately preserve and extend the knowledge of realized salvation.[7] "Such acts of salvation and gifts of grace are alien to Judaism; it does not pretend to bring heaven to earth."[8] Judaism is without dogma; it lacks and does not seek an authoritative head who can determine and impose dogma;[9] it repudiates any form of ecclesiasticism which would imagine itself empowered to reveal in the language of time the ineluctable nature of the eternal. Creation is given, the locus of man is defined, the ambit of his acts is described; however, at the heart of Judaism is the insistence that the future is still open. What remains open—what joins the givenness of the beginning to the indefinite but confident expectation of the end—is what Baeck calls "the eternal task" of man. It is to the eternal task that Judaism calls mankind.

The Judaism which Baeck confronted—the Judaism of the late nineteenth century—was one oppressed by the strictures of a self-conscious Protestant biblicism intent upon locating and limiting the Hebrew contribution to Western religion; a *Wissenschaft des Judentums* which, though uncovering hidden resources and forgotten dimensions, had made Judaism an *object* of history rather than life itself; a cacophony of Jewish religious movements, Reform, Conservative, Orthodox—each committed to an absolutizing version of the Jewish truth. The dilemma of Judaism, which Baeck acknowledged, was that it was no longer seen as a whole: as a unity which had not only emerged from history and been shaped by it, but whose essential character not man but God[10] had defined.

[7] Baeck, *The Essence of Judaism*, p. 13.

[8] *Idem.*

[9] *Ibid.*, p. 15.

[10] About this there can be no mistake. Baeck was no liberal if by liberalism is meant the reduction of Judaism to the vagaries of historical adjustment. God convoked Israel. The covenant is real; the election is real; the chosenness is real. The liberalism of Leo Baeck consists, not in an indefiniteness regarding the origin of Judaism, but in an uncertainty regarding the form of its unfolding.

To define the "whole" of Judaism, to articulate and display that "unity" which is Judaism and the Jewish people, does not require that one press beyond history. History defines all that the Jew need know of Judaism. It discloses his origins, stamps upon him the seal of obligation, casts him forth upon the sea of discovery and pursuit, and sets him down upon the hard rock of chastisement and judgment. Judaism is a morphology. Its wholeness is present only in its unfolding, in its historical past, in its historical present, in its conviction about the historical and ultimate future. It is definable by its consequences rather than by its doctrines, because its primary concern is with "man's attitude toward the world,"[11] its purpose is the reformation and perfection of that attitude, its image of beatitude is the divine confirmation of the truth of its intention and the virtue of its pursuit. Judaism is, in short, ethical monotheism. The God of the prophets (and, as for Hermann Cohen, Judaism is fully manifested only with the prophets) is the God of ethical intention.

Ethical monotheism is not left by Baeck to the desiccating sirocco of liberal rationalism or to the sentimentality of the social reformer who would reduce it to mere good works. Such a reduction of Baeck's position would do scant justice to the scope of his understanding of Jewish history and his awareness of the exigencies of Jewish tradition. Baeck neither evaporates the authority of the commandments, nor explains away the mystery. *Gebot* (commandment) and *Geheimnis* (mystery) remain central terms of his thinking; but as with many such pairs of concepts their relation to one another is polar, dynamic, and fluid. They form the basis of the Jewish dialectic. But the terms of the dialectic are less important than the movement which passes between them. Although this leads to considerable vagueness and imprecision in Baeck's definition of concepts, it does compel a certain

[11] Baeck, *The Essence of Judaism*, p. 60.

recognition of the vitality of religious existence which more formal theologies often fail to transmit. The movement between mystery and commandment is less a movement between God and man as such, than it is a movement within man.[12] What concerns Baeck is that man should achieve not precision in understanding but sublime involvement in the work of creation and redemption. Theology is therefore restricted by him to pedagogy. A concept is useful only if it instructs life; a doctrine is valuable only if it functions in the ordering of human ends. Baeck exhibits Jewish life. He rarely argues it. Judaism is never a problem; but it is always a task.

It is ironic that Leo Baeck is most telling in his attack on Christianity. It is ironic for no less a reason than that it illustrates the difficulty of most contemporary Jewish thought. Baeck is opposed to dogma; he is opposed to formal theology; he is less concerned with knowing God than with affirming the Jewish understanding of God. His argumentation always pivots upon the human coefficient to truth—What does truth mean here and now? How does it function in life? What meaning does truth have by *my* standards, my *human* standards? It rarely makes the effort to push behind personal truth to an apprehension of truth itself. In effect, it sees God in man's universe and not man in God's. Although Baeck might disagree profoundly with such a formulation, we can find no evidence to contradict our conviction that God functioned for him somewhat as He functioned for Cohen—the reality who validates human effort. God is the all for man: He is the reason of man, the motive of man, the argument for human enterprise. God gives man the task, sustains man in its pursuit, and encourages man to press forward to its fulfillment.

[12] Leo Baeck, *Wege im Judentum: Aufsätze und Reden* (Berlin, Schocken Verlag, 1933), pp. 33–48; "Geheimnis und Gebot," English translation: "Mystery and Commandment," in *Judaism and Christianity*, pp. 171–84.

To the open universe of Jewish trust and labor, Christianity comes with an assertion of decisive finality. Shocking as such a thesis might appear to Christians, Baeck considers Christianity a romantic religion. As he has argued in his essay on "Romantic Religion," there is a continuum which runs from St. Paul to Friedrich Schlegel. Romantic religion, paraphrasing Schlegel's definition of the romantic, "seeks its goals in the now mythical, now mystical visions of the imagination. Its world is the realm in which all rules are suspended; it is the world of the irregular, the extraordinary and the miraculous, that world which lies beyond all reality, the remote which transcends all things." [13]

If indeed romantic religion transfers the expectations of man from this world to another, it would follow, Baeck suggests, that "romanticism lacks any strong ethical impulse, any will to conquer life ethically." [14] Romanticism —a surrender to the divine, an evaporation of effort into feeling, a rejection of the moral imperatives of the immediate historical task—is present in all religions. "Every religion has its dream of faith in which appearance and reality seek to mingle; each has its own twilight valley; each knows of world-weariness and contempt for the factual." [15] But where in one religion it is a current which runs weak, a mere tremolo amid the roar of life, another religion will dam up more powerful waters in order to give the eddy artificial strength.

Christianity is a religion which has made the romantic dominant. Its essential romanticism lies in the fact that it believes itself to have fulfilled life—it turns the believer from the immediacies of life toward an apocalyptic future; it trains the believer to forgo the real demands of this world for the promises of the next; it admits the be-

[13] "Romantic Religion," pp. 189 f.

[14] *Ibid.*, p. 192. Rudolf Bultmann agrees with such an interpretation of early Christian thought: cf. *History and Eschatology* (Edinburgh, The University Press, 1957), p. 36.

[15] "Romantic Religion," pp. 195 f.

liever to a mysterious life that is gained by "faith in a force of grace, entering the believer from above through a sacrament,"[16] and promising him redemption from the bonds of guilt and death. The triumph of Christianity is the triumph of romanticism.[17]

"Romantic Religion," like any apologetic polemic, oversimplifies. Its power derives from the uncompromising scope of the attack, from its unwillingness to acknowledge temporizing qualification. All Christianity disappears before Baeck's assault—what is most profound and true in Christianity, its Jewish ancestry, is held debased by a doctrine which commences with St. Paul and proceeds through St. Augustine and the Reformation. The essential failing of all romantic religion—from the cults of Isis, Adonis, and Osiris to the sacramental system of Christianity—is that man is rendered superfluous. Man is created, endowed with intelligence and will, those elements of freedom, invested with obligation, and charged with the commandments; but in a later moment creation is judged corrupt and beyond salvage, and the advent of a divine savior is demanded. What becomes of intelligence and will? They are henceforth passive receptacles of the divine. Reason does not avail ("In all who have faith in Christ," says Luther, "reason shall be killed; else faith does not govern them; for reason fights against faith."[18]) nor do commandments ("What are the Ten Commandments to me? Why should I require the law or good works for blessedness? When the nourishment of Christ does it, I may not do any good works to attain eternal life."[19]); works are demeaned; neither effort nor accomplishment count before a God who can create and recant his creation. Man is borne on sufferance—faith and grace supply what man cannot provide.

The romantic dimension of religion is that man is encouraged, if not compelled in the interests of his own salvation, to abandon reason, to abjure freedom and deci-

[16] *Ibid.*, p. 197.
[17] *Ibid.*, p. 198.
[18] *Ibid.*, p. 207, cf. note 4.
[19] *Ibid.*, p. 277, cf. note 33.

sion and cast himself helpless before God. In Luther's phrase, the true believer is to become "as one paralyzed." [20] Indeed, what is essential to romantic religion and essential to Christianity is the passivity of man before God. "Man is no more than the mere object of God's activity, of grace or of damnation; he does not recognize God, God merely recognizes him; he *becomes* a child of redemption or of destruction, 'forced into disobedience' or raised up to salvation." [21] The characteristically paradoxical formulation of the Gospels, the losing in order to find, the forgetting in order to know, the abandonment in order to discover—all these announcements are but so many examples of what romantic religion always requires: the sacrifice of intellect and the sacrifice of will. It is summarized in that famous apostrophe: "Do not seek, for to him who has faith all is given." The will exists only to subdue the world, to blunt its temptations, to tranquilize its abundant vitality. What is an essential dimension of all religion, "a religious consecration or even seizure," is taken by romantic religion for the fulfillment of religion and for its ultimate truth.[22] The romanticism of Christianity could not give birth to other than an exclusivist church. If indeed the miracle of the sacrament is the guarantor of salvation—if indeed faith cannot be won, but can only be bestowed by grace—then surely a church, the sole and continuous guardian of the sacrament, becomes indispensable. "It alone has faith and it alone makes blessed; it is the vicar of God on earth, and only those are with God who belong to it; it shuts and opens the gates to the Kingdom of Heaven. It is everything, and the individual in his striving and searching is nothing; he is absolutely dependent on it and can only share its faith. Whatever would be different and independent, is separated from salvation and turned over to the abyss." [23] One cannot help but speak of such a church as St. John spoke: "No one cometh unto the Father, but

[20] *Ibid.*, p. 205, cf. note 3.
[21] *Ibid.*, p. 204.
[22] *Ibid.*, p. 210.
[23] *Ibid.*, p. 228.

by me." [24] Thus the exclusivity of salvation, to which St. Augustine (always enthusiastic) felt compelled to add: "I should have no faith in the *gospel*, if the authority of the Catholic church did not induce me." [25]

It should come as no surprise that Baeck considered St. Paul to be the fountainhead of Christian romanticism. Paul, confronting the unfulfilled dreams of pagan mysteries—the dying God and the returning God—and the traditional expectation of Israel—the redeeming God and the suffering servant who prepares the way of redemption—found in Jesus of Nazareth the Christ who unites Israel and the pagan. "The significance of Jesus, who had become the Christ of his people, could not be that he had become the king of the Jews, their king by the grace of God, their admonisher, comforter, and helper, but his life and his power signified the one, the greatest thing, that he was the resurrected, miracle-working, redeeming God. . . . And for all who owned him, who had faith in him and possessed him in sacrament and mystery, the day that was promised had become today, had been fulfilled. In him Jew and pagan were the new man, the true Israel, the true present." [26] Paul, beholding in childhood and youth the inheritance of Judaism and the mystery cults of paganism, fashioned a doctrine which united them. His religion "became victorious in a world which had become weary and sentimental. . . ." [27] But in Pauline Christianity, Baeck contends, "what had been most essential in the ancient mysteries is preserved." [28] The fate of a god becomes the inescapable lot of man and the substance of all life. Not the created order nor the moral order, but a pageant of salvation, "a heavenly-earthly drama," [29] is unfolded. What triumphs in Pauline Christianity is, in Baeck's judgment, "romantic myth." [30]

Friedrich Nietzsche, an older contemporary of Leo

[24] John 14:6.
[25] "Romantic Religion," p. 233, cf. note 13.
[26] *Ibid.*, p. 201.
[27] *Ibid.*, p. 202.
[28] *Idem.*
[29] *Idem.*
[30] *Ibid.*, p. 203.

Baeck, died in 1900. Nietzsche's language may well have differed from that of Leo Baeck, but in their assessment of Jesus and Paul and the romantic myth of Christianity they shared much.

It has been well observed that Nietzsche's repudiation of the Christ may be considered under two aspects:[31] the opposition of faith to action and the opposition of faith to reason. Indeed Nietzsche characterizes with bitter satire the hypocrisy of Christendom. He describes "the miscarriage of falseness"[32] which divides the Christian by profession from the Christian by act. As Nietzsche expresses it in *The Will to Power*, "*the Christian acts like all the world* and has a Christianity of ceremonies and *moods*."[33] Whereas Jesus left an inheritance of action, a *praxis* which "will be possible at all times,"[34] the Christian religion is founded, not upon the instruction of Jesus, but upon the institutions of Paul. Paul substituted faith for life, projected *fides quae creditur*—the faith which one believes as a given, a required and objective datum—in place of living faith, the *fides qua creditur,*[35] the faith *with* which one believes, with which one undertakes the task of life. Paul is for Nietzsche, as for Baeck, "the first Christian."[36] As Walter Kaufmann has commented: "Unable to fulfill even the Jewish law—not to speak of Jesus' so much more demanding way of life—he [Paul] conceived of faith in

[31] Walter Kaufmann, *Nietzsche* (New York, Meridian Books, Inc., 1956), p. 292.

[32] Friedrich Nietzsche, *Der Antichrist,* in the Musarion edition of the *Gesammelte Werke,* 1920–1929, p. 38; Kaufmann, *Nietzsche,* p. 293 and Key to Abbreviations and Bibliography, p. 361. All translations from Nietzsche quoted in these pages are by Walter Kaufmann and appear on those pages of his work, *Nietzsche,* to which reference is made.

[33] *Der Wille zur Macht,* in *Gesammelte Werke,* p. 191; Kaufmann, *Nietzsche,* p. 293.

[34] *Der Antichrist,* in *Gesammelte Werke,* p. 39; Kaufmann, *Nietzsche,* p. 293.

[35] Baeck, "Romantic Religion," p. 230.

[36] Friedrich Nietzsche, *Der Morgenröte,* in *Gesammelte Werke,* p. 68; Kaufmann, *Nietzsche,* p. 294.

Christ as a substitute." [37] Nietzsche sees Pauline Christianity, not as the fulfillment of the teaching of Jesus, but as the manifestation of resentment, inability, romantic failure. Paul could not fulfill the *praxis* of Jesus; his escape from failure, his transformation of the Jesus of life into the Jesus of the Cross and the Jesus of the Resurrection was the rejection of life. "The 'glad tidings' was followed on its heels by the *very worst:* that of Paul. In Paul was embodied the opposite type of that of the 'bringer of the glad tidings,' the genius in hatred, in the vision of hatred, in the inexorable logic of hatred." [38] Nietzsche opposes Paul as the apostle of a vengeful myth —a myth of repudiation and escape; he considers the transformation of such a symbol as the Resurrection into dogma to be ultimately destructive of life, a devaluation of human effort and activity; he judges the unworldly romanticism of Christianity to have provided a rationalization for human destructiveness: man, weakened by resentment, indulges his anger and hostility in the confidence of divine support; Luther, in the tradition of Paul, could choose to elevate faith only because of his "incapacity for Christian works." As faith triumphs over action in the judgment of Nietzsche, so faith triumphs over reason. Conviction is no proof of truth; martyrdom and suffering no confirmation of clear understanding. To bring the act of faith as evidence of truth—the willingness to suffer and fanatic imperturbability—is as much evidence of deception and folly as of truth.[39]

Friedrich Nietzsche and Leo Baeck condemn Christianity: Christianity is for both a debasement of life. And yet, in reflecting upon this remarkable concurrence—the anguished herald of the death of God and the serene rabbi of Theriesenstadt—it becomes clear that Nietzsche

[37] Kaufmann, *Nietzsche*, p. 294.
[38] Friedrich Nietzsche, *Der Antichrist*, in *Gesammelte Werke*, p. 42; Kaufmann, *Nietzsche*, p. 295.
[39] Cf. Walter Kaufmann's discussion of Nietzsche's attitude toward Luther and the Reformation (*Nietzsche*, pp. 300–309).

contra Christiana would be, before Leo Baeck, an *adversus judaeos*. For what is it that Leo Baeck opposes to romantic religion? What is the vaunted classical religion of which Judaism is progenitor and Christianity the corrupted descendant? It may be that Baeck felt that his exposition of classical religion had been completed in his *Essence of Judaism,* that there was no need to go beyond the definition of Judaism which he had offered there ("Judaism is the religion of ethical optimism").[40] If, indeed, that was his conviction, it was one which he might have reconsidered, for before the intensity of his criticism of Christian romanticism his discussion of Judaism seems eminently pallid and uneventful. In "Romantic Religion," as in *The Essence of Judaism,* what is characteristic of Christianity is the repudiation of time, history, and the created order—hence the impossibility of taking the ethical task seriously. The act bows to grace, the moral decision weakens before promises that only faith can justify. But the reverse—when the attack ceases and the defense begins, when Christianity is vanquished and the power of Judaism must be displayed—is unconvincing. Judaism is the commandment, the task, freedom, self-affirmation, dynamism, openness.[41] "In classical religion, man is to become free through the commandment . . ."[42] The commandment —an exceedingly Jewish word—is given a meaning, however, which is more explicitly Kantian than Jewish. The commandment, the *mitzvah,* is in classical Judaism that which God demands. The demand of God, the rabbis were well aware, may sometimes be confirmed by conscience and justified by reason, but it may often transcend reason and seem to revile conscience (one has but to recall the considerable difficulty which Abraham's sacrifice of Isaac gave rabbinic commentators). Baeck, however, finds the commandments confirmed by the argument of Kantian ethics. Baeck's citation of "Kant's pure consciousness of

[40] Baeck, *The Essence of Judaism,* p. 84.
[41] *Ibid.,* p. 21. [42] *Ibid.,* p. 22.

duty"[43] is as much opposed to Luther's conception of man's nature as is his citation of Rabbi Ben Azzai's apothegm that "the reward of a duty *is* the duty" in opposition to any subjective eudaemonism.[44]

Judaism is undeniably the partisan of the created order. We do not question the legitimacy of Baeck's affirmation of the Jewish will to life, the conviction that history is open before God, that God presents the task, that man accepts the task, that God offers His Kingdom, but that the price of the Kingdom is "the yoke of the commandments." Where the difference comes is in the assumption that the description of error and imbalance in Christianity is sufficient to make the truth of Judaism transparent. But Judaism does not triumph as a *pis aller.* It is as liable as early Christianity to the Nietzschean rebuke of a "resentment" morality—by the time of the return from the Babylonian exile and the composition of Deutero-Isaiah the self-assertiveness and vitality evidenced in the historical books of the Bible had passed. In its place the searching out of divine reasons for human pain and punishment, the quest for a justification of suffering and oppression, is pursued, the transmutation of poverty and humility into virtues is completed. What is most characteristic of Leo Baeck—the combination of Biblical love with Kantian ethics—will receive a double portion of Nietzschean scorn.

To be sure, we need not bring Nietzsche onto the scene. However, he serves Judaism, as well as Christianity, as therapist. He makes as clear the deficiency of Baeck's defense of classical Judaism as Baeck has made clear the inadequacy of romantic Christianity.

Leo Baeck serves Judaism with an ultimately unsatisfactory but profoundly moving example of hortatory theology. Judaism takes creation seriously; Judaism is confident of the ultimate triumph of the good; Judaism insists upon the final vindication of divine justice. His-

[43] *Ibid.*, p. 66.

[44] *Ibid.*, p. 180.

tory will somehow unfold the divine intention. Toward the achievement of this vindication man must strive; the ethical commandments afford him the instruments of the pursuit. The Sabbath, the festivals are pedagogic devices for strengthening man's resolve to continue the pursuit. Can this be any more than a transitional theology? Are we any longer certain that the sermonic inculcation of virtue is sufficient to convince the modern world that the eternal task still holds promise? What is finally lacking in Baeck is argument: either to convince us that the ethical obligation may be grounded in the universality of reason and good will or to reconsider the possibility that ethics is, at best, but a precarious deduction from God's disclosure of himself as the Holy One.

The skepticism with which one confronts the presentation of Judaism as an ethical religion is far-reaching. Indeed, one may even question whether its ethical intuitions constitute its most profound contribution to man's religious understanding. The concept of ethical monotheism is a peculiarly nineteenth-century formulation—a formulation fashioned, moreover, in that never-to-be-repeated spectacle of Jewish competition with Protestant Biblical criticism and German liberal nationalism. The Jew had to give something to the West. Since he could give only what he found in common with Christianity he was compelled to see himself as the sire of authentic Christianity. Authentic Christianity was of necessity pre-Paulinian; it was inescapably the morality of the Gospels; hence that considerable literature of late nineteenth- and early twentieth-century liberal Judaism—the common sources of Judaism and Christianity. The Judeo-Christian tradition (from the Jewish side) was to be found in ethics. From that time forward Judaism became the religion of ethics, confidence, and optimism.

The perspective of liberal Judaism which Baeck articulates with such moving conviction is finally unconvincing. Baeck conceives the fundamental movement of God and man to take place in the sphere described by divine mystery and divine commandment. Mystery projects the promise; commandment defines the task. It is evident that if the ethical commandment is founded upon the testimony of the Bible, then God is *not only* inscrutable mystery; the ethical command is an effect of the divine personality, a witnessing to his presence and concern. Man's acknowledgment of the divine mystery is affirmed by his acceptance of the task of the commandments. The commandment is then no simple deduction of reason in reflection upon the universality of good will and the unavoidable demand of moral duty. If the commandments were only rational the evidence of the Bible would serve man as no more than venerable testimony; it would serve only to confirm the antiquity of moral concern; it would be but one more link in the chain of rational authority which instructs man in his task. The dilemma of Leo Baeck is that by insisting upon the divine mystery he insists upon the power of God as Person. As Person, God is more than the sum of his commandments; the commandments do not exhaust all that we may know or understand or intuit to be the Person of God. God is the Holy One: as such he is more than the moral law, for the moral law cannot exhaust his holiness. Clearly, if Judaism is simply commandment it could be founded completely (whether convincingly is another question) upon an argument from nature; God becomes little more than an instrument of pedagogy, an idea which expresses and rationalizes the totality of moral aspiration. If religion is more than this—if God is a subject before subjects—then God is not only mystery (which is to say his personality is not wholly unknown to faith) nor do the moral commandments exhaust his nature (which is to say that revelation discloses more of the divine nature than moral directives).

The task of Jewish theology is to interpret, not merely to state, the tension between mystery and commandment. There can be little question that one way to the answer lies in deepening one's understanding of the community which perceives the mystery and preserves the commandments. Such a community is not only an heroic minority, an index of world culture and civility: it is a holy community. Indeed this is what the Jewish people was called to be—a holy community. The holy community mirrors the holiness of God. Its mystery lies in the fact that it is not, as God is not, the sum of its obligations. The holy community is, as God is, a holy person. Its corporate destiny is formed out of the multiplicity of its obligations —the variety and extent of its commandments—and the singularity of its end, which is to reflect the holiness and personality of God.

This holiness which is accessible only to the oblique consciousness of faith cannot be the coefficient of the moral law. The moral law is too plausible, too reasonable, too direct to encompass a history of anguish, suffering, and martyrdom. As God exceeds his commandments, so the Jewish people exceeds its acts.

IV. FRANZ ROSENZWEIG (1886–1929)

All thought is derivative. It responds to the pressures which culture elaborates and tradition transmits. We should have to recover the innocence and pristine sophistication of the pre-Socratics to achieve a form of underived speculation; to discover at this moment that the essence of the universe is "water" or "number" would be to make ourselves one with the pre-Socratics, while admitting our hopeless ineptitude as modern thinkers. We cannot retrace the path to that innocence which would announce truth with wonder, fascination, and gnomic obscurity.

We are bound to the past, to successive ages of thought which have arisen and vanquished their predecessors. The language of thought is spun through the delicate ambience of time, in the continuous *durée* in which no single word remains reliable. All thought tends to submit to the vicissitudes of its ancestry. The pathos of language —its inability to sustain the continuity of the past while naming and describing the experiences of the present— creates a rupture within language, an inadequacy, an unreliability, a failure to maintain within the flow of time a fixity which is enduring. Each of us is aware that perhaps a portion of our despair arises from the fact that we no longer possess a language which is adequate to express our feelings. Pain, suffering, the meaningless are preserved as a hard core of unknowing, for adequate language deserts us. Neither the classic language of wisdom and reason nor the Biblical certainty of God and revelation suffices to set our experience upon the rock of the real. All tends to float loose and unfixed. We are liberated indeed from the vested sureties of the past, but it is a liberation purchased at high price. Our skepticism and indecision, our critiques of religion and philosophy are carried on either in the high style of intellectual muckraking or in the careful, precise, and limiting discourse of logical analysis. The former acknowledges the real but conceals it by rendering all language unequal to its display (somewhat as an amateur magician who knows how all the tricks are done but cannot perform them convincingly); the latter limits the real to the narrow purview of language, making language the ultimate reality, but an ultimate which is impoverished, unimaginative, and barren of relevancy. It is acknowledged on the one hand that language points to the real, while on the other hand the real to which language points is so trivial and unyielding as to leave us as unknowing as before.

The medieval Christian tradition was able to speak of "things" and "people" as *vestigia Dei et imagines Dei.* Presuming a connection between speech and reality, the medieval was able to accredit language. Language was no veil shrouding reality, vague, insubstantial, elusive. Language pointed to reality. In pointing to reality it was capable of articulating the unity which sustained the variety intellect had described. Language expressed the world, man, and God which speculation had distinguished and which culture had brought into living unity. Art, science, philosophy, and religion were not, as they are at present, distinct, autonomous, and uncommunicate disciplines. The artist of the Middle Ages was not intent upon the expression of a portion of reality; the philosopher was not embarrassed by the enormity of his visions; the religious were not indifferent or hostile to the manifestations of the *saeculum*. The medieval architect was as responsive to philosophy and theology as the theologian was respectful of the power of reason and the glorification which architecture sought to bestow upon creation.[1] Culture was an intellectual unity in which all moved toward the articulation of ultimate concerns.

The twentieth century cannot appeal to such unities. Culture is fractionalized and dismantled. The unities of purpose which enabled artist and philosopher to gather in the courtyard of Abbot Suger or centuries later to inaugurate the decline of homogeneous culture in the salons of eighteenth-century Berlin or Paris have disappeared. Artist, philosopher, scientist, and theologian have had little to say to one another for half a century. Retired into the privacy of their meditations, turned inward from the glare of the world's tarnish, the theologian has become a symbolist, the philosopher has become a diamond cutter, the artist has become an analyst of color, form, and motion.

Franz Rosenzweig was born into a world already ministering to the wounds of its division.

The European world of the twentieth century, as Rosenzweig consistently described it, was one in which Hegel had completed philosophy. The philosopher was no

[1] Erwin Panofsky, *Gothic Architecture and Scholasticism* (New York, Meridian Books, Inc., 1957).

longer a pagan, a *discipulus Graeciae,* as the Church Father Tertullian had called him. The philosopher par excellence was no longer the heretic who stood outside the door of the Church caviling against her irrationalisms. The philosopher had succeeded, at last, in identifying revelation with history, Christianity with the fulfillment of the divine spirit. The daily unfolding of historical events was not indifferent to providence, but was, as Hegel argued, "essentially His Work." [2] Mind and spirit became one; the concrete was absorbed by the unfolding of Mind; history was merely the scene on which the Spirit was realized and God justified. Christianity was triumphant, division was past, incompletion was overcome, the stranger and the heretic were vanquished.

The triumph of Christianity is, however, problematic, for it is purchased at the price of its fundamental nature. Christianity, which must continue to retrieve the world from paganism, has taken the pagan to itself, and in Christianizing the pagan, Rosenzweig suggests, it has itself been paganized.[3] The Church neither missionizes the external pagan as did the Petrine Church; nor does it baptize with the Pauline sufficiency of faith the inner pagan that the Renaissance produced. Both the Petrine and Pauline churches which Joachim of Flora and Rosenzweig's precursor, Schelling, had described have perished. What follows in the wake of Hegel is the universality of the Church of the Holy Spirit, the Johannine Church. The modern Church is no longer in submission to the Holy Roman Empire or the authority of the secular state. According to Rosenzweig modern nationalism is the "complete Christianizing of the concept of people-

[2] G. W. F. Hegel, *The Philosophy of History,* trans. by J. Sibree (New York, Willey Book Company, 1944), p. 456.

[3] The Petrine, Pauline, and Johannine moments of Christian history are elaborated in Alexander Altmann's brilliant essay, "Franz Rosenzweig on History," in Alexander Altmann, ed., *Between East and West* (London, Leo Baeck Institute, East and West Library, 1958), pp. 194–212; cf. particularly pp. 195 f.

hood."[4] The split which Luther enforced between the pure inwardness of faith and the external world, independent of the authority of the spirit, removed Christianity from control of the world. The idealism of Hegel made the Protestant error into an objective truth—spirit can really, it would appear, produce the world out of itself. The moment paganism comes to reassert the primacy of the individual, to initiate the Christian soul into freedom, the Pauline power of faith is dispersed by the free spirit of Johannine universality.

Rosenzweig undoubtedly constructed the history of his times. It was neither as self-evident nor as neatly divided into periods as he described it. His description was not intended, however, to be mere cavalier conceptualization. Rosenzweig's intellectual development must be seen against the background of his passage from philosophy through Christianity to Judaism. Rosenzweig was characteristically dissatisfied with partial turns of the soul—he could not maintain mixed allegiances. Each life decision was accompanied by a transformation of his vision of the universe, each stage of his life shaped the next and was carried forward into the future to be refashioned and transcended. As life had destiny, so the convictions which activated life enjoyed a destiny, an historical purpose and ultimacy. The particular life was not a disinterested and uninvolved appendage of the universe, but its agent. Judaism was to be located in the universe against the background of philosophy and Christianity. If Hegel ended philosophy, if the Johannine Church was post-Hegelian Christianity, then Rosenzweig was no mere respondent to events, but a providential occasion of a new beginning.

To begin anew, the past must first be appraised, its insufficiencies described and abandoned. Nineteenth-cen-

[4] "Die vollendete Christianisierung des Volksbegriffs." Franz Rosenzweig, *Briefe*, ed. by E. Simon and Edith Rosenzweig (Berlin, Schocken Verlag, 1935), p. 686. See also Altmann (ed.) *Between East and West*, p. 199.

tury German philosophy generally adopted one of two alternate conceptions of the universe: either man and the world were assimilated into the Absolute—Mind, Spirit, Being, and Thought being considered parallel and mutually defining terms—or else the individual, rising in protest against the aggrandizing Absolute, protested that he would not be considered a transitory moment in the universe. The Absolute surpassed revelation and overwhelmed man and history.

The individual, finding "an Archimedean fulcrum outside the knowable Whole," dissented.[5] Sören Kierkegaard, acknowledging with irony that however much he might be "pure being," a mere moment, pause, gasp in the Absolute, he is also a sinner, preoccupied with his sin, aware of his redeemer, and infinitely distant from his redemption. Kierkegaard affirmed that not the Whole, not the Absolute, but the private passion and subjectivity of the person alone mattered. If indeed philosophy could not, as Rosenzweig understood the Kierkegaardian demurral, encompass the person; if it had truly disqualified itself from accounting for the condition of man, then the comprehensive posture of the Hegelian system was an empty pretension. Thought might indeed triumph, but man escaped. Kierkegaard, as Rosenzweig summarizes his view, disputed "the right of philosophy to enter a territory whose existence it denied . . ."[6] Having denied philosophy's competence to treat of men, the new philosophers—Schopenhauer and Nietzsche—appeared even to question the right of philosophy to traverse its previously uncontested domain: the world. Schopenhauer declined to accept the world as it had been presented to him, refused indeed to acknowledge the criteria of validation which philosophy had transmitted for centuries. Rather,

[5] Nahum N. Glatzer, *Franz Rosenzweig: His Life and Thought* (New York, Schocken Books, Inc., and Farrar, Straus, & Young, Inc., 1953), p. 185; Franz Rosenzweig, *Der Stern der Erlösung*, 3rd ed. (Heidelberg, Verlag Lambert Schneider, 1954), p. 12.

[6] Glatzer, *Franz Rosenzweig*, p. 186; Rosenzweig, *Der Stern der Erlösung*, p. 13.

"he describes as the content of philosophy the reaction of an individual mind to the impression made upon it by the world. 'An individual mind'—it was after all the human being, Arthur Schopenhauer, who here occupied the position that . . . should have been occupied by an abstract problem." [7] Since life was, as Schopenhauer once described it to Goethe, "a sorry thing," life—not the Whole, not the world—became the object of thought.[8] Schopenhauer the man, not the ratiocinator, chose to confront the world and, in the process of thinking of the world, could not help but reflect upon himself and the pitiable condition of men. With Nietzsche, whom Rosenzweig adjudges a complete "integer to the very last" [9] (poet, saint, and philosopher) "the individual human being—or rather *an* individual, a very definite individual—gained ascendency over philosophy. . . . The philosopher ceased to be a negligible quantity in his philosophy." [10]

Having described the course which runs from Hegel to Nietzsche, from the objective mind to the subjective integer, Rosenzweig is not content with the spectacle of intellectual debris. If the one had made the world, man, and God into functions of thought and the other had succeeded in destroying such specious unity, it remained true that they were still *facts*. The affirmation or denial of objective thought, the disappearance or reaffirmation of subjectivity in itself, did not demonstrate that the *world* and *man* and *God* were other than real and obdurate facts.

In his famous essay "The New Thinking," [11] written toward the close of his tragically brief life and some three

[7] Glatzer, *Franz Rosenzweig*, p. 187; Rosenzweig, *Der Stern der Erlösung*, p. 14.
[8] *Idem.*
[9] Glatzer, *Franz Rosenzweig*, p. 188; Rosenzweig, *Der Stern der Erlösung*, p. 15.
[10] *Idem.*
[11] Franz Rosenzweig, "Das neue Denken," *Kleinere Schriften* (Berlin, Schocken Verlag, 1937), pp. 373–98; partially translated in Glatzer, *Franz Rosenzweig*, pp. 190–208.

years after he had prepared the second edition of his masterwork, *The Star of Redemption,* Rosenzweig summarizes the principles which *The Star* exemplified.

Rosenzweig conceives of the world, of man, and of God as facts. Philosophy may seek to make one the function of the other—to absorb world and man into God as do the ecstatic mystics; to objectify man and God as but necessities without which nature could not function; or to spin God and the world out of the caverns of the self. The passion of philosophy—perhaps its sole passion—is to locate the essence of the universe.[12] To accomplish this task it must necessarily avoid an Aristotelian discrimination of pertinent facts and relevant sciences, independent disciplines and operative principles, in favor of a characteristically Platonic reduction. Philosophy is an alchemist, working out "all possible permutations" [13] of the single reduction. It is reluctant to grant even hypothetical validity to a position which denies that everything is capable of being assimilated and reduced to something else.[14] This dilemma is as accurate in the case of the mystic who discovers all in God as of the psychologist who makes of nature and God but the reflection of the self. And yet, as Rosenzweig is acutely aware, these very reductions point the way beyond themselves, for however one manipulates the abacus of the universe, one always confronts "the human in man, the worldly in the world, and the godly in God. And it will find the godly only in God, the worldly only in the world, and the human only in man." [15] Shift and turn, the thinker will always return to the facts. In trying to discern the nature of man, world, and God he must first consider them independently, *as they are,* isolated and bracketed off from all other experience.[16]

[12] Rosenzweig, "Das neue Denken," p. 377; Glatzer, *Franz Rosenzweig*, p. 191.

[13] *Idem.*

[14] *Idem.*

[15] Rosenzweig, "Das neue Denken," pp. 378 f.; Glatzer, *Franz Rosenzweig*, p. 192.

[16] The consideration of the facts as they are in themselves, shorn

The corrupting influence which philosophy has had on common sense is traced by Rosenzweig in his little book *Understanding the Sick and the Healthy*.[17] In this work Rosenzweig describes the paralysis of common sense before philosophy, its inability to see what it sees and, more crucially, to trust what it sees and build upon its sight and trust a structure of meaningful relations, a unity fashioned from the discreteness of the facts of life. Could philosophy indeed reduce and permutate if it did not first seize the world in its separateness? It knows something that is world, man, and God; it means something by these names; it must understand something of their character even to speak of them. Rosenzweig restores a version of the classic Anselmian ontological proof [18] for

of their constitutive relations, is reminiscent of Husserl's method of "phenomenological reduction"; although where Rosenzweig is preoccupied with defining the facts as they are in experience and as they appear to common sense, Husserl will seek "to set aside the limitations to knowledge essentially involved in every nature-directed form of investigation . . . until we have eventually before us the free outlook of 'transcendentally' purified phenomena. . . ." (Edmund Husserl, *Ideas*, trans. by W. R. Boyce Gibson [London, George Allen & Unwin, Ltd., 1931], p. 43). What is significant is that both Rosenzweig and Husserl, with vastly different objectives, were aware that the object had to be recovered and investigated before truths about it could be defined.

[17] Franz Rosenzweig, *Understanding the Sick and the Healthy* (New York, The Noonday Press, 1953). This work, written by Rosenzweig during July, 1921 (see introduction by Nahum N. Glatzer, p. 9), was entitled in German *Das Büchlein vom gesunden und kranken Menschenverstand*. To have been more in keeping with the significance of the work and its intention, its title should have been translated, *On the Sick and Healthy Understanding*. It is important to note that this little work—which is not only a popularization but an untheological version of *The Star of Redemption*—was written after *The Star of Redemption* and before "The New Thinking."

[18] One of the classic proofs for the existence of God was formulated by St. Anselm of Canterbury in the eleventh century. If all things possess some degree of perfection, the mind can conceive of that which possesses all perfection. But if the conception of that perfect being lacks existence (which is a perfection), then it is imperfect, the mind being capable of conceiving that being who not only possesses all perfection hypothetically, but possesses as well the perfection of existence. This argument can be pressed until it is granted that if existence is perfection and the mind can comprehend the

the existence of God, but uses it with such daring as to suggest a double point: if indeed our names for world, man, and God mean something, if we seem clear about the significance of world and man, but deny significance to God, we call equally into question world and man. Language draws no distinction between these entities. In ascribing truth to man and world, it gives them life and reality. In speaking of God, in using his name as concept, it makes him no more remote than man or world; as life and reality he is as close and near as man or world.[19]

This understanding of common sense will not strike Anglo-Saxon readers as familiar. It is not the common sense which English empiricism generally endorsed. Actually it will be found, however, on close reading of his *Dialogues on Natural Religion,* that Hume's skeptical common sense shared much with Rosenzweig's passionate avowal of the universe of facts. Hume's unwillingness to go beyond a strict construction of the facts would indicate not that he conceived the facts differently than Rosenzweig, merely that he was unprepared to draw the self-confident conclusions characteristic of eighteenth-century rational theology. The *erfahrende Philosophie* of Rosenzweig, the philosophy "based upon experience" [20] (which Rosenzweig has called elsewhere "absolute empiricism"), takes the world, man, and God as data available to common sense. Hume might argue that Rosenzweig derives

---

all-perfect, then a God who exists outside the mind is more perfect than one who exists only as an idea within the mind. Cf. Étienne Gilson, *La Philosophie au Moyen Age* (Paris, Payot, 1944) pp. 245–48. Anselm's argument is developed in his *Proslogion* (circa 1063 when he became prior of the Abbey of Le Bec) and buttressed in his answer to the objections of Gaunilon. Cf. also Karl Barth's enormously suggestive *Fides quaerens intellectum. Anselms Beweis der Existenz Gottes im Zusammenhang seines theologischen Programms* (Munich, Kaiser Verlag, 1931).

[19] Cf. Rosenzweig's illuminating commentary on his own translation of Jehuda Halevi's poem, "Der Fern-und-Nahe." Franz Rosenzweig, *Jehuda Halevi. Zweiundneunzig Hymnen und Gedichte,* 2nd ed. (Berlin, Verlag Lambert Schneider, 1927), pp. 143–88.

[20] Glatzer, *Franz Rosenzweig,* p. 192; Rosenzweig, "Das neue Denken," p. 379.

more from his experience than the facts warrant, but he cannot accuse Rosenzweig of ignoring the facts.

Common sense is for Rosenzweig the medium of our encounter with the universe. It is not a faculty of intellect nor the storehouse of feeling; neither objectivity as such nor subjectivity as such mean anything to it. Common sense is a mode of cognition peculiarly suited to creatures of time. The New Thinking of common sense cannot occur other than in time. Cognition which would seek to transcend time, to seize objects in the timeless pincers of thought, must perforce divest them of what is most preciously theirs: their presence in the flow of time. Temporality is of the essence of experience. The world comes in my way, a human being comes in my way, God comes in my way; all passes before and through me, and only if experienced within its medium of passage does it truly enter my experience *to be* experienced. Every event has its history within time. The world cannot be within me, for then to love the world would be to love myself; I cannot be within God, for then there would be no "I" with which to love. Subjects must be preserved; objects must have their station—but all must move from birth to death in the slow procession of time.

As time is the medium in which common sense encounters the events of life, so speech is the faculty by which these events are connected and related. Speech prizes the event and confers upon it the eternity which raises it beyond evanescence and death. Speech is different from the timeless process of thinking, for where the thinker has framed experience outside the flux, making it timeless before its proper time, speech is "bound to time and nourished by time, and it neither can nor wants to abandon this element." [21] The thinker presses argument through the mesh of thought—all is anticipated, all is discovered in the mind. Speech is, for the thinker, but a

[21] Glatzer, *Franz Rosenzweig,* p. 199; Rosenzweig, "Das neue Denken," pp. 386 f.

concession to the deficiency of others—the speaker's pride in thought and contempt for the hearer's inability to think. The new thinker is the "speaking thinker." [22] The speaking thinker is not, as Rosenzweig makes clear, one who has abandoned logical thought for "grammatical thinking" so much as he is one who requires the presence of him who hears. Hearing—the response to speech—is not silence. The hearer is not silent, though he may not speak. He is the presence who demands of the speaker that he apprehend the hearer as he speaks, that he know that thought arches over time to a living being who requires speech. Speech binds existence to existence. As such it is the medium which compels thought to retire from the separateness and atomic reality which it perceives to be man *in himself*, world *in itself*, God *in himself*. Speech binds man, world, and God into the union which theology calls creation, revelation, and redemption.

Philosophy will identify and discriminate the parts of the universe. It will describe what experience reports of the uniqueness of man, world, and God. Yet these three are not alone and separate. They are joined together. They are arranged in the stations of time, but are joined together by the agencies of hope and trust. Where philosophy will see but separateness, theology will build a bridge. "For, within reality, and that is all we can experience, the separation is spanned, and what we experience is the experience of spanning. God veils himself when we try to grasp him; man, our self, withdraws, and the world becomes a visible enigma. God, man, and world reveal themselves only in their relations to one another, that is, in creation, revelation, and redemption. . . ." [23] Common sense becomes the medium of both philosophy and theology. What the philosopher will require "in the

[22] *Idem.*
[23] Glatzer, *Franz Rosenzweig*, p. 198; Rosenzweig, "Das neue Denken," p. 386.

interests of objectivity will—for theology—prove to be a demand in the interests of subjectivity." [24]

Metaphysics is the turning-point of Rosenzweig's thought. *The Star of Redemption* will commence by establishing the discreteness of world, man, and God and proceed to activate their stasis, displaying each in the agony of its inner movement and unfolding. All life passes from gestation to birth, moving from the Nothing to the Something, from the No to the Yes. In the final affirmation, the great Yes will continue to preserve the denial of the No and the limitation of the Nothing.

God begins with the Nothing and moves to infinite fullness. With impassioned language reminiscent of the seventeenth-century German Protestant mystic Jacob Boehme, Rosenzweig sees God passing through the anguish of the *Mysterium Magnum;* the small spark catches fire and burns, the *ungrund* locates its *grund,* the No of the Nothing is denied and out of denial God affirms Himself. Within God the fundamental polarity of speech is found which denies and limits, affirms and spreads out infinitely to encompass the universe. The limitation, the refusal of the infinite expanse is the divine fiat of freedom and power, the refusal to be other than Self, the freedom which in God is always the potentiality to create.[15]

The *metalogical* world, no different in its separateness than God, passes through the same rhythm of affirmation and limitation: the No of the world is the infinite uni-

[24] Glatzer, *Franz Rosenzweig,* p. 209; Rosenzweig, *Der Stern der Erlösung,* p. 24.

[25] Rosenzweig, *Der Stern der Erlösung,* pp. 33–55; cf. particularly the crucial methodological passages, pp. 33–36. A different and less technical summary of the doctrine of *The Star* is to be found in Steven S. Schwarzschild's valuable pamphlet *Franz Rosenzweig: Guide for Reversioners* (London, The Education Committee of the Hillel Foundation, no date), pp. 15–20; for a philosophic analysis of Rosenzweig's doctrine and sources, see Else Freund, *Die Existenz Philosophie Franz Rosenzweigs* (Hamburg, Verlag von Felix Meiner, 1959).

verse of particular phenomena—limited by their unrelatedness and isolation. The world of objects seeks form. Form is conferred by the Yes of the world which presses down upon formless particularity the order and structure of conceptualization. Finite phenomena are gradually embraced by the pure Logos and lose their limitation and individuality. The No of the world is joined to the Yes of the world and the way is traced from a negative estimate of the cosmos to knowledge of the world.[26]

The procession of man from the recognition of his uniqueness and logical identity to the emergence of the self, individuality, character, and personality describes the emergence of the *meta-ethical* separateness of man. The acknowledgment of the being of man brings with it the awareness of infinite freedom (infinite in will, however limited in action). Man's inability to ever fully actualize his freedom brings him to the awareness of the self—born as the self is out of the union of the defiant will and the finitude of individuality. Rosenzweig unravels the implications of this negative psychology for the *meta-ethos* of man: trapped by his limitation and the reaches of the infinite will, man shuttles between the alternatives of immersion in the world or transcendence of it.[27]

The God of the *meta-physis,* the world of the *meta-logos,* and the man of the *meta-ethos* define the atmosphere of pagan mythology. The pagan world is not, however, for the fact of being pagan an untrue world. The pagan world is the world of stasis and isolation. All is brought to the threshold of vitality and left to lie. The mythic world which man constructs for himself shows forth the lines of truth, for man may see God and the world, as he sees himself, locked in the universe of self-affirmation and denial. Man employs timeless mythological images to bracket his experience. The mythology allows

[26] Rosenzweig, *Der Stern der Erlösung,* pp. 55–81.
[27] *Ibid.,* pp. 82–108.

him to see the universe in its separateness and isolation. We confront "the mythical God, the plastic World, and the tragic Man." [28]

Autonomous thought (philosophical idealism is for Rosenzweig a primary example) traditionally rejects any reality it does not create. It would appear, however, that thought can yield little beyond the achievement of a broken universe, for God, world, and man are set apart from one another. The task of philosophy and theology is to lead thought out of the realm of the timeless into the ambient of time. God, world, and man can pass into each other's dominion, imparting vitality, communicating love, bringing reality to its fulfilled being only when God is led out of his privacy into relation with the world and with man, and man is restored to his community with God and the world. To accomplish this end the interweaving lines of creation, revelation, and redemption must be imposed upon the static individualities of God, world, and man.

While traditional philosophy will define concepts and seek to achieve their formal interrelation, *The Star of Redemption* passes from philosophy to theology. To give mankind that taste of eternity which is its own and the world's proper destiny, concepts must be introduced into time. The *end* of philosophy—the articulation of concepts—is the *beginning* of the New Thinking. Where God, world, and man end, creation, revelation, and redemption begin. Where Greek thought ends, Biblical thought begins.

Rosenzweig's use of Biblical thought is unconventional. In the second part of *The Star of Redemption,* it is not Rosenzweig's concern to be Jewish as such, to validate Jewish sources by their simple incorporation into a theological apologetics. Biblical sources are quoted to adumbrate and suggest, but not to confirm. Although Rosenzweig stands firmly within the Biblical tradition he never

[28] *Ibid.*, p. 109.

abandons his critical awareness of the symbolic apostrophes of Scripture. Greek thought testifies no less to the serenity of the courageous intellect for the presence of elaborate myths; Biblical thought is no less the source of all true theology for the presence of the unhistorical and hyperbolic. Biblical faith testifies but does not prove. It would be foolish to ask that the Biblical record of the meeting of man and the living God supply also proof and confirmation. It is less important whether the text survives as unimpeachable *sanctum* than that the text displays the living unity of God, man, and world.[29]

It is just, therefore, to consider Rosenzweig's conception of creation, revelation, and redemption as originating in Biblical faith. The faith of the theologian, that is, of him who holds his whole being open before reality, does not make the theologian unresponsive to philosophy and science.[30] The theologian is merely one who guards against a blasphemy to which philosophy and science are liable—the blasphemy of making life over into thought, of emptying the temporal of significance by having prevented eternity from entering into time.

Biblical faith discerns that God moves out of his metaphysical isolation into creativity. Impelled by his power and by the wisdom which qualifies his power, God both chooses and is compelled to leave his seclusion. The meeting of divine creativity and the unactualized Logos of the world defines for creation its ongoing, ever renewing,

[29] The holiness of Scripture does not arise from the *what,* but from the *that* of divine address and human rejoinder. Holiness is an aspect of persons, not of things. The place is sanctified because a person gave it presence and moment: the piece of earth because a messenger of God conversed with Moses or with Joshua; the Ark which condemned Uzzah because God was present in it; the Temple because God was present in its inmost place. But equally important is the *what,* because it is the content of the divine word which makes holiness into an imperative, converting it from the power, presence, and terror of the divine into the conditioning directive.

[30] Rosenzweig, *Kleinere Schriften,* pp. 128–33. Cf. particularly p. 133. Glatzer, *Franz Rosenzweig,* p. 210. "And the word *believing* does not signify a dogmatic tying oneself down, but having a hold which holds one's entire being."

never ending task. Creation spans time from beginning to end, for creation always acts to bring the world to its completed *being*.[31] Creation brings the world and man into a unity. Man, however, beholds God with dumbness, being wrapped in the ample cloak of the private Self. The substance of man is the creation of God, but his meta-ethical isolation prevents him from acknowledging his creator. It is from revelation that the conscious reciprocity of God and man proceeds. Creation is the beginning of God's speech, but the actuality of his speech is revelation.[32] Creation is a mute act; it contains the subject matter for which revelation is exegesis. What creation manifests as the flow of destiny, revelation brings forth as love. Revelation draws forth the ego from its shelter into the light of God. As the Logos is brought to being by the repeated movements of creation, the self is formed and shaped by each thrust of love.[33]

The meta-ethical man, brought forth from the isolation of his private rapture and pathos into the day of revelation, may succumb to the sufficiency of revelation. The love of God which descends upon the individual may so capture his spirit that God becomes his sufficient goal. The sufficiency of God's love, rather than the unity of

[31] It would appear that Rosenzweig holds a doctrine of the eternity of matter: that creation is merely that divine act by which a pre-existent matter is endowed with form. Such Aristotelian alchemy, although suggested by Rosenzweig's painfully difficult language, is really foreign to his thought. It must be understood that the description of the three subjects of reality is one carried on against the background of a conscious act of philosophic conceptualization. The question which Rosenzweig asks is not how reality unfolded in time, but how the mind conceives of reality when it addresses it with thought alone. Thought spins out the movement within God, world, and man; timeless thought causes its objects to enact a dumb show in which what is causal and successive in the order of time and relation is frozen and separated from its vital connections. The indwelling Logos of the world would appear to pre-exist creation only because the solutions of thought are partial and incomplete without the fulfilling relations which creation, revelation, and redemption supply.

[32] Rosenzweig, *Der Stern der Erlösung,* Part 2, p. 30.

[33] *Ibid.,* pp. 88 f.

God, world, and man, becomes his only task. The love which God plants in the individual soul must, however, be opened before the world; the individual must bring his love from the secret places of the heart into the society of men. When love moves from God to the *Nebenmensch*—to one's neighbor, to him who "happens in my way"—when love passes out of the mystic community into the community of the world, when it goes forth and transforms, the work of redemption is begun.

The redemption of the individual is coextensive with the redemption of the world. The creature stands amid the tension of life and the lifeless; for some death comes to give serenity, for others it comes to complete the absence of life. Although love restores the self to life, the self must struggle against the lifeless that surrounds it. Redemption would properly consist of that kingdom in which each creature has received and imparted the vitalities of love—when love has bestowed life and each creature has loved. The redemption of the *Nebenmensch* is the redemption of the world; as each man turns to his neighbor, the world awaits its next moment. In each turning and each fresh moment the eternal coming of the Kingdom is presaged and anticipated.

Time is juxtaposed to the timeless, but time is not set in contrast to eternity. Time is but the curtain before which the procession of life moves from birth to death. God's time, however, is eternal life. Eternity is not undifferentiated sameness, the endless repetition of familiar forms, the same truths, the uniform quality of existence. As life is the presentness of vitality, novelty, new discovery, and enrichment, so eternity is the quality of undiminished life achieved only in the consummated relation of God, world, and man. The ever coming Kingdom of redemption is presaged in historical time. Rosenzweig acknowledges that it has been anticipated in the historical communities of Judaism and Christianity.

Rosenzweig is characteristically unable to indulge the

merciless and barren apologetics that have described historic Jewish-Christian communication. Christian apologetics, corrupted by secular power, and Jewish apologetics, alternately beside the point or compromising, can yield history little illumination. The transition from the arguments of theology to the historical reality of Christianity and Judaism marks the passage from the personal experience of faith to the historical embodiment of faith—revelation becomes historical revelation, the redemption of the neighbor and the redemption of time become the redemptive communities of Jew and Christian.

Something is to be learned—in the order of providence—from the fact that the Jew is dispersed, that he covers the earth but nowhere enjoys power,[34] whereas Western Christianity is everywhere in power, or in search of power.[35] These are historical facts: the Jew is powerless but endures, the Christian is powerful but has not yet triumphed. The paradox of the historical condition of Judaism and Christianity would suggest that both Jew and Christian are metahistorical communities, that they participate in an order of experience which binds them to an eternal redemptive purpose. Judaism and Christianity are, according to Rosenzweig, communities of love. As such they may equally fulfill the requirements of redemption, that eternity enter and be embodied in time. The presence of both communities is not evidence of incommensurability, that one be higher and the other lower, that one be superior and the other defective. Their presence is rather an indication that, however God's

[34] It should be noted, not without a sense of tragedy, that Rosenzweig wrote before the coming of Hitler and the fulfillment of Zionist aspiration.

[35] Rosenzweig is both uninterested in and uninformed about the religions of the East. He is interested in but uninformed about the religion of Islam. His tendentious views of religions other than Judaism and Christianity, though they may compromise his scholarship, are characteristic of many great minds—the intuition is so powerful, the vision so full that facts (and they are really so often unimportant) are blunted to conform to the intuition.

truth be one, history may fulfill His truth by different means.[36]

The difference of Judaism and Christianity is not, however, a difference of emphasis and aspect, but a radical and uncompromising difference of being.

The eternity of Judaism is that of eternal life and the eternity of Christianity is that of the eternal way. The eternal life of the Jews is the life of a people of faith who have been with God since their birth. The people transmit the faith: from one generation to the next the eternal word is borne as a movable treasure, fixed neither by the customs of nations nor by the transitory conditions of history. Peoples of the world live in time; as servants of time they grow up and pass away. They are formed by events and circumstances, kings and climates; they mature culture and fashion character, but ultimately their fortunes are telluric, arising from the earth and destined, with the passage of time and the shiftings of influence, to return to the earth. An eternal people, by contrast, is sustained beyond the fortunes of history. Its essential style and its enduring character are imposed as a command and transmitted as a teaching. Revelation is addressed to the six hundred thousand assembled at Sinai to receive the Law as a command to them *to do and to hear*. It is only because of their passion *to do* forever and to recall forever that they transform the commandment into law.[37] The Law gives cohesiveness and order to what might flash forth from God and be lost. The Law becomes

[36] Our own exposition of this view may be found in "The Natural and the Supernatural Jew: Two Views of the Church," in Philip Scharper, ed., *American Catholics: A Protestant-Jewish View* (New York, Sheed & Ward, 1959), pp. 127–57.

[37] The discussion of *Gebot* (commandment) and *Gesetz* (law) in modern Jewish thought is particularly heated and significant when placed in the context of the Emancipation and the attrition of Jewish observance which followed upon its completion. One should read carefully the thoughtful correspondence of Rosenzweig and Buber on "Revelation and Law," which is presented in Franz Rosenzweig, *On Jewish Learning*, ed. by Nahum N. Glatzer, trans. by William Wolf (New York, Schocken Books, Inc., 1955), pp. 109–18; pp. 119–24.

the junction of God's love and God's justice.[38] It is the link of eternity which binds the people from the moment of its birth to the completion of its redemption.

The Christian community is not formed by any natural tie nor renewed and strengthened by the order of eternity which the festivals of the Jewish year impose upon time. It is rather an association of believers who are joined by their common faith in the redemptive life, death, and return of Jesus the Christ. The Christian faith is understood to partake of an eternal dimension in that both the birth of Jesus and the return of Jesus have their instance in the activity of an eternal God. The Christian moves from the beginning to the end as indifferent to time as is the Jew, but whereas the Jew will cultivate separateness from the world, the Christian will seek to penetrate it. The contrast of eternal life and eternal way results from the fact that the Jew is always with God whereas the Christian is always on his way to Him. This is but to say, as Rosenzweig has said, that the Christian, unlike the Jew, was once pagan—the pagan is subdued only to reappear and be repeatedly expunged.[39] The Christian passes through a never ending cycle of appropriation and loss, submergence and recovery. The Christian is, it would appear, in tension with eternity; the Jew is at peace with it.

Rosenzweig has been called the last Jewish thinker of

[38] Rosenzweig does not draw the conventional distinction between the just God and the gracious God. God is one person; as such, distinctions of qualities and aspects, whatever their significance for theology, are irrelevant as devices of Jewish self-justification.

[39] Rosenzweig's remarkable understanding of the pagan essence of Christianity derives not only from his observation of early Christian history and his interpretation of the Pauline literature, but from his more fundamental insistence that Judaism and Christianity reflect absolute and disjunct embodiments of providential intention. The Jew and the Christian, although complementary, are dialectical antagonists. Their conflict can be stated dialectically; the substance of the dialectic is ontological; the actual manifestation of the dialectic is historical. Cf. Rosenzweig, *Der Stern der Erlösung*, Part 3, pp. 178–82.

the Exile.[40] This is undoubtedly so in the limited sense that his thought matured and his life ended in that brief period after Zionism had been defined as an urgent alternative for European Jews and before intensive Jewish colonization of Palestine had begun. There is, however, a deeper sense in which Rosenzweig may be accounted the last thinker of the Exile, for his doctrine—however much it reacts to the history of the Jews amid the nations of the West and the impact of Christian history upon the external life of the Jews—is directed toward the life of the Jew independent of normal categories of time and history. The Jew creates his own time and his own history in order to maintain himself with God and to make known to Christendom the reality of its dialectical counterpart.

Rosenzweig's insistence that the time and history of the Jew is radically different from that of the Christian is initially alarming. In what sense can this be true? and, more significantly, if it is not true, for what reason did Rosenzweig nevertheless insist upon its truth so passionately? It is possible to argue that time is a wholly subjective dimension of experience, that each man's time (and space) is but the medium through which the individual encounters the world. If time and space are only categories through which the individual meets, apprehends, judges, and remembers his experience, they are assuredly subjective. If, however, they are *only* subjective it is not only impossible for individuals to *share* experience in any meaningful sense, it is questionable whether an historical community can really enjoy a communal time (and space) which unites all of its members. If time is subjective—and therefore personal and individual—it is hard to understand how there can be a time which is either Jewish or Christian. But this is precisely what Rosenzweig seems to insist there is. The Jew has his own

[40] Schwarzschild, *Franz Rosenzweig: Guide for Reversioners,* pp. 29, 31, 36.

sense of time which is given to him with his being Jewish. The Jewish sense of time is revealed time; it is time already anticipating redemption; it is, to introduce again that ungainly term, eschatological time—time which carries within it, as Jehuda Halevi suggested, the seed from which the fruit of redemption grows. Jewish time, as Samuel H. Bergman described it, is "static eternity while Christianity is eternity within time." [41] Such a view of time has the consequence of annihilating the relevance of history. It ceases to matter, as it ceased to matter for Rosenzweig, where the Jew lived, whether the Jew regained Zion, or re-established his connection with a national land or a spoken language. The annihilation of history moreover enabled Rosenzweig to put aside Christianity, not only to blunt its claim, but to counter it with the conviction that whatever its enormous relevance to unredeemed time it has no relevance to the redeemed time in which the Jew perseveres.

The annihilation of history and the establishment of the Jewish community as a mysterious eschatological enclave within natural time has, whatever its visionary and moving character, a devastating consequence. Rosenzweig not only accepts and rationalizes the discontinuity of the Jew with the history of the West—in this we would agree with him—but he tacitly accepts the verdict of the West upon the Jew and seeks to turn it to the advantage of Jewish existence. The Christian had for centuries destroyed the natural historical time of the Jew, affirmed his irrelevance to European culture, denied his integral relation to the development of Western history. Rosenzweig not only accepts such a verdict, but locates and defines a metaphysical hypostasis in which this verdict ceases to be unjust and capricious and becomes in fact a metaphysical necessity and truth. History is vanquished and in its place Rosenzweig enthrones a

[41] Samuel H. Bergman, *Faith and Reason: An Introduction to Modern Jewish Thought* (Washington, D.C., B'nai B'rith Hillel Foundation, 1961), p. 67.

pageant, epic, mystery-play version of history in which the litany of Jewish life not only sanctifies time and nature but replaces them. The Christian lives within time in order to redeem it, while the Jew is eternity rooted in time. The Jewish community is a permanent eschatological community, a community which lives through millennia in the face of the last days, a community which sustains what Pauline Christianity had to overcome—namely, the failure of the parousia. Judaism does not have to rationalize its life with God, whereas Christianity must always rationalize that its Christ has not returned. Rosenzweig dissolves the challenge of Christianity by both neutralizing its thrust and incorporating its strength. He is no longer threatened by Christianity—as he was in the days of his magnificent exchange with Eugen Rosenstock-Huessy [42]—because Christianity is rendered irrelevant to the Jew. At the same time, however, that Christianity becomes irrelevant for Judaism, Rosenzweig counters the Christian disqualification of Judaism by formulating his remarkable doctrine of parity truth—the truth of Christ and the truth of Torah.

It is questionable whether Judaism can be restored—whether Judaism can be "smuggled into" general culture, as Rosenzweig thought, if general culture is really unnecessary and authentic Judaism is obliged to be indifferent to it. Rosenzweig's cure tends, it seems to us, to further debilitate the patient by sundering precisely those connections to the real world, man, and God which he had so painstakingly reconstituted. The metahistorical community which Samson Raphael Hirsch and Isaac Breuer described and which Rosenzweig fully equips with the habiliments of endurance may perish for lack of involvement, dedication, and responsibility to the whole of culture. It is here that the strong, however innocent and

[42] Rosenzweig, *Briefe*, pp. 638–720. Cf. also Alexander Altmann, "Franz Rosenzweig and Eugen Rosenstock-Huessy: An Introduction to Their 'Letters on Judaism and Christianity,'" *The Journal of Religion*, Vol. XXIV, No. 4 (Chicago, 1944).

disarming, moralism of Hermann Cohen and Leo Baeck would have been a valid tonic to Rosenzweig's image of the paradigmatic holy community. Judaism is—and this Rosenzweig understood well—life itself. Judaism is not its force, its law, its regimen—it is nothing less than the whole of life drawn into and around a community. The new time of the Jew (eternity fixed amid time) is the life of the Jew within Judaism; it is not the life of the "Jewish" Jew in the world.

Clearly Rosenzweig's marvelous position—a position which, it should be noted, eternalizes the prophetic notion of the "remnant"—emerges out of a double entrapment: Christianity and the Law. Where his rejection of Christianity is fashioned out of the insistence that Jew, as well as Christian, have existence with God, his interpretation of the Law is his effort to texture and give quality to that existence. It is clearly central to Rosenzweig to understand the Law as that which man "can" do to serve God.[43] He does not deny that the Torah is an integer in which abstract discrimination and selection is both facetious and dishonest—in this he stands with the Orthodox. However, he debars the judgment of the nineteenth-century Orthodox counterreformation by insisting that however much the Law be an absolute demand it is not for that reason a demand which is fixed and frozen. The Law comes down upon life; it is confronted by the Jew; and the Jew asks, if he is serious about his Judaism, *What can be done?* Once the Jew decides, the Law (*Gesetz*) ceases to be Law and becomes commandment (*Gebot*). The Law becomes apodictic through life—it cannot compel life, but life compels it to become *a command to do.* This should not be confused

[43] For a comprehensive discussion of Rosenzweig's doctrine of Law and teaching see the crucial volume *On Jewish Learning*, particularly the essays, "The Builders: Concerning the Law," "Revelation and Law (Martin Buber and Franz Rosenzweig)" and "The Commandments: Divine or Human?" As well note the discussion of Bergman, *Faith and Reason*, pp. 72–79; Schwarzschild, *Franz Rosenzweig: Guide for Reversioners*, pp. 40–42.

with the position of liberal Judaism, except insofar as this view opens itself to an anarchic subjectivism,[44] for Rosenzweig has the profoundest trust in the honesty of the Jew before God. He could not readily believe that an individual who seeks God would betray both God and himself to ease the burden which in conscience he is prepared to assume. The existential decision to hear the command and obey is decision out of the whole of existence and is therefore valid and truthful if it is made out of the whole of existence. If the price of such trust is that all Jews will obey differently (even if authentically), that price is not too high as long as the Law remains *the* objective reality for the Jew and all Jews hear something and obey something and that "something" is done with all their heart, with all their soul, and with all their strength.

This is not the occasion to review Rosenzweig's theory of Jewish education, his efforts to establish the foundations of adult Jewish instruction, the patterns of his personal piety, the history of his rich and productive relations with Martin Buber. These form the substance of his life—the interweaving of conception and practice—but to recite them necessarily restricts us to the narration of events. Our concern has been and remains not the writing of the lives of Jewish saints nor an exercise in Jewish piety but an attempt to suggest the forms which Jewish thought has taken when, caught between the world and its own true destiny, it seeks to understand itself.

The closing words of *The Star of Redemption* (words to which Rosenzweig made frequent allusion) are: "Into Life."[45] *The Star of Redemption* was written in the effort to instruct life, to impart to the diversity of experience that order and coherence which thought demands. Having led philosophy into the embrace of theology, having drawn both philosophy and theology into the circle of

[44] Bergman, *Faith and Reason*, pp. 78–79.
[45] Rosenzweig, *Der Stern der Erlösung*, Part 2, p. 211.

life, what remains to thought? Nothing but that it should become in *fact* what it affirms in thought. The command into life is no longer the command to philosophize, but the command to live.

Rosenzweig's vision of life as the flowering of eternity was shared by another poet of Jewish existence: Jehuda Halevi. It is gratuitous to speak of Rosenzweig as poet if indeed one respects the poetic imagination. Where poetry is set in opposition to life, where one conceives it as the inability of conception and the deformation of intellect, then indeed poetry becomes a scarecrow, casting crippled images on the landscape.

Poetry was for Rosenzweig, as for Halevi, the language of existence—the means by which the paradoxes of theology can be rendered into life. The intellect will fashion the conditions of poetry: whether Halevi describes the organic responsiveness of the Jewish community to truth (its witness to Torah, its wandering and exile, its relations to Christendom and Islam—those triumphant communities of time) or Rosenzweig traces the rays of the redeeming star of Israel, what is apparent is that the *Kuzari* and *The Star of Redemption* are works that prepare for life. The *Kuzari* prepares Halevi to desert Spain for the holy wanderings that bring him to his death. *The Star of Redemption* gives Rosenzweig the courage to sustain that elevation of the spirit which he possessed during his long years of illness. The intellect prepares both Halevi and Rosenzweig for the heroism of life.

If our conviction is justified, it is not remarkable that Rosenzweig should have turned in 1922–1923, during the early years of his fatal illness, to the translation and interpretation of *Ninety-Two Hymns and Poems of Jehuda Halevi.* Rosenzweig is not concerned with Halevi's theology as such, nor is it his concern to establish Halevi's stature as a thinker, or to locate him in the procession of Jewish thought. Neither his translations nor his commentary are intended to return the dead to life, to resurrect the forgotten, to prove that this twelfth-century personality can breathe the air of twentieth-century Germany and survive. This was no exercise in intellectual embalming. Rosenzweig had only one task: to make Jehuda Halevi his own. His task was not to imitate, not to fake the rhythms of the medieval Hebrew, not to preserve the original for the sake of its authenticity, but to demonstrate that truth is viable where the perception of truth is the same; the sense of God and Israel which animates Halevi can avail modern Jewry because that sense is true and universal.

"Jehuda Halevi was one of the great Jewish poets in the Hebrew language. . . . These translations are not intended to induce the reader to forget even for an instant that these are not my poems which he reads. They are poems of Jehuda Halevi and Jehuda Halevi is neither a German poet nor a contemporary." [46] As surely, however, as the translator dare not pretend that he is the creator of the words he renders, as surely must he avoid the illusion of absolute fidelity. Experience inescapably shapes the word in its passage from medieval Hebrew to modern German. It is not only that German creates exigencies which Hebrew does not anticipate or that Hebrew enjoys an existential concreteness which German cannot achieve; rather it is that the translator has lived. The living man comes to the language and revives it. Not only is Halevi rendered into German but German is infused into Halevi. The poet and the translator pass through the stream of address and response. The essential act of the translator is the same as that which each man must perform that he himself may live. The translator must hear and speak. Translation is speech; it matters little whether one renders Goethe or Halevi, the task is the same: the word must be heard and it must be spoken as it is heard. The hearing constructs the spoken

[46] Rosenzweig, *Jehuda Halevi,* "Einleitung zur Anmerkungen," p. 153.

as profoundly as the speaker fashions his speech. Speech is relation: the life of the speaker enters the word and the life of the hearer amends what is heard.

What is true of the speech which passes between Halevi and Rosenzweig is true of the word which passes between the divine and the human, between God and Israel. Halevi and Rosenzweig form a horizontal continuum which echoes to the pounding Word of God. Rosenzweig finds in Halevi all that which brings eternity into the life of Israel—the anguish of the near and distant God, the ineluctability of God's name, the indwelling presence of God, the soul in exile, the soul in praise, the election and misery of the Jewish people. These are the themes of faith as well as themes of poetry; they are equally the grammar of that language which the Jew must speak if he is to restore the timeless to time, eternity to the community of man, and the vitality of "eternal life" to the life of Israel.

Writing of Franz Rosenzweig the year after his death Martin Buber observed that he "does not flee, but stands firm just there where he, the Jew, stands. . . . This standing firm where one stands must not be understood as a renunciation of the approach to truth, but as the opening out moment by moment of the one approach that exists; for it exists at every moment when a person really stands there where he stands." [47]

To be willing to take our place, to accept what providence has honored us with being—Jews amid the nations—and not to flinch from the fact that the demands of destiny always disqualify us from the impermanent satisfactions of time: this is to take our reality as it is. It was to this reality and to the training of the Jewish person to step into the life which opens before him, that Rosenzweig was consecrated.

[47] Martin Buber, *Pointing the Way,* trans. by Maurice Friedman (New York, Harper & Brothers, 1957), p. 92.

V. MARTIN BUBER (1878–   )

The "death of God" has been a commonplace in Western thought for nearly a century. Nietzsche's announcement was but one assertion amid a history of assertions. Two centuries earlier Pascal had described "the lost God" and Hegel, in his essay "Faith and Knowledge," had affirmed that "God himself is dead." [1] It required but half a century beyond Nietzsche for Heidegger to observe, commenting on Hölderlin's apostrophe: "Our generation walks in night, dwells as in Hades, without the divine," that the dawn may return and "the appearing of God and the gods may begin again." Western man has passed through the ages of security, when God was familiar and accessible, to the present moment when He appears to be wholly abscondite.

The devices of intellect which would fasten God to his universe, divest him of mystery, and expose him to the critical examination of mathematicians, scientists, and philosophers appalled Pascal—for the immediate God vanishes and only the traces of "the lost God" remain. Pascal renounced philosophy and returned intellect to an older path. Spinoza, believing that the human demand for the concrete results in the humanization of the divine, elected to protect the inaccessibility of God by making of him an infinite substance with infinite attributes, two of which—"extension" and "thought"—are sufficient to exhaust the universe of man's experience. Yet even Spinoza could not forgo contact with the merely human, for God's love of himself is identical with our love of him; the most sublime love is manifest through man's incomparably defective love.

[1] G. F. W. Hegel, "Glauben und Wissen" (1802), *Werke,* Vol. I (Berlin, 1832), p. 157. "Gott selbst is tod(t), (dasjenige, was gleichsam nur empirisch ausgesprochen war, mit Pascals Ausdrucken: la nature est telle qu'elle marque partout un Dieu perdu et dans l'homme et hors de l'homme). . . ."

Man had begun to drive God from the world. It mattered little whether God survived as an indispensable function of the philosophic system or was pronounced "slain," the Hegelian or Nietzschean alternatives achieve the same consequence: whereas the one binds God to the rack of the mind, the other acknowledges that such a God—if he lives only for the sake of the System—is already dead.

God does not perish, however, because he has been eclipsed. Although "eclipse of heaven, eclipse of God" is surely "the character of the historic hour through which the world is passing" [2] God is not slain by proclaiming his mortality. He does not die merely because it is determined that he cannot survive his own theodicy or that he is vulnerable to the pain of his world. Pascal describes the lostness of God and Spinoza protects him from his world; however, both elevate him beyond the pain of the world. Kant rediscovers him as the peg on which to hang the virtue of man, and Hegel affixes him as a figurehead upon the prow of the System; however, both make him into a philosophic requirement. A God dispossessed of his world is surely lost to the world.

The peculiarity of our times is that although God is absent he is nevertheless rediscovered as the one "problem" which focuses the task of man, the crisis of thought, and the dilemmas of time and history. Sartre may repudiate him with confidence, affirming "he is dead. He spoke to us and now is silent." [3] Heidegger, with a calmness in striking contrast to the proclaiming madman of Nietzsche's *The Gay Science,* may observe, "Because we hark back to Nietzsche's saying about the 'death of God,' people take such an enterprise for atheism. For what is more 'logical' than to consider the man who has experi-

[2] Martin Buber, *Eclipse of God* (New York, Harper & Brothers, 1952), p. 34.

[3] Jean-Paul Sartre, *Existentialism and Humanism,* trans. by Philip Mairet (London, Methuen & Co., Ltd., 1947). Cf. Buber, *Eclipse of God,* p. 88.

enced the 'death of God' as a Godless person." [4] C. G. Jung, modifying the atheism of Sartre and the ontic paganism of Heidegger, may make God a "function of the unconscious," a projected reality which "does not exist 'absolutely,' that is, independent of the human subject and beyond all human conditions." [5] Yet it is clear that the death of God is but a metaphor for a more profound death, for this God did not die a natural death—he withered, contracted, starved to death. He is no longer a constructive power in human existence; he is among the displaced and unemployed. Not only are the traditions of Biblical Judaism and Christianity discarded—this could well be tolerated, for historic forms, to the extent that they are merely historical, can be reviewed, amended, or abandoned. It is rather that God as the Other, he who in his being is wholly independent of the world and yet related to it as creator, revealer, and redeemer, is dead. The death of God is the death of the Absolute. Henceforth each man is considered free to authenticate his own existence (Sartre), each man is responsible for the rescue of Being (Heidegger), each man fashions his own God according to the deepest requirements of his psyche (Jung).

There is a pathos in the concept of the "death of God" which cannot be ignored. The twentieth century—the century least able to dispense with God—has, in fact, dispensed with God. It is understandable for the eighteenth and nineteenth centuries to have abandoned God—the enthusiasm of the Age of Enlightenment and the complacent self-assurance of nineteenth-century society could well destroy religion. The assault of intellectual scrutiny or the smugness of conventional religion is

[4] Martin Heidegger, *Briefe über den Humanismus* (Frankfurt am Main, Vittorio Klostermann, 1947; 3rd ed., 1949); "Nietzsches Wort 'Gott ist Tod,'" *Holzwege* (Frankfurt am Main, Vittorio Klostermann, 1950), pp. 192–247. Cf. William Barrett, *Irrational Man* (New York, Doubleday & Company, Inc., 1958), pp. 184–212, for a lucid discussion of Heidegger.

[5] Buber, *Eclipse of God,* pp. 106 f.

enough to eclipse even the most articulate of divinities. Where the one slays God by argument, the other slays him by boredom.

The twentieth century is a postreligious century, a century which has seen the end of religion. Rational religion is gone; God is not a function of the mind, an object of feeling, the buttress of good will, the foundation of ethics, or the serviceman of values and standards. The conventional God is surely dead. But Sartre and Heidegger dispense not only with the God of convention and the God of religion; they dispense with the God who is Absolute Other.

In 1932 Martin Buber wrote a brief, characteristically elliptic and evocative essay[6] in which he described an exchange between himself and a worker who had attended a special discussion that had been arranged after his formal lectures on "Religion and Reality" had been concluded. Having argued back and forth for many hours, this worker arose and, in a manner heavy with deliberation and seriousness, said, "I have had the experience that I do not need this hypothesis 'God' in order to be quite at home in the world!"[7] What had been until that moment a casual exchange of minds—each exposing concern and interest, but concealing the self and its torments from the engagement of argument—became, with this question, an issue of urgency. An unprepossessing worker had announced what had been announced for nearly a century: God is unnecessary. As Buber comments: "It came to me that I must shatter the security of his *Weltanschauung*, through which he thought of a 'world' in which one 'felt at home.'" The argument which Buber schematically recounts is one with which

[6] *Ibid.*, pp. 11–15.

[7] Buber's philosophic anthropology is most comprehensively sketched in his essay "What Is Man?" in which the history of philosophy is presented as an extended commentary on man's security or "homelessness in the world." *Between Man and Man*, trans. by Ronald Gregor Smith (New York, The Macmillan Company, 1948), pp. 118–205.

we are familiar—it is familiar, though none the less telling for its familiarity. Buber unfolded the primitive uncertainty of the world—the unsureness of perception, the inadequacy of our knowledge, the imprecision of our language, the evanescence of our experience, the limitation of our comprehension. If all is then unsure, if the world is not the place where man can feel at home, "What was the being that gave this 'world,' which had become so questionable, its foundation?" After a painful interlude of silence the worker—whose face had been lowered throughout Buber's reply—looked up and with the same deliberateness as before acknowledged, "You are right."

It appeared that the argument won, the securities of a vulnerable naturalism exposed, Buber would have been gratified. And yet characteristically he rebukes himself, for only an argument had been won, a formulation of language that issued from the life of a living man had been destroyed, an admission of defeat had been secured —but what conversion had been effected? It had been shown that the world had an unperceived foundation, that the *Weltanschauung* of natural science afforded but partial truth (and therefore a useless ideology when it pretended to all truth and adequacy), that the God of the Philosophers indeed had merit and significance. But, Buber asks, was it to the God of the Philosophers that this worker should be led? "Had I not rather wished to lead him to the other, Him who Pascal called the God of Abraham, Isaac, and Jacob, Him to whom one can say Thou?" [8] It was evidently not enough to locate the God who is principle and foundation, criterion and value. Whatever his life as principle, foundation, criterion, or value, God remained above all *an object* and as object he is still most effectively and profoundly eclipsed. As object he can be manipulated and used, he can be thought and conceived, and—as object, he may be discarded as are all

[8] *Ibid.*, p. 14.

worn-out objects. New objects—new gods, new psychological requirements, new demands of will and feeling—may come to occupy God's accustomed place. What was abandoned by Nietzsche and even by Kierkegaard—the God who is corrupted by religion—is now, *post Hegel mortuum,* no longer useful even as principle.

The relocation of the Absolute who is not object but subject of man's subject, the Being who is always *there* and *at hand,* has been Buber's lifelong preoccupation. But this task has not been undertaken as a philosophic task; the arguments which Buber has developed to disclose the Absolute as eternal Thou have been essentially moral, not metaphysical; the arguments of an "existential humanist," not the arguments of one who battles through the obstinacies of thought and reason to a truth.[9] This, in itself, is not a criticism. It has been thought by some that the description of Buber as a "philosophic anthropologist," or as we now prefer to call him, "an existential humanist," is intended invidiously. Quite the contrary. The question of philosophic anthropology which Buber raises at the opening of his essay "What Is Man?" commences not with an exposition of historic

[9] The suggestion of Albert Salomon in his review of the author's *Martin Buber* (*Social Research,* Autumn, 1958, p. 372) that Buber was to be understood as a Jewish humanist, crystallized the reaction which had earlier been defined by Jacques Maritain in a letter to the author. On that occasion Maritain agreed with the author's and Buber's own estimation of his work as a philosophic anthropologist (cf. "What Is Man?" in *Between Man and Man*). Maritain went on to observe that "a 'religious thinker' who lingers over the flavor of philosophy and theology and claims he is neither a philosopher nor a theologian will sometimes seek in prophecy an alibi for his neglect of hard and genuine philosophical and theological problems." The suggestion of Albert Salomon and the observation of Maritain are both sustained and developed in a brilliant essay by Ernst Simon, "Martin Buber and Judaism" (Martin Buber v'Emunat Yisrael), *Iyyun,* Vol. IX, No. 1 (January, 1959), pp. 13–50. Simon assesses, without the restraint of narrow discipleship, the inconsistencies and contradictions which beset Buber's theological position. Those unfamiliar with Hebrew will profit from Steven S. Schwarzschild's summary of Simon's essay in *Judaism* (Summer, 1959).

doctrines of philosophic anthropology—that comes later —but with the assertion of Rabbi Bunan von Przysucha, one of the last distinguished teachers of Hasidism: "I wanted to write a book called *Adam,* which would be about the whole man. But then I decided not to write it." [10] Buber understands Rabbi Bunan's decision to originate in the recognition that although Man is the most fitting subject of man's own reflection, to treat of man as a whole is the most awesome, challenging, and difficult enterprise which can be undertaken. As likely as not philosophers, theologians, and social thinkers have taken the risk only to be "overpowered" and "exhausted" by the immensity of the task, falling back on the familiar and characteristic solutions of thought: either to consider all things except man, or to departmentalize the human subject, considering him exhaustively in some respects but ignoring others.[11] The whole man, who only in his wholeness is valuable, is never comprehended, for the whole man can never become an *object* of study. Whenever man is studied—whether the psychologist considers his emotions, the moralist his conduct, or the theologian his beliefs—the whole man recedes and in place of the living man emerge abstracted emotions, actions, and beliefs.

There is, it would appear, an eclipse of man which accompanies the eclipse of God. The living God cannot be perceived other than by the whole man. The recovery of God requires the revived spontaneity, self-awareness, and openness of man before the world. The philosophic anthropologist exists to press for this recovery, but philosophic anthropology—the discipline—does not exist. Kant posed the question, "What is man?" in his notes to his lectures on logic.[12] The answer to this question was to have been given by a philosophic anthropology, and yet, as Buber notes, this philosophic anthropology was never

[10] Buber, "What Is Man?" p. 118. [11] *Idem.*

[12] *Ibid.,* p. 119. Ernst Cassirer, ed., *Immanuel Kants Werke,* Vol. VIII (Berlin, Bruno Cassirer, 1922), p. 343.

composed. The discipline which Kant believed capable of compassing the concerns of metaphysics, ethics, and religion (for if we understood the nature of man, we would know what it is that man can know, do, and hope) could not be established. Whereas metaphysics will locate the proper objects of thought, and ethics will describe the modes of right action, and religion will posit the expectations of faith, they can do so only by ignoring the wholeness of man. "The possibility of its achieving [the philosophical branch disciplines] anything in thought rests precisely on its objectification, on what may be termed its 'de-humanization.' " [13] The establishment of philosophic anthropology would of necessity destroy the wholeness which it is intended to describe. To consider man as a whole, the anthropologist must consider himself (for surely he is, in his subjectivity, part of man and his subjectivity is indispensable to the human situation). By considering himself, by remaining faithful to his subjectivity, he can never project the principles required by an objective discipline.[14] The discipline cannot be defined; it can exist, but its principles cannot be posited. Rabbi Bunan decided wisely not to write of the whole man, for it cannot be written. Man cannot become a science. It might be possible to suggest what authentic wholeness would consist in; it might be indicated what qualities of person and immediacy are requisite to that wholeness, but Buber is not concerned with projecting a descriptive science, whatever its existential concreteness. The problem of man is not merely that he does not know, but that knowing insufficiently he does not dare to risk that meeting which, although guaranteeing nothing, is capable of revealing all.

World cataclysm, the dessication of the community, the trivialization of religion and ethics, the confusion of love and Eros—all these are symptomatic of the more fundamental condition of our life which defines the cor-

[13] Buber, "What Is Man?" p. 122. [14] *Ibid.*, p. 124.

relative eclipse of man and God. The alternatives which modern man has projected for the resolution of his precarious state are unavailing: individualism, which would restore man to freedom and spontaneity, is capable of understanding only a part of man, whereas collectivism, which would force unity upon man, surrenders man to the interests of the "just" society.

> Both views of life—modern individualism and modern collectivism—however different their causes may be, are essentially the conclusion or expression of the same human condition. . . . This condition is characterized by the union of cosmic and social homelessness, dread of the universe and dread of life, resulting in an existential constitution of solitude such as has probably never existed before to the same extent. The human person feels himself to be a man exposed by nature—as an unwanted child is exposed—and at the same time a person isolated in the midst of the tumultuous human world. The first reaction of the spirit to the awareness of this new and uncanny position is modern individualism, the second is modern collectivism.[15]

It is clear that modern thought considers God to have died. But it is possible that what man views as the death of God is, from God's side, a withdrawal from the world. The manifest God is also the concealing God.

The rejection of God is accompanied by the effort to recover man. Having repudiated the Absolute, man seeks to define anew the significance of his own existence. Buber contends that man cannot be located other than through God; the whole man cannot be disclosed except through that which reveals man to himself. God is, as the light, that without which we cannot see. The human effort to recover man requires that we rediscover God.

[15] *Ibid.*, p. 200; *Paths in Utopia*, trans. by R. F. C. Hull (London, Routledge & Kegan Paul, Ltd., 1949), pp. 1–15, 129–49.

Buber's description of God and man in the twentieth century depends upon the absence of God and the incompleteness of man. Man is isolated—sequestered in loneliness or assimilated to the mass. The sense of God is withered and the holy is abandoned. The essential condition of our time is divestment and alienation.[16]

The concern for man, the preoccupation with man's predicament, was not emphatically expressed in Buber's thought until he had passed through a severe and protracted period of withdrawal and self-reflection. In language reminiscent of the *illuminati* of all times and ages, Buber recounts the course of his own involvement in the world, his disenchantment with and retreat from it, his reappearance as mystic, his repudiation of mysticism, and his discovery of truth.

A note of self-consciously constructed charisma marks Buber's autobiographical writing.[17] Each work announces its biographic moment, the hour which evoked it, the issue to which it is addressed. Buber has an historic sense—a sense of his own history and of the history of the times. It is this sense which makes his work so fascinating, for he is unconcerned with problems as such, only with their immediate consequences for life, his own life and the life of man. His own life becomes an exam-

[16] Although it is inappropriate at this juncture to extend the point, it may be noted that Buber's emphasis upon the lostness of man in the world is a universalization of the category we have stated earlier and to which we will return (cf. pp. 6–7, 182–88), that Exile is the symbolic affirmation of man's unredeemed condition. Lostness in the world, as much as Exile, is a hypostasis, for no man is lost (except insofar as he is clinically deranged) and yet all men may be lost, even though they have home and community, if these relations are but the imposition of formal, ordered structure upon a life at whose heart is emptiness and meaninglessness.

[17] This strain of personal and self-conscious exposure is marked in Buber's untranslated works *Daniel* and *Ecstatic Confessions*, as well as in his "My Way to Hasidism" (trans. by Maurice Friedman, *Hasidism and Modern Man* [New York, Horizon Press, Inc., 1958], pp. 47–69), "Dialogue" (trans. by Ronald Gregor Smith, *Between Man and Man*, pp. 1–39), and the numerous texts of Eastern mystics and Hasidic masters which Buber has edited.

ple of how life can be paralyzed by inauthenticity and how life can be regenerated and restored. Out of the personal experience of incomplete dialogue and its consequent tragedy,[18] Buber discovers the insufficiency of mystic abandonment and intuits the marks of true meeting. The personal experience of "conversion" which took place during the years of his withdrawal—when he was already famous as a mystic and a writer on mysticism—supplies him with the germ of understanding which becomes, in 1923, *I and Thou.* The lostness of man and the repudiation of God to which Buber's thought constantly returns has its center and significance in the essential inauthenticity of man's attitude toward the world. The fact that modern man can no longer encounter the world as Other while yet retaining the apprehension of the Other as Thou results in a constriction of human vision and understanding.

The intuition of the twofold attitude of man is indispensable to Buber's thought. It is significant that Buber describes man's twofold position before the world as an "attitude." The German word *Haltung,* which is rendered as "attitude," has a number of clarifying echoes which should be noted. What is really implied by it is the manner in which a man comports himself before the world, how he stands, fixes himself, presents himself to the world. In our day, "attitude" carries an ideological implication which is misleading, for what is important is not how man, reflecting upon himself, determines his view of the world, but how man, in the *wholeness of his being,* opens himself before the world. The *Haltung* of man is not a view, an outlook, a position before an abstraction, but an attitude before the world. The world is not a principle, a mind, but a concrete Other, a living being, whom one encounters. The attitude of man is twofold before the Otherness of the world.

[18] Buber, "Dialogue," in *Between Man and Man,* p. 13. Cf. also the author's discussion of this conversion, *Martin Buber* (New York, Hillary House, 1958), pp. 41–46.

> The attitude of man is twofold, in accordance with the twofold nature of the primary words which he speaks. The primary words are not isolated words, but combined words. The one primary word is the combination I-Thou. The other primary word is the combination I-It; wherein, without a change in the primary word, one of the words He and She can replace It. Hence the I of man is also twofold. For the I of the primary word I-Thou is a different I from that of the primary word I-It.[19]

It should be observed that Buber consciously avoids the intellectual strictness and precision of customary philosophic language. He speaks not of concepts but of "words"; he does not even introduce the interruptive and bifurcating "and" to describe the immediacy of the combined words: to man all is the directness and spontaneity that the hyphen—that merest breath of distinction—suggests in I-Thou. Language, as with Rosenzweig, becomes the means of articulating the transitive character of all relations. Subject and object emerge under scrutiny and analysis: the *I* may discern that it speaks and another hears, that a stone is handled, that a sunrise is seen; but the moment of intellectual judgment turns the *I* out of the path of immediacy into the charted road of objectification: *Thou* becomes object and the *I* becomes the abstract consciousness of traditional philosophy.

It may be wondered why Buber has seen fit to employ such language—the grammatical simplicity, the avoidance of relative clauses and qualifications, the one-sentence paragraphs. Simplicity is indispensable because what is by nature primary must be stated with the decision and directness of the pristine—the I-Thou is described but it is also spoken, for if the reader be not

[19] Martin Buber, *I and Thou*, trans. by Ronald Gregor Smith (Edinburgh, T. & T. Clark, 1937), p. 3.

Thou, the argument is lost. Man is addressed as a Thou that he may learn from this address how Thou may be spoken. The language of *I and Thou* discloses, it would appear, its fundamental intention. The primary "attitude" of man derives its metaphysical and religious power not from the fact that man is to be convinced to speak, that disciples are made and believers are instructed, but that each man henceforth goes before the world with the openness of an I to its Thou and the awareness of guilt which attends a relapse into the "dead" world of objectification.

Buber's intention is essentially moral and prophetic. A theory of knowledge, a philosophy of history, a doctrine of interpersonal relations, a sociology, a politics, an ideology, have been founded upon Buber's primary intuition. But such theories, however valuable and convincing, transfer insight from the field of action to the normative kingdom of theory. Buber is not interested in becoming a new philosopher; he is concerned with directing the actions of man. A theory of relations may enjoy the distinction of enabling interpretation and analysis, but clearly Buber's use of such intense and evocative language is designed to *convert* man—to turn him out of the accustomed ways of beholding and using the world and to nourish in him the passion to risk himself before the world.

The familiar language of existentialism—"daring," "risk," "the sense of danger"—characterizes Buber's writings before the appearance of *I and Thou.* The familiar language of mysticism—"concentration," "ecstasy," "unification"—also characterizes his writings before the appearance of *I and Thou.* Before *I and Thou* the condition of man was, according to Buber, besetting paradox: man's goal was elsewhere than the present moment and the recognition that it was elsewhere gave to life its quality of failure, despair, and danger. This world was unprofitable and the world of grace was unattainable. The early writings of Buber were suffused with the heavy perfume of Stefan George's romantic pessimism and the predictable gnosticism of an undisciplined mystic.

With the publication of *I and Thou* and the elaboration of its principles in *Between Man and Man,*[20] his translation of portions of the Bible with Rosenzweig, his Biblical studies, *Moses* and *The Prophetic Faith,* his essays on Hasidism and Judaism, his works of political reconstruction, *Israel and Palestine* and *Paths in Utopia,* and his apologetic work, *Two Types of Faith,* it becomes clear that Buber is a reformer. We have called him an "existential humanist." The polarity of existentialism and mysticism which characterized his early writings disappears in a higher order of insight and combination —the mystic touches the existential and the dialogue is defined. Man and God, the temporal and the eternal, the historic and the messianic are brought together in dialogue.

The dialogue—that which is most completely human—is defined against the background of existential incompletion. The humanism—and we mean by this nothing more than the effort to recover and emphasize the importance and meaning of man—is joined with the existential: for our purposes, the concrete and irreducible immediacy of human life. The humanism of Erasmus—the critic of picayune formalism, the opponent of hypocrisy, stupidity, and intellectual arrogance[21]—and the existentialism of the twentieth century are joined in Buber.

The existential humanism of Buber has its center in

[20] *Between Man and Man* contains five works of major significance to the elaboration of Buber's understanding of I-Thou: "Dialogue" (1929), "Education" (1926), "The Question to the Single One" (1936), "What Is Man?" (1938), and "The Education of Character" (1939).

[21] We are aware that one element of Erasmian humanism—the revival of the classics and a preoccupation with Greek and Roman literature as normative to the exposition, style, and method of Christian argument—is absent in Buber. What the classics were to Erasmus, Goethe and Kant would appear to be to many contemporary German thinkers, including Buber.

God. "The extended lines of relation"—which join man with man and man with nature—"meet in the eternal Thou." [22] The terrestrial relations of men do not, however, merely reflect divinity; they are not images or shadows of God nor do they imply God, the way one concept implies another. "Every particular *Thou* is a glimpse through to the eternal *Thou;* by means of every particular *Thou* the primary word addresses the eternal *Thou.* Through this mediation of the *Thou* of all beings fulfillment, and non-fulfillment, of relations comes to them: the inborn *Thou* is realized in each relation and consummated in none. It is consummated only in the direct relation with the *Thou* that by its nature cannot become It." [23]

The concrete Thou—the creature who is greeted without reserve, the mute glance of understanding, the animal whose pain is apprehended—is approached and created (turned from object into living subject) in the image of that which alone validates the reality of the Thou. Each Thou is Thou precisely because God is Thou: each Thou points to God—"is a glimpse through to the eternal Thou" and the speaking of the Thou "addresses the

[22] Buber, *I and Thou,* p. 75.

[23] *Idem.* The inborn Thou mediates the I of every man to his eternal Thou. Upon this somewhat vague and insubstantial peg much of Buber's opposition to the substantive content of revelation, the role of Torah as mediate interpreter of God to man, rests. Buber will trust no substantive idea of mediation. Anything, whether it be Person (obviously incompatible with Jewish tendency), Word (more compatible with Jewish tendency), or the Teaching, is suspect because they are genuinely mediate interpositions between I and Thou. Although the "inborn Thou" is in some sense real, one is tempted to believe that it is simply a literary means of suggesting the bond which unites man and God. If the inborn Thou is really an image or an ego-configuration then it is somehow unreal and its function is only heuristic. If it is substantive and real, then this is pantheism, which Buber professes to disavow. If it is, however, *that* in man which God created (as in "the image of God created He him"), then it has a mediating function only to the extent that man becomes conscious of his being created by God and being united with Him. If this latter, then the phrase "inborn Thou" is unnecessarily portentous and somewhat misleading.

eternal Thou"—and yet no concrete Thou embodies God. The eternal Thou is present in every particular Thou, but only under its aspect of incompletion. God is called Thou only when he is encountered directly. And yet since all relation leads to Him Who is never object, the halting address of love, the chance gesture of mercy may turn man to Him Who *is* love and mercy.

Each man enters the world vested with the loneliness of individuality. Before him there is another. He may turn away, refuse the glance, withdraw the hand—or he may approach. The act of approach which surpasses the procedures of handling and manipulation, which greets without motives or interests, which greets merely because the other is Other who also approaches to be greeted and return greeting—this action of the spirit takes place in what Buber has termed "the sphere of 'between.' " The "between" is actual, a reality; it "is not an auxiliary construction, but the real place and bearer of what happens between men"; it is fluid, deteriorating and arising "in accordance with men's meetings with one another." [24] The "between" world is not neutral. It is the charged atmosphere which surrounds real meeting. It is the "between" which brings forth a new whole out of the meeting of two independent beings. The "between" is intended as a category of being rather than as a psychological category. The "between" draws into the life of man with man that which functions on the "narrow ridge" between creatures.[25] It is a reality born out of the reality of meeting—the medium, the aether, the new whole which is the foundation and achievement of meeting. The between is the "dialogic"—the Word which joins together and is itself given life by the speaking of Thou.

The dialogic, the "between," manifests the "eternal and eternally present Word in history." [26]

[24] Buber, "What Is Man?" pp. 203 f.

[25] *Ibid.*, p. 204.

[26] Buber, *I and Thou*, p. 119.

V. Martin Buber (1878–   )

> The times in which the living Word appears are those in which the solidarity of connection between *I* and the world is renewed; the times in which the effective Word reigns are those in which the agreement between *I* and the world is maintained; the times in which the Word becomes current are those in which alienation between *I* and the world, loss of reality, growth of fate is completed. . . .
>
> But this course is not circular. It is the way. In each new aeon fate becomes more oppressive, reversal more shattering. And the theophany becomes ever *nearer,* increasingly near to the sphere that lies *between beings,* to that Kingdom that is hidden in our midst, there between us. History is a mysterious approach. Every spiral of its way leads us both into profounder perversion and more fundamental reversal. But the event that from the side of the world is called reversal is called from God's side salvation.

What commences with the diagnosis of our times—the death of God and the incompletion of man—ends with the anticipation of redemption. With the reconstruction of man, the foundation of the *zwischen-mensch*—the "between-man"—and the projection of the image of true dialogue and the growth of dialogue, the great turning comes to pass, the Word is empowered and appears, and the eclipse of God ends.

Many sectors of the Jewish community, difficult as this may be to understand, have not received Martin Buber with affection. Often it would seem the Jewish community has not seen fit to read, much less to understand him. It has accused him of betraying Jewish sensibilities; of being overly sympathetic to Christianity; of being what he most certainly is—an existential thinker; of being what he most certainly is not—an irrationalist; of being what he once was, but is no longer—a mystic.

Jewish incomprehension is not without its foundations. Buber has none of the atavism which often masquerades, with conspicuous self-righteousness, as "Jewishness." Buber has not been narrowly nationalistic; if anything his Zionism has been courageously eschatological—*Eretz Yisrael* is more than a land of rescue and terrestrial hope (though Buber is well aware that it must be these first in order to become more than these). Buber's understanding of Christianity and personal affection for Jesus of Nazareth is misunderstood by Jews who do not acknowledge a difference between Jesus of Nazareth and Jesus Christ; the former Buber considers to be "his great brother," but the latter, as anyone reading the work in which this affirmation of fraternity appears will note, is incomprehensible to him.[27]

Critics of Buber who found their criticism upon a reading of his acts and affections, his imputed loyalties and disloyalties, do him a profound injustice. His acts and affections have their unity in his thought and it is his thought—his whole thought—which gives to disparate acts and solitary gestures (incomprehensible, perhaps, by themselves) their fundamental coherence and reasonableness. It is hard, admittedly hard, for a community whose destiny is tied to a litany of acts to understand one who professes his limitless affection for that community and yet refuses, with conviction and self-assurance, to be bound by its traditional litany. Jewry tends to have a monolithic view of loyalty: one is either in the community or outside it; one is either Jewish nationalist, Jewish culturalist, or Jewish believer, or he is outside the community. It is hard to comprehend someone who is believer but does not practice, a scholar of Jewish history and letters but also a passionate student of Western history and letters, a Zionist and yet a supporter of *rapprochement* with the Arab and a loyal opponent of Israeli nationalism.

[27] Martin Buber, *Two Types of Faith,* trans. by Norman P. Goldhawk (London, Routledge & Kegan Paul, Ltd., 1951), p. 12.

V. Martin Buber (1878–   )

Buber is not a "practicing" Jew. What does this, in fact, mean? Construed narrowly, it means that Buber does not obey Jewish law: does not observe the festivals as they are observed, does not pray as prayer is defined, does not fulfill the grammatical requirements of Jewish discipline and obedience. Broadly understood and broadly stated, Buber's action involves a more fundamental question: Is God a lawgiver? It is true and it is accepted by Buber as true that God reveals. The content of revelation is, however, at issue. What does God reveal?[28] Does he only reveal *himself?* Is the content of God's revelation revelation itself, as Rosenzweig wrote in a letter to Buber (June 5, 1926),[29] or is revelation prescriptive? In the former, what God discloses is that he is God—it is his person, its majesty, grandeur, and glory, that overwhelms us; it is our poor imagination, however, that would transform glory and the service due glory into law and regulation.

In "Herut"[30] (1919), Buber argued for a resurgence of primal religious forces which would enable modern man to recover the sense of the Absolute. Inherited religious categories of thought and action had to be abandoned, Buber argued, if man was to live before the face of the divine. As Nahum N. Glatzer has suggested, this essay is the origin of Buber's "metanomianism."[31] But metanomianism is not, as some Jewish critics have argued, antinomianism. Buber does not repudiate Law: he does not suggest that Law is evil, that Law perjures the divine; rather it is that Law inhibits openness before the divine,

[28] One of the author's essays deals with Buber's conception of revelation: cf. "Revelation and Law: Reflections on Martin Buber's Views of *Halachah,*" *Judaism,* Vol. I, No. 3 (July, 1952), pp. 250–56.

[29] Franz Rosenzweig, *Briefe*, ed. by E. Simon and Edith Rosenzweig (Berlin, Schocken Verlag, 1935), p. 435; *On Jewish Learning,* ed. by Nahum N. Glatzer, trans. by William Wolf (New York, Schocken Books, Inc., 1955), p. 117.

[30] Martin Buber, "Herut," in *Reden über das Judentum* (Berlin, Schocken Verlag, 1932), pp. 199–235.

[31] Introduction to *On Jewish Learning,* p. 22.

restricts the power of God, limits the possibilities of human encounter. Law is, one may suggest, that which man interposes between his terror of the numen and the numen itself. Law becomes a retreat from God, a contentment with the devices of human inadequacy. Law is devised because man cannot risk living freely before God.

Rosenzweig opposed "Herut" with his significant essay, "The Builders." [32] However, Rosenzweig's position was incomprehensible to Buber. The passage of Rosenzweig from acknowledgment of the commandments to observance of the Law, from the aspirations of faith and the dramas of the spirit to the sober speech of liturgy and the patient and implicit messianism of the commandments, could not be communicated. Yet what Buber has argued regarding the Law, what Buber has argued regarding the Bible, what Buber has defined as the essential nature of Hasidism, is wholly consistent with his fundamental position. It is his genius and it is consistent with his genius and his task. As with Erasmus, the plateaus of time and the routine must be elevated to the peaks of the spirit; man must be raised up to God. As Erasmus understood Christianity to be the consummation of all that was knowledge to the Greeks and wisdom to the Apostles, so Judaism was to become all that had been the directness of the patriarch and prophet before God. The rescue of modern man was to be effected through the recovery of his freedom and capacity to face God without mediation and artificial self-limitation.

The challenge of Buber's position, and it is a challenge with which Judaism must reckon, is that *religion* as such falsifies that which is most characteristically Jewish: that a religious community *can* achieve sanctity and perpetuate sanctity by addressing each event, each moment, as Thou. This position, however it exceeds the narrowly Jewish, is after all inescapably Jewish. It is that which calls out to us from the Bible. Surely the risk,

[32] *On Jewish Learning*, pp. 72–92.

daring, immediacy, and passion with which the life of Israel was pursued before God testified to a form of spontaneous and unmediated sanctity which, according to Buber, has been achieved only one other time in the history of Western man: in the communities of the *Hasidim*.[33] As surely, however, as religion turns the Thou into the formality of regulations, freezing the word and stopping the open mouth of revelation, as surely is Buber's position open to danger.

God is distant and concealed, Buber argues, when man seals him out of the world. Divine self-disclosure, revelation, the promise of redemption are open to man, but only in response to the speaking of God and the acceptance of God's speech. God cannot be present except in conjunction with man's openness. In a certain sense, it would appear, Buber resolves the problems of theology—the objective content of revelation, the historicity of Biblical experience, the reliability of divine promise and election—by locating God in the flux and unpredictability of divine promise and meeting.

The danger of Buber's humanism, the obverse of its power, is that God is made a respondent of man. Although Buber everywhere insists that God acts, that God reveals, what in fact does God do that is not in response to man? Where is the initiative of God before which man —sullen and unbowed—*must* yield?

In Buber's famous and spirited attack upon Kierkegaard, he repeatedly makes the point that Kierkegaard succumbed to a position which, at the same time that it elevated and centralized the lonely, individual believer, had the consequence of obliterating his obligations to his

[33] In a long-awaited essay Gershom Scholem has strongly criticized Buber's interpretation of Hasidism as being a misrepresentation of the actual life, doctrine, and history of the movement. He claims that Buber has introduced into the Hasidic literature assumptions "that have no root in the texts—assumptions drawn from his [Buber's] own very modern philosophy of religious anarchism." "Martin Buber's Hasidism: A Critique," *Commentary*, October, 1961, pp. 305–16.

fellow men. Kierkegaard, Buber believed, had destroyed the world around him in order to free himself of those encumbrances which obstructed his clear path to God. Quite correctly, it seems to us, Buber affirmed that God cannot be found by subtracting from Him all that which is not God, by distilling God from the world by denying the world;[34] rather God is found by extending man's unity with his world, by embracing all, and locating within all the Thou which leads to God. It would seem that such a position resolutely identifies Buber with the enterprise of an historical community: the individual lives among men and must share with them the task of revealing the now hidden person of God.

At the same moment that Buber defines the task of the individual within the community, it is somehow a timeless and an ahistorical universe in which both pursue their destiny. Buber would, of course, insist that his view is eminently historical, that he is enormously sensitive to the historical moment, the present demand, the evocative call of each hour. And yet, although this might be true in the broadest sense, such a claim is undeniably refuted by Buber's position on Jewish tradition. One cannot help but feel, as one of Buber's most astute critics and warm disciples has suggested, that Buber's image of the Jew in community is somehow defective.[35] The Jew is shaped by tradition but never stands within it; it is his atmosphere, the texture of his situation and longing, the source of his language and his manner, but it is not the giver of his spirit.

If tradition cannot make demands of the Jew, it is divested of its two authorities: it is not the disclosure of God and it is not the command of history. Where tradition cannot gnaw at conscience it is a dying tradition, for

[34] "The Question to the Single One," *Between Man and Man*, p. 58.
[35] Ernst Simon, "Martin Buber and German Jewry," *Year Book III*, Leo Baeck Institute (London, East and West Library, 1958), pp. 34–36. Simon's analysis of Buber's implicit reply to Rosenzweig in the persons of "the Yehudi" and Yeshaja is brilliantly suggestive and contains the germ of our argument here.

it has neither God nor history behind it. Rosenzweig has made clear that he believes God to be behind tradition, but we have questioned whether his view carries as well the force of history. It is our contention, however, that for Buber there is *neither* God *nor* history behind tradition, for the God of Buber and the moment to which He speaks are always in the present. There can be no tradition and certainly no Torah if all is in the present, if the meeting of man and God is limited to that instant in which an individual man goes forth to meet God. The past—and we think it is notable that Buber always narrates the past in an almost mythical atemporality (where dates, persons, sources, and the appraisal of events are overwhelmed by the *message* of the past)—serves Buber as example, paradigm, instruction, but never as genuine past in continuous flow and connection with the present moment and the future to come. The past is simply there to be drawn upon to sustain and give courage to the present. The result is that the Jew can never be in the Jewish community as such. He can address the community, he can partake of the community, he can pass through the community, but if he stands within it and takes its character to be his own he runs the risk of drying up the spirit. Clearly Buber, unlike Rosenzweig, was a victim of the monolith into which Samson Raphael Hirsch had turned the Law. The Law confronted Buber as an objective datum, and as a mere datum Buber quite correctly (and one feels, quite obtusely and without wholehearted effort to do otherwise) rejected it. Where Rosenzweig allows a real tension between the Law and the tradition, the brute demand of the Law and the living option of those who obey it, Buber refuses the tension because he refuses to acknowledge that the Word of God transmits more than the person of God.[36] Rosenzweig removes the Jew from actual history to sacred history, cutting his moorings and connection with the life and culture of the nations in

[36] Cohen, "Revelation and Law."

order to intensify his paradigmatic (and almost mythological) existence. Buber, on the other hand, identifies the historical past with sacred tradition, making both the sources of spiritual decay; for when sacred tradition feeds upon living history it destroys its spontaneity, and when the sheer "pastness" of events encourages the unimportant and the inconsequential to be venerated and memorialized, history gives way to idolatry. The historical past can only be, for Buber, a conditional instruction to the present; what God has said and what tradition transmits have only a contingent status in the present hour.

From both sides, from the side of tradition and from the side of the consummate present, real history becomes irrelevant to sacred history. Where Buber accuses Rosenzweig of affirming but a partial view and Rosenzweig can speak of incompletion in Buber, we feel obliged to say that the defect of both is that the inseparable unity of real history and the person of God has been compromised. The supernatural Jew of Rosenzweig, static in his eternal life amid time, disdainful and superior to the pathos of his natural condition, is inadequate; the natural Jew of Buber, always seeking to escape the enclosures of the present into genuine meeting with God, is also inadequate. If there is a truth, trapped like a unicorn in these dialectical thickets, it can only be found by clarifying how the natural and the supernatural interpenetrate and define each other *at every moment* and *throughout all history.*

The intuition of the *I* and *Thou* restores man to eminence and significance, and opens God to meeting. The Thou cannot be spoken, however, without interruption—love perishes or is transformed into hate. The Thou declines in the world; the Thou increases in the world; God nears; God recedes; redemption approaches; redemption becomes distant. But time endures and history goes forward. The endurance of time and history requires that a line drawn from creation to redemption be sustained. Not only the vertical line of revelation which bisects time, but the horizontal line of order which binds creation to the future must be maintained, while man struggles toward sanctification. The commandments of the revealing God and the Law of the receiving community do not perjure the power of man's freedom or compromise the overwhelming necessity of dialogue. They make certain, however, that man never forgets that it is before God that he lives, that God requires as well as gives. The commands of God—not alone commands to right conduct but commands to sanctity—are not to be obeyed merely because God is the eternal Thou in whom we have our center, but because in some sense God addresses history as well as the individual heart.

VI. CONCLUSION

The thought of Hermann Cohen, Leo Baeck, Franz Rosenzweig, and Martin Buber posed no questions foreign to the historical experience of Judaism. The distinctive quality of their thought arises not from the novelty of their questions but from the unparalleled conditions of Jewish life to which their answers testify. The nexus of traditional Judaism and Western culture which their thought exemplified produced perforce a new Judaism. It is a new Judaism in precisely the sense in which the development of Jewish philosophic theology from the tenth to the fourteenth century projected a new vision and compelled redefinition of all earlier ones. As the centuries from Saadya Gaon to Maimonides were characterized by the effort to establish the viability and truth of classic Judaism before the intellectual challenge of Islam, so the Westernization of Jewish culture, the emergence of the emancipated Jewish intellectual, the attempt to forge a union between the religious patrimony of Judaism and the appealing universe of eighteenth- and nineteenth-century rationalism and enlightenment called Judaism to self-examination and apologia.

Cohen, Baeck, Rosenzweig, and Buber sought the recovery of Judaism and the authentication of Judaism *before*, not *in spite of*, the West. The task was no longer the protection and insulation of Judaism from the West nor was it, like the Eastern European *haskalah*, the popular and often indiscriminate glorification of culture. It was clear that Judaism could not avoid the West. In previous ages it had been willing to meet the challenge of the alien and subverting—to meet the threat of Moslem theology with the development of a "philosophy" of Judaism; for nearly six hundred years on the stage of European history it had been content to remain in the obscurity of the wings, to avoid notice, to be spared the notoriety as well as the danger of publicity.

The egalitarian dictatorship of Napoleon and the insistent liberalism of post-1848 Europe forced upon the Jews of Western and later Eastern Europe the civil, legal, and social institutions of a secular society. The acceptance of a secular version of civic concord in place of the legal provisions of Talmudic law introduced a serious gulf between the secular and the sacred order, between those areas of life to be governed by the State independently of classic Jewish civil law and those areas of life still bound to the authority of Jewish law. Granted the legitimacy of the claim of the secular order and granted the unavoidability of Jewry's acquiescence, it was henceforth impossible to keep Judaism—the religion and the culture—a secret. The Jew was public; Judaism became public with him. Christian Biblical scholarship had now penetrated the arcane domain of rabbinics; the occasional phenomenon of sixteenth-century humanists such as Reuchlin who were familiar and sympathetic to Jewish studies and the Hebrew language became a relative commonplace. The nineteenth century found inquisitive and learned Christians characterizing with generosity and intelligence—Hermann L. Strack—or with hostility and animus—the distinguished Julius Wellhausen—the patrimony of Judaism. The Jew was public. So was Judaism.

It was not remarkable, therefore, that the thinkers with whom we have dealt—thinkers who were creative, original, profound, and influential—should have in common a commitment to Western culture. For both Cohen and Buber the commitment was and remained both primary and prior, informing and shaping their inquiry into Jewish literature and belief. The West was prior: in spite of being the son of a cantor or being raised in the home of Salomon Buber, a distinguished *maskil,* both Cohen and Buber had first to refurbish Judaism from the discarded equipage of youth; philosophy preceded for the one, literature and mysticism preceded for the other. Although the West was equally prior for Baeck and Rosenzweig, the efforts of both thinkers to subdue the West, to bring European influence and Christian history under the domination of the Jewish spirit, tended to moderate the emphatic centrality of Western influences. Kant is never finally Judaized by Baeck, and Rosenzweig's often apologetic stance *contra Christiana* suggests that he was never wholly convinced that Hegel or Christian Europe had been overcome.

The presence of Europe, the challenge of Europe, the temptation of Europe—surely greater for the twentieth-century Jew than Islam had been for the Jew of the twelfth century—shapes the Judaism which the thinkers of the German Jewish renaissance project. Europe—vast, embracing diverse cultures, bound by the communality of Christian beliefs and assumptions, shaped by the unifying secularity of nationalism—gave to modern Judaism its terror. And it is this terror which has been realized and refracted with particular poignancy and despair by Rosenzweig and Buber; with enthusiastic innocence by Cohen; with heroic optimism by Baeck. The

European phenomenon lies at the heart of the malaise of the Jewish Emancipation. The ordered hierarchies and dominions of a universe arranged according to an Aristotelian discrimination of spheres and disciplines, principles and faculties, moral balance and distributive justice, had passed. The Jew was dislocated; his philosophic language, the only philosophic language he had seen fit to mature, was centuries old, geared to an age long since vanished. The scorn and despair of Jehuda Halevi's *Kuzari* and the political ironies of Ibn Verga's *Rod of Judah* were of the past; Maimonides' elaboration of Talmudic stricture regarding the obligations due a Gentile majority, though morally instructive, were beside the point. The Gentile neither sought to overwhelm nor to convert, neither to perjure nor to corrupt. Europe was no longer an enemy. It was fact, a presence, a given, a reality that had to be reckoned with.

What is clear is that Cohen, Baeck, Rosenzweig, and Buber tried to think out a way for modern Judaism: to define the Jewish situation *in* the West, to locate the genius of Judaism *amid* the nations, to sustain what is imperishably true in Jewish belief *in spite of* the presence of Western indifference and negation. In the process they sought to mark out a new ground for Jewish ethics, to locate the existential coefficient of the rabbinic man and the catholic breadth of Jewish uniqueness. For each Jewish reality they sought to find a Western corollary; for each Western reality they sought to find a Jewish corollary. The Jew and the West were made companions in the dialectic of history. The emergence of the dialectic was accompanied by the emergence of the modern Jewish intellectual. The modern Jewish intellectual sustained and bore the dialectic. He was within Judaism and within the West—he challenged one with the other and was alien to both.

It would appear that the German Jewish renaissance is dead and forgotten, that European Judaism is but a memory. The present Jewish age—the age to which we shall shortly turn—is the age of American Judaism.

The ferment and intellectual intensity of the Judeo-Islamic Age was succeeded by the social homeostasis of European Judaism. The stabilization of Jewish life throughout its European Middle Ages was succeeded by the disaster of intellectual and religious unpreparedness which overtook it in the days of the Emancipation. To this challenge the work of modern German Jewish theology was a partial, though failing, response.

The continuity is broken. There is no chain of succession which binds the traditions of European Jewry to the traditions of American Judaism; no neat lines of transfer and influence. All is *de novo*—Orthodoxy was transplanted; Reform was transplanted. The transplantations neither communicated nor fashioned one another. American life and American opportunity contrasted to European disability and European poverty were, it would appear, an unmixed blessing. America fashioned Judaism, and Judaism, it is lamentably but unassailably true, fashioned not a bit (until but recently) the intellectual and spiritual life of America.[1] The passion of Judaism was adaptation; that passion has been relieved of its characteristic frenzy. American Judaism has entered a new period, a period in which something appears to be

[1] One could easily challenge this assertion if we did not elaborate the basis upon which it is made. The Jewish passion for social and political reform, which has undoubtedly contributed to the American ethos, is at once a recognition of the demands of justice as well as a realistic desire to conserve Jewish progress in American life. The Jews have been agitators when they were least secure, and archconservatives, strongly behind the status quo, when they were most secure and well established. The Jewish capacity for adaptation has been most articulate in American life when political and economic security have been supported and rationalized by an undemanding version of Jewish faith. Where either or both components have been lacking the Jews have been either militantly un-co-operative with the established order or devoutly alien in their orthodoxy. The natural Jew has surely contributed to American life; the supernatural Jew has not at all (but could he *sive natura?*).

happening. Whether the Jewish genius for religion will display the tensility, urgency, and creativity to make of American Judaism something more than a boring legacy of conservation remains to be seen. It is clear, however—painfully clear—that if it fails, only God (and perhaps always *only* God) will be responsible for the survival of Jewry in the Exile that endures.

3

Judaism in Solution: The American Moment

I. EXILE AND DIASPORA: A POSSIBLE METAHISTORY

The Dispersion of the Jews and the Exile of the Jews are both facts. They denote the same phenomenon, but their intention and meaning are different.

The Dispersion of the Jews is an historical fact. Jews left Palestine, were driven forth from the Holy Land and settled in the nations of the East and West centuries before the destruction of the Temple. Commencing with the days of the Babylonian Captivity (586 B.C.E.) they were not only dispersed but in Exile. However, Ezra returned from Babylon and the Temple was rebuilt; and whether Jews remained behind in Babylon or Jews traveled forth to settle in Alexandria, Tyre, Rome, or Athens, their focus was restored to Jerusalem. Annual pilgrimages to the Temple, the giving of tithes, the collecting of the half-shekel continued. Though the Jews lived among the nations, spoke their languages, entered into their lives, they refused the nations that transcendent loyalty which bound them still to Jerusalem and to the community of the God of Israel. Theirs was not the despair of incompletion and unfulfilled trust, for Jerusalem lived, the Spirit of God was present in the Holy of Holies, the priests and Levites served and sang, the sacrifices were offered, and prayers for their own well-being were spoken without interruption. The culture of the Dispersion was shaped by the intermixture of Biblical ordinance and textured and interpenetrated by the accentuations of Greek and Roman civilization.

The destruction of the Temple, the abortive uprisings of the communities of the Dispersion, and the final obliteration of the Jewish community of Palestine by the Emperor Hadrian transformed the Dispersion into disaster and thrust the reality of Exile into the foreground of Jewish consciousness. In the archaic past God had covenanted with Israel that it would become his people and he would become its God. A bond of trust and obligation, fidelity and confidence had been sealed. The Temple, however, was now destroyed, the nation dissolved, the people banished, and the millennial Exile commenced. It could not be other, historical Judaism counseled, than that God saw fit to try those he loved and chasten those whom he had called. The rabbis could not but see the destruction of Jerusalem as both a judgment and a trial: a judgment upon the nation's inadequacy and a trial of its vocation.

The introduction of God into the interpretation of historical disaster marked off Israel from the nations. The oracles to whom, Herodotus records, the rulers of Greece repaired for judgment were not called upon to moralize the conduct of the Greeks but to prognosticate their fate, to anticipate the defeats or consummations which the gods had already sealed into the potency of events. The oracles discerned and announced. The prophets did otherwise. Though they prognosticated and predicted, their evocation of the future was intended to instruct. The future was destiny, not fate; it was evitable, not inexorable. They read the conscience of the times, tested its strength and character, and judged. They were, at best, moral realists, uncompromising in their certainty of God's presence and power, conscious of his justice, confident that he would judge history with truth and rectitude. Amos was called to announce justice, Isaiah to proclaim destruction and the surviving remnant, Hosea to affirm love, Jonah to plead reluctantly for Nineveh. The prophets traced the lines of providence already implicit in events, defined their portent, and interpreted their consequences.

It came as no surprise to the people of Israel that after centuries of ambivalent maneuvering, failure, and indecisiveness, God should become weary of its irresponsibility and judge it. The judgment might well be hard and the burden heavy, but this people was as no other people, for as Amos (3:2) emphasized: "You only have I known of all the families of the earth, therefore I will visit upon you all your iniquities." What befell Judaism in the days of its destruction was chastisement, and recall. The nation—a congerie of religious and political ends, a culture bound to a land, a civilization embracing terrestrial ambition and eternal hope—was destroyed. What survived the destruction of the Jewish commonwealth, what has survived until the present day, is the religious culture of the Jew. The survival of that culture is a reflection of its having acknowledged its political destruction to have been the work of God. Had the Jew allowed the possibility that the policies and repressions of Vespasian, Titus, and Hadrian were but historical fortuities, that the ravaging of the Holy Land was but the misfortune of war and the triumph of superior power, it is questionable whether Judaism would have survived. Judaism never countenanced the possibility that what befell it was without ultimate intention and meaning. God revealed himself in his chastisements as well as in his mercies, and his chastisements were but postponed appointments to a future glory and regeneration. Moreover the Jew did not imagine that God destroyed His Temple, desolated His nation, and ejected its inhabitants in a mood of stern and dispassionate rebuke. The rabbis imagined God mourning over His decision, repenting of the necessities of providence, full with remorse and weeping over the requirements which He must exact of His beloved. The Jew is sent into Exile and God goes with him.

The Dispersion is but the historical fact. The Exile transposes that fact into a different order of apprehension, and a construct of faith emerges. The Arch of Titus, a monument of ancient Rome, testifies to an historical triumph of the Empire and an historical destruction of a people. The fast of the ninth of Av, the poems of lamentation, the juxtaposition of suffering and redemption in the liturgy, the martyrologies of the Day of Atonement, the thousand and one allusions to destruction and Exile which thread the litany of acts incumbent upon the Jew witness to the transformation of terrestrial event into a cosmic disaster.

The Exile is a cosmic, not an historical, event in Jewish tradition. The Jew goes forth among the nations. This is God's action. The nation receives the Jew, grants him asylum, establishes his station, defines his limitations, and fences his universe. This is the action of secular history. What has been to the nations a response to an alien, unassimilable people in its midst is to Israel the consequence of Exile. The historical catastrophe is elevated to a metahistorical reality.

The Jews amid Islam and Christendom refined the conditions of their historic religious culture. They accepted the limitations imposed by their external environment, and acknowledged the sovereignty of non-Jewish authority to define its hegemony; and within the universe to which they were granted free access and control, they fashioned a new culture. It was, to be sure, a ghetto culture. This is only to define pejoratively what was in context a voluntary and desirable self-enclosure. Gentile society had no wish to be penetrated by the Jew and Jewry was prudent enough to recognize that free contact and intermingling was a precarious adventure. It was content to maintain its faith, explore its wisdom, and leave redemption to God. But, what—alone upon the sea of Islam and Christendom—did the Jew understand by redemption? Redemption meant, if it meant anything at all, the end of the Exile. And what, if anything, did the end of the Exile signify? It meant the coming of the Messiah, the restoration of the people to its appointed land, the rebuilding of the Temple, and the conversion of the nations to the one, true, and holy God of Israel.

The Exile was the pivot on which the creativity or conservation of Jewish religion and culture turned. When it was deemed that the Exile would be long and unrelenting, tradition was conserved, the adaptation of Jewish law to the requirements of the nations and the exigencies of time and place was undertaken, centers of authority and teaching were established. Redemption was distant and the people of Israel must live on. Tradition must be sharpened and defined so that it might be transmitted to the next generation whose turn it was to await the Messiah. But apocalyptic waves swept over the Dispersion, visions and portents were announced, cataclysmic wars shook Europe, and seers, prophets, and madmen rose out of Israel to proclaim the coming of the End and to declare that the Exile was shortly to be commutated. This dialectic of expectation and despair, conservation and perpetuation, unfolded many times in the two-thousand-year Exile of the Jew. It was the Exile, however, which cadenced the rhythm of Jewish existence, elevating it to expectation and bringing it low to the funereal despair of renewed waiting.

The apocalyptic view of history which flows from the overwhelming awareness of Exile is possible only as long as decisive events, the true matter of history, remain remote, distant, and obscure. It was possible for the Jew —secreted in his ghetto, concentrated in his prayers or

Kabbalistic combinations, believing himself to conserve a purer and more exalted ordinance than the nations—to scan secular history with a supernatural eye. The Jew was trained by his sequestration and loss of nexus with the primary dramas of history to locate in the events of the world signs and indices, anticipations of crises and calamities which would befall not only himself but all history.

The moment that the history of the nations becomes the history of the Jew, that the fortunes of the nations become the personal fortunes of the Jew, apocalyptic history disappears. The assimilation of the Jew to Western history, or rather the Westernization of Jewish history, accelerates with the Enlightenment and the advent of Emancipation. At that moment the Jew breaks into Western history. The emancipation of European Jewry in the nineteenth century ended the hermetic isolation of the Jew. It defined new alternatives and natural choices which served to undermine the integrity formed of the image of the Exile and the historical condition of the Jewish people. It made of the Exile a conscious, separable, and expendable principle, where previously—for eighteen centuries—it had been the valence of Jewish culture. It was obviously foolish to maintain such a mysterious, obscure and private notion as "Exile" when the terms and conditions of normalization had been accepted. To be sure, it was still possible to speak of Diaspora—a harmless Greek substitute for the word "Exile" —but Diaspora no longer filled the consciousness of the people, but had become a description of its historical situation.

"Diaspora" and "Dispersion," describing, as these terms do, the *physical* separation of the people from its land, the removal of a people from the source of its cultural integrity, was deprived of its symbolic power. The Dispersion is an event of history. The Dispersion ends when the people are restored. The Zionist movement and the triumph of Zionism in the founding of the State of

Israel consummate the natural return of the people to its home. The physical incubus of Diaspora is ended. Even if Jews choose not to return, determine not to be gathered into the Land, decide to remain in the countries of the Dispersion, it cannot be doubted that Diaspora has ended. The question still remains, and indeed it is the question which underlies the ideological postures of American Jewish life: Is the Exile ended?

There is little question but that the doctrine of the Exile was formed against the background of actual dispersion. Nations do not anticipate disaster, formulating doctrine to account for the disaster that has not occurred. Nations act retrospectively, reading into history the illuminations of theology, transmuting the past in the interests of the present, reconstructing history to interpret the given moment, the current crisis, the immediate need. St. Augustine constructed the City of God in the face of those events for which he sought to account; the barbarians were already at the gates of Rome and the Empire was crumbling when Augustine recalled the Christian from his terrestrial ambition to his eternal hope.

Israel has a somewhat more ambiguous and mysterious tradition of historical reflection. It does anticipate disaster. It constructs the future, as much as the past, in the light of the present. It comprehends its destiny under the Kingship of God and construes its historical course under his dominion. The prophets foresaw disaster, warned of the Exile, described the surviving remnant. Israel has the harrowing distinction of having defined a doctrine of history which anticipates and builds into the life of the nation a recognition of the consequences which defection and spiritual waywardness, idolatry and paganism entail. The doctrine of the Exile was not determined *post facto*. To be sure, the sophistication of the doctrine, its innumerable ramifications and eddies, were defined in rabbinic tradition after the Dispersion had taken place and the Temple was destroyed. The heart of the doctrine can be located, however, not in the observations of the Pharisees and their descendants, but in the writings of Jeremiah, Isaiah, and the Psalmist (familiar as they were with the Babylonian Exile).

The Exile is a principle of exegesis which may be used to interpret the destiny of the Jew from the destruction of the Temple to the coming of the Messiah. The Exile is active, not passive: God judges, Rome acts, Israel is exiled and remains exiled. God restores, the descendants of Rome repent, the exile is ended, and the anointed of God, his Messiah, the bearer of divine tidings of regeneration and restoration, enters history. The Exile is an eschatological principle. It is meaningless as an historical category; however, as a metahistorical category it enables the eyes of the believer to be opened and understand, to sustain and bear, to be patient and wait. Like all religious realities, the reality of the Exile is something tangible, immediate, active for him who lives with it, who is penetrated by it and in turn works upon the world in response to it.

The Exile is of immense importance to the interpretation of the Jewish mind precisely because it has textured its unfolding in the past, marked it with an unrelenting sense of burden and significance, shaped its pride and formed its prescience, defined its vulnerability and its characteristic indignation. The Exile, at worst, has transmitted a recognition that the world is not right, that it is unfulfilled and incomplete. The Exile, at best, is a recall of history to transcending obligations. It is a constructive reality because it signals the beginning of redemption as much as it marks the end of a pristine and ancient homogeneity. The driving forth is the first moment of recall. This is but to project the old and marvelous paradoxes upon which religious enthusiasm lives—the losing which is finding, the despair which announces hope, the end which begins anew. The Exile is the end which begins the final, ultimate, and consummate end.

I. Exile and Diaspora: A Possible Metahistory

If, indeed, the Exile and the sense of the Exile are the groundwork upon which the Jewish mind has fashioned the religious culture of the Jew, we must ask what must befall the Jewish mind—its passion, its authenticity, its creativity—if this motive concept is abandoned. What happens if the Exile is "over"? It might be answered that the Exile is simply not over, the alteration of historical fortune having no bearing upon ultimate categories. The essential character of man and history is not altered by any temporary penance or conversion. The fact that the nations of the West have exhibited revulsion before the crimes of Hitler, that they have co-operated in the fulfillment of Zionism, that Anglo-Saxon society presently considers anti-Semitism to be vulgar and insupportable, gives one no cause to assume that man's capacity for corruption is lessened. It is dangerous to renew optimism. It is at the very least unrealistic to assume that the contemporary improvement of attitudes toward Jews and Jewish aspiration has any bearing upon the reality of the Exile. To consider such alteration relevant is to mistakenly construe the Exile to be but a parochial, limited, private category. The Exile is a universal category; its significance is universal; its scope and pertinency are universal. Exile is surely bodied forth out of the experience of a peculiar people—but a peculiar people which holds itself and is held by others (notably Christians) to be unique and chosen, an index of the world, a cipher of transcendence and divine intention. To that extent, again holding with the assumptions which Jews have immemorially believed and which the nations of the world believe concerning it, the Exile of the Jew is a symbol of the "sin" of the world. If you will—and we suggest this with a sense of its liability to misconstruction—the concept of Exile is the Jewish doctrine of the Original Sin, an animadversion upon the corruptibility of all history, the violence of all events, and the defection of all nations. What Original Sin imputes to the individual sinner, the Exile imputes to the collectivity of all nations.

And so we have sought to transform the Exile from interpretation of history into a judgment upon history, a judgment which suggests something of the Jewish understanding of *all* history—the profane history of all nations and peoples. From this point of view the Exile continues to be an indispensable reality for the Jew. It enters into the immediate life of the Jew; it underwrites his awareness of history, expresses his consciousness of the formlessness, transiency, and insubstantiality of all history that is separated from God.[1]

It is exceedingly difficult for the Jews of America to keep present before their minds the reality of the Exile. They can understand the harassed and persecuted Jews of all ages and times living out the meaning of the Exile. They can imagine them—those distant and despairing Jews—projecting phantasms of Messiah and Israel *redivivus* and sustaining on their behalf the humiliations of each day. It is difficult, however, for the Jews of America to behave like these remote ancestors. The reminders of Exile amid security, the allusions to disaster and incompletion in an environment of incomparable lushness and sanguinity, seem bizarre, incongruous, if not somehow ungrateful. To the extent that Judaism insists that, if it is a religious culture, religion is no less obligatory than culture, it seems unyielding, irredentist, and vaguely fanatic. And finally, to the extent that it founds its

[1] Recently Emil Fackenheim observed—and we hold with his views—that "had their hope [the hope of the Jews] been nothing more than a national hope, the Jews of the Diaspora would have been forced many times to abandon it. It was precisely because it was more than a national hope that they could retain it. Hence, although it may seem paradoxical, it is nevertheless true that it was precisely because of their messianic sense of kinship with all the nations that the Jews did not lose their identity among the nations. . . ." Of course, Fackenheim is concerned here with a somewhat different problem, that of Jewish survival. He shares with us, however, the conviction that Jewish survival is unavoidably religious and not a consequence of group loyalty, social identity, or characteristic Jewish stubbornness. See Emil Fackenheim, "Jewish Existence and the Living God," *Commentary*, August, 1959, p. 132.

religious culture upon transcendent claims and commitments, it seems dogmatic, unscientific, and irrational.

The predicament of Judaism stems from an historical irony: it has nobody but *born* Jews upon whom to depend for sustenance and survival. It has enjoyed no periodic infusions of new peoples and cultures; it has not benefited from the reception of new adherents and the renewal of passion, vigor, and intensity which the convert usually brings to his adopted faith. Judaism and the Jew have been historically on suffrance to the immediacies of events and environment. The act of perpetuation has been a gesture of conservation before the alien, survival in the face of social and political depredation. Until the nineteenth century, Judaism survived by stubborn indifference made possible by social distance and voluntary self-limitation. The twentieth century has put an end to such isolated self-dependence. It has become impossible to play off historical Judaism against the incursions of secularism and remain reasonably confident that Judaism will emerge the victor. Gradually the Jew has cast off Judaism and Judaism has retired into sullen resentment, European Orthodoxy becoming increasingly inflexible and intransigent,[2] and American Reform becoming increasingly confident and ambitious. It could not have been otherwise. The Jew and Judaism were increasingly polarized and set in opposition. The assimilated Jew vanished into the anonymity of the cultures of the world,

[2] It has been observed—not without justification—that the tendency of classic rabbinic Judaism to be lenient and forbearing in its interpretation of the Law has been reversed in recent centuries. The rabbis of the Talmud, great legists though they were, were infinitely more sensitive than their modern descendants to the necessity of adaptation without change, leniency without compromise, modification without corruption. The legal ideology of contemporary Orthodoxy has been on the side of inflexibility: all adaptation, leniency, and modification are seen as breaches in the wall of tradition. The assumption seems to be that prevailing ignorance and indifference (and the Orthodox often succumb to the temptation of considering all nonobservance to be merely the consequence of ignorance and indifference) will, given encouragement by leniency, willfully trample the vineyards of the Law.

setting his mark upon his adopted culture but rarely marking it with anything identifiably Jewish.[3] The religious Jew, resisting the temptation and opportunities of secularization, retreated into conservation, hostility, and annoyance with those who did not have the "courage" to survive as religious Jews.

The vast majority of Jews do not make conscious and articulate decisions as do the assimilators and the traditionalists. They neither choose nor are chosen; they neither assimilate nor retreat; they have neither self-hatred nor pride. It is to these, because they are the majority, that the ideologists of assimilation and the new theologians (and in this latter category we include ourself) direct their attentions. The decisions of these millions of American and English Jews[4] will determine

[3] As we have said elsewhere, it is trying, to say the least, to have both Jew and non-Jew seeking to identify the characteristically Jewish qualities of sundry Jewish worthies of science, literature, and the arts. Three years ago, *The Times Literary Supplement* devoted an article in its special supplement "The American Imagination" to "The Jewish Part in American Literature." The anonymous author of this essay is to be congratulated for having undercut the admiration of Jews for Jews at any price and the popular and unsophisticated philo-Semitism of many Christians. The writer observed quite wisely that the prevailing mark of the Jewish contribution to American letters is that, as the postwar years wear on, it is ceasing to be observably Jewish; that the Jew is better assimilated than ever before; and that what a generation ago would have been unmistakably Jewish is now so commonplace as to be unexceptionable. The Jew tends, to the extent that he wishes to remain an eccentric in the secular order, to look for wilder causes than Judaism or Jewish ancestry to mark him out (say Norman Mailer's passionate effort to de-assimilate, not through a return to Judaism, but through an identification with yet another unassimilated culture, that of the American Negro). "The Jewish Part in American Literature," *The Times Literary Supplement*, November 6, 1959, p. xxxv.

[4] We single out American and English Jews and fail to mention the Jewish communities of South America and the atrophied and dying communities of Europe, because the former have the following significant characteristics in common: (1) they participate in a single Anglo-Saxon language and culture, (2) they have enjoyed an incomparably tranquil history, and (3) they are rich, secure, and well-educated communities. From them the Judaism of the Exile

the future of Judaism. If they depart the Jewish community and none appear to replace them, the community's richest resource shall have vanished. Their disappearance from the Jewish community will not of itself destroy Judaism, since their quantity will not offset quality—if, indeed, quality of purpose and intellect remains with the religious community that survives. The tragedy is that it seems unlikely that the community that survives such attrition will retain the independence of spirit necessary to persevere. This is so precisely because American Judaism is so much a reaction to what its least religious elements demand. In the last fifty years, the uninformed, the religiously illiterate, and the socially assimilated have succeeded in affecting, if not shaping, the religion offered by the synagogue. Judaism is more than ever a reaction to the disinterest and embarrassment of the already secularized Jewish majority. It is inescapable that this should have been so: the Jew has become, in matters Jewish, doggedly and uncritically American. For a moment let us put aside reproach and ask a somewhat different question: What precisely does it mean for the Jew to become an American? This is not asked against the background of what he has neglected or forgotten in order to effect his Americanization. The problem is not to parade before him the shades of his disappointed ancestors, for we have no desire to encourage Jewish survival out of some necrophilic obligation

---

will derive strength or perish. It is doubtful, very doubtful indeed, if the State of Israel can give strength to the Exile at the present moment. The contribution of Israel may well be creative—at this moment anything fresh, inspiriting, and to the point can be accredited as creative. The question is: Can Israel, functioning under the conviction that it has begun the days of the Messiah, that the political restoration of Israel fulfills the requirements of a nationalistic messianism, address itself to those outside who believe, firstly, that the Exile endures and, secondly, that Israel, in spite of being homeland, is—as are all things Jewish until their proper consummation—in *galut?* Cf. pp. 183–84, where we have discussed the difference between the exile of the physical nation and the exile of the spirit.

to honor the memory of the dead. It is evident, however, that something has occurred in the United States (and perhaps even in Israel) [5] which had not occurred previously in Jewish history.

In centuries past Jewish communities assimilated and were forgotten. In our days Jewish communities assimilate but do not disappear. In centuries past, ten of the tribes of Israel vanished into an encompassing paganism; thousands of Jews who were dispersed to Babylon with the destruction of the First Temple did not return; myriads of Jews were Hellenized and Romanized and only inscriptions and manuscripts testify to their ethnic origin; and in modern times thousands of European Jews—German, French, Italian, and to a lesser extent, English—converted to a status Christianity, pocketed their baptismal certificates, and vanished into Christendom. To be sure, many of these passed through the trauma of Fascist total recall, but many have remained finally, successfully, and devoutly non-Jews.

The pattern of conversion and assimilation has not been the American pattern. If anything, precisely the reverse has been the case: assimilation to prevailing American values is so commonplace, acceptable, and virtuous an alternative that it is no longer productive of explicit cultural crisis. Many of the most thoroughly assimilated American Jewish families are among the most devoted supporters of Jewish religious institutions. How can this be, one might ask? It is simple. Judaism is so taken for granted, so conventional, so unexceptionable in our times—in these post-Hitler, post-Israel days of pride—that assimilation can go side by side with ostensible religious conformity. We cannot afford in these days to deal with heretics, disbelievers, and malefactors with

[5] If one questions the extent and seriousness of the problem of the de-Judaization of the Israeli Jew, the brilliant articles of Ernst Simon ("Are We Israelis Still Jews?" *Commentary*, April, 1953, pp. 357–64; and "What Price Israel's 'Normalcy'?" *Commentary*, April, 1949, pp. 341–47) will prove alarming.

the same degree of authority and discipline with which they were treated by the Babylonian Exilarchate, the Spanish *Aljama*, or the Polish Council of the Four Lands. In those days failure to accept the authority of the Jewish court, the flouting of its decisions, the bringing of dishonor to the community of Israel, religious heterodoxy, and, in such cases as those of Uriel Acosta or Spinoza, theological heresy, elicited the varying decrees of excommunication which the Jewish courts could impose. In those days the individual Jew needed the Jewish community; he could not afford to transgress boldly and wildly because the community possessed the power to disown him. To be cast forth on the nations was more perilous then than it is now, for there was no secular community willing to receive him.

The social and political power of the Jewish community was not alone in ensuring conformance to tradition. This would be to interpret the power of excommunication as a mere device of coercion. It was not. Beneath power lay belief: the power of the community was valid because the beliefs upon which it rested were acceptable. The generality of Jews, until the middle of the nineteenth century, accepted the structured system of beliefs and actions which the Torah defined, which tradition elaborated, and which the consensus of the Jewish community enforced.

The condition of Judaism in America is not without its reasons and explanations. These reasons and explanations are familiar; they are also just. They describe the necessary response of the natural Jew to the invitation of a congenial environment. All reasons and explanations reduce themselves to one: the American environment and the American tradition of democratic freedom have made it possible for the Jew to become an American without ceasing to be a Jew. There can be nothing objectionable in this historical good fortune. The natural Jew—the Jew of affections and humors, conventional needs and normal wants, the Jew who, like the natural Christian, is a product of nature and a creature of history—has found the American scene so pliant, tractable, and robust as to be able not only to welcome him but to absorb him.

The paradoxical triumph of Americanism lies in the fact that it received the Jew from the very beginning. The Jew, however, entering as he does each new environment with a sense of danger and suspicion, initially reacted by anticipating hostility and disarming his seeming "enemy." Many Jews divested themselves of that which they considered most noticeable, provocative, and embarrassing, namely, their religion. It is discovered now, fifty years or more after the process of divestment had commenced, that America never wished the Jew to sacrifice his Judaism, that his religion was a positive asset, indeed, the most respected and laudable asset he possessed. His ethnic peculiarities, his lingual eccentricities, his social mores, the American environment was patiently willing to abide until they quietly vanished. Today, nearly two generations after the last wave of Jewish immigration subsided, Yiddish has become a dying language, the Eastern European beard and caftan are but a discomforting archaism, those habits of mind and behavior characteristic of *shtetl* society have already been bred out of the second- and third-generation Jew.

America was tolerant of the Jew; the Jew was conspicuously intolerant of himself. He did more than the environment demanded; he paid a higher price than was asked.

II. THE STAGES OF AMERICAN JUDAISM

It is possible to speak, with loose attention to the specifics of historical events, of four significant phases in the unfolding of American Judaism and the definition of its characteristic habits of mind.

II. The Stages of American Judaism

Firstly, the era of colonization, which extends from the arrival of a community of Portuguese Jews from Recife, Brazil, in 1654 to the late eighteenth century. These were the days when intrepidity emboldened by religious persecution brought to the United States Jews of Spanish and Portuguese descent. These Jews, elegantly traditional, formed in the gentler, more pliant atmosphere of Sephardic Judaism, sought on the American scene religious toleration and the opportunity to pursue their commercial enterprises untrammeled by the religiopolitical agents of Old World autocracy. They came in search of freedom, and they wished, not a life of pious exaction like the Puritans of New England, but pious peace. They built a number of splendid synagogues, several of which stand to this day; they arranged communal charities to succor their own; they were sniffy and disdainful of poverty (confusing it, as good Americans were often to do, with indigence); they were, in deference to their marrano ancestry, opposed to Christianity and attentive to the coming of the true Messiah; but they were not overly learned or punctilious in their practice of Judaism.

Secondly, upon the thin foundation of Sephardic Judaism the heavier, more consequential, stubborn, and ambitious immigration of German Jews was to be laid. The earlier immigration of German Jews, those who arrived prior to 1840, were overwhelmingly younger men from the poor rural areas of Germany, Yiddish-speaking in the main, unsophisticated and observant. They were appalled by the frightening proximity and comparative accessibility of Gentile society and the cold aloofness of their Sephardic coreligionists. In time they performed as might be expected: they either intermarried with the Sephardic community and assimilated to their mores or formed communities which reflected both their German ancestry and a more familiar Ashkenazic liturgy.

By the 1840s changes in the German Jewish community had begun to take place. The overthrow of Napoleon and the victory of the Holy Alliance, followed by the abortive revolution of 1848, and the growing agitation within and without German Jewry for Jewish emancipation brought to the United States a mixed Jewish immigration: political dissenters, intellectuals, the representatives of a nascent Reform movement, and a further influx of young people formed by the rural traditions of Jewish Orthodoxy. This amalgam produced within a short span a significant cultural movement indigenous to the American scene, but reflective of nostalgias, alienations, and hopes which Jews cut off from their German environment, but passionate to locate themselves in the New World, might be expected to develop.

The German Jewish religious intellectual supplied the leadership from which the Reform movement, a distinctive product of German Jewish immigration, emerged. The Reform movement crystallized the ambition of German Jewry—distorted and arrested in the post-Napoleonic reaction—and gave it a peculiarly acceptable American form. The history of Reform Judaism in America is complex but fascinating, marked as it is by the formidable influences of such figures as Isaac Mayer Wise (1819–1900), David Einhorn (1809–1879), Bernhard Felsenthal (1822–1908), and Samuel Hirsch (1815–1889). Although accented by differences of stratagem and variations of emphasis and rhetoric, these leaders of Reform Judaism (first in 1869 at Philadelphia and later in the enunciation of the Pittsburgh Platform in 1885) succeeded in creating a new Judaism. The abortive and tragically unsuccessful efforts of Isaac Mayer Wise and the passionate religious journalist Isaac Leeser to form a co-ordinated Judaism in America had failed. In place of a Judaism which would strike a balance between the authority of tradition and the guaranteed secularity of American society, Reform Judaism—encouraged and abetted by its teachers and supporters who had remained abroad—chose the radical alternative. The Jew must be separated from his restrictive limitations—limitations which no longer had a foundation in nature (much less super-nature) or history (much less eschatology), but were so many retardations of the unfolding spirit which Hegel had bestowed upon Reform Judaism as the final gift of Christian culture to the wandering Jew. Whatever the many virtues of Reform Judaism, one virtue which it did not possess was intellectual self-consciousness. Although it claimed to exalt the critical and historical intelligence, it failed to scrutinize the philosophic foundations upon which it wished to build the mausoleum of historical Judaism. We need not rehearse what Reform Judaism saw fit to discard: its *disjecta membra* included the Hebrew language, the traditional prayerbook, the obligation of the commandments, the specific institutions of the Sabbath and the festivals, the personal Messiah, the restoration of Zion. What it saw fit to retain—the election and mission of Israel—reflects a thoroughly uncritical acceptance of a Hegelian intellectualization of the universe. The irony of the Jewish situation (and it is a not uncommon irony) is that where Hegel reads the Jews out of history at a rather early stage in the unfolding of Western culture, nineteenth-century Jewish thought reinstalls the Jew at the very peak of the Hegelian system. Hegel discharges us, but with insistent and stubborn folly we accept Hegel for what he thought himself to be: the incarnation of the fulfilled Logos; and since the truth is independent of its spokesmen (particularly when a tradition is casting about for a good and useful truth), we take on Hegel's Absolute Idealism as though it were our own.

The incision of the German philosophic intellect—notwithstanding the significance of pragmatic Reform in the economy of American Judaism—into the American Jewish community left a wound which has only in these present decades begun to heal.

Thirdly, without documenting the vast inundation of Eastern European Jewry which commenced in the late decades of the nineteenth century and did not ebb until the early twentieth, it is enough to say that more than two million Jews were admitted to the United States in a period of fifty years.[1]

The Eastern European immigrant was by no means *one* immigrant. His motivations were external: persecution, famine, poverty, the increase in discriminatory legislation, and impressment into foreign armies were to be numbered among them. But there were, as well, internal longings and concerns which a closed, static, and inflexible environment was no longer able to fulfill. Eastern European Jewry was profoundly traditional; it was learned and it was pious; it was also illuminated by the lightning flashes of the *haskalah* and political radicalism. The German Jew was already familiar with Gentile society by the middle of the nineteenth century. The era of the French Revolution was over, the German romantics had already admitted the Jew to their society, baptism and assimilation were the familiar compatriots of emancipation. Jewish society had already given to the West Moses Mendelssohn, Solomon Maimon, Rachel von Varnhagen, Ludwig Börne, and Heinrich Heine by the time the first light of the West was to penetrate the dense atmosphere of Eastern Europe. What was already a fact and a mission for Western Judaism was but a remote and fabled dream for the East. It is quite understandable, therefore, that the Enlightenment and Emancipation shook Eastern Europe as profoundly as they did. However, they would not of themselves have brought millions of Eastern European Jews to American shores. Jews would have been content, as millions were, to remain in the familiar environment of Warsaw, Vilna, and Odessa. But Russian and Polish anti-Semitism did not spare the poor and unenlightened: the pogroms of the 1880s, culminating in the Kishinev Pogrom of 1903, accelerated mass emigration. The Jews who arrived in the United States in

[1] Anita Libman Lebeson, "The American Jewish Chronicle," in Louis Finkelstein, ed., *The Jews*, Vol. I (New York, Harper & Brothers, 1949), p. 338.

those decades were fleeing from one society rather than seeking the certain promise of another. The United States was a myth to Eastern Europe. It was surely a land of promise, but promise unconfirmed and unknown. It is not surprising, therefore, that these migrant millions should have quickly despaired: the poverty that greeted them—for they were mostly unskilled workers—was appalling; the language was unfamiliar and difficult to acquire; the slum areas in which they congregated were desperately congested and noxious; the society which they entered was formidably cold and stern. From the point of view of the religious development of American Jewish life, however, the appearance on the American scene of millions of nominally observant Jews was an unexpected fortuity. It explicitly challenged the regnant religion of Reform Judaism. It made impossible the triumph of Reform and the defeat of the traditional Judaism defended by Isaac Leeser, Marcus Jastrow, Sabato Morais, and their supporters.[2] Although for a number of decades the transplanted Orthodoxy of Eastern Europe fought a holding action against the erosive influence of both American secularity and Reform Judaism, its presence provided the occasion for the development of a middle ground between traditional Judaism, in its Western European mode of *Wissenschaft des Judentums,* and what, for want of a more accurate phrase, might be termed "historical Judaism." [3] The Conservative Juda-

[2] Moshe Davis, "Jewish Religious Life and Institutions in America," in Louis Finkelstein, ed., *The Jews,* Vol. I (New York, Harper & Brothers, 1949), pp. 379–97; see in particular pp. 379 f.

[3] It would seem appropriate to consider at length the thought of Solomon Schechter (1849–1915) in the development of American Judaism. In one sense it is desirable to do so, but in another wholly impossible and out of place. Schechter was a great scholar, teacher, and apologete—in the exemplification of these roles one could construct his view of Judaism; but it would only be a construct. One cannot turn to Schechter, as one would to Kaplan or Heschel, with the expectation of finding an articulate and developed statement of ideas. For Schechter the ideas are immanent in the historical situation—there is the broad, overarching, unquestioned commitment to God, Torah, and the Jewish people and then there are the novelties

ism which emerged never thought of itself as a middle way. It was pushed into the middle way because its own understanding of traditional Judaism proved unacceptable to the hardening position of the Orthodox community. By contrast with Reform Judaism, Conservative Judaism was, however, outspokenly traditional. Its traditionalism emerged as a not quite articulate, clear, and convincing compromise of what it construed to be the extremes. It defined the protest of an already Americanized upper-middle-class Judaism to the supernally abstract and idealized Judaism of the Reformers. It distinguished itself, both in the character of its moving spirits and in its institutions, from the literalistic Talmudism that characterized the defensive Orthodoxy that opposed it.

In the decades that have elapsed since the early part of the twentieth century much has changed. Reform is less Reform. Conservative Judaism is, in its varied aspects, both somewhat more Reform and somewhat more Orthodox. Orthodoxy is more intellectually self-conscious and self-critical, although no less absolutistic and unqualified. The decades that intervened between the establishment of Reform, Conservative, and Orthodox modes of Jewish religion in America and the present, somewhat altered and complaisant, attitude which each assumes toward the other, are a result of the crisis through which American and world Judaism have passed, but which they have not yet survived.

Fourthly, the crisis of which we speak—and it was a fundamental and as yet unanalyzed crisis—was formed by multiple tributary influences.

In the decades from the 1910s to the end of World

---

and discoveries embedded in concrete history. At one and the same time, therefore, we are obliged to consider Schechter the most suggestive and searching mind that American Judaism has produced (and for that reason he is the only thinker with whom we deal in the closing theological chapter of this book) while considering his conceptual formulations as such to be too interstitial and schematic to be extracted—that is, too implicit, too unanalytic, too rooted in history to be considered abstractly with ease or point.

War II, the American Jewish community changed character: the first generation of poor immigrants have produced at least two generations of well-educated, adjusted, and thoroughly acculturated American Jews. To arrive, however, at the present generation of middle-class Judaism, it was necessary to pass through a period of intellectual awakening that left little of traditional Judaism unaffected. In the decades of the twenties and thirties, Jews of any intellectual aptitude—and they were uncommonly numerous—were querulous and dissatisfied. The securities that defined their ancestry had been weakened and the American society to which they turned was demonstrably unjust. Neither Judaism nor American democracy was adequate to the needs of that younger generation. In those decades the techniques of flight and alienation were perfected: Jews left Judaism for the anonymity of the American middle class or the commitments of American radicalism.

Much as we might wish to ignore it, both assimilation and radical protest are indigenous extremes of American life. Those who are assimilating make the vastness, generosity, and tolerance of American life into an excuse for discarding the worn-out ties which bind immigrants to ancestral European society. America rationalizes assimilation for the assimilating. The radical makes the native passion for justice and equity into the foundation for Americanizing European models of protest. Both assimilation and radicalism were the extreme techniques by which Jewish self-alienation was temporized by the American experience.

Whatever America gained by the vigor of Jewish intellectual reaction to America, Judaism assuredly lost. In the twenties, thirties, and forties Jewish intellectuals affirmed their distance from Judaism. There is an indescribable pathos in their fury and their incomprehension, their impatience and their longing. They were, however, alienated from a tradition which was equally alienated from them. It is not only that the Jewish intellectual deserted Judaism; Judaism deserted the Jewish intellectual. To be sure, there were moments of halting recall and *rapprochement*. The death of six million Jews and the vindication of Herzl's Zionism affected many, but the effect has not proved enduring. If anything, it served to underscore alienations already well defined: some saw in the victory of Zionism the last excuse for remaining Jewish in the Diaspora, whereas others interpreted the juxtaposition of disaster and renascent nationalism with the continuing necessity for affirming the Exile.

In all events, the intervening decades which separate our own from those of the immigrant generations witnessed the attrition of Judaism in America. During those decades no Judaism—whether Reform, Conservative, or Orthodox—prospered in the spirit (however much they may have improved in the flesh). Yet they were not decades without inner transition and movement. The plight of Judaism, the obvious testimony of empty synagogues, declining interest in religious education, and uninspired leadership, moved a number of Jewish thinkers to shift their emphasis from conservation to the search for the conditions of Jewish survival in America. The ideologists of Jewish survival—we will consider Mordecai Kaplan and his younger but dissenting disciple, Milton Steinberg—have defined an American Judaism founded upon the strongest elements of an enlightenment and a democratic tradition and the most malleable and accommodating elements of historical Judaism. It was their intention to make Judaism contemporary, and acceptable doctrine for Jews who had passed into the secular world without having used their secularity as a conscious rationale for assimilation. The reconstruction of Judaism was an effort to induce the disaffected to return. It was directed outward to the community, for only upon the revitalization of the community, it believed, could an authentic Judaism be refounded.

There were others, however, who came later; who entered the life of American Judaism after the ideology of reconstruction had begun to run its course. Judaism had survived, but the quality of its survival remained questionable. These others—we shall consider Abraham Joshua Heschel and Will Herberg as distinct but related thinkers—turned from the task of ensuring survival to the assessment of its quality.[4]

III. JUDAISM AND SURVIVAL: MORDECAI M. KAPLAN

It would be folly to deny that Judaism is in crisis. It would seem, if one attends to the literature of the past century, indeed to the literature of a millennium, that Jewish history has been a continuous and unrelieved succession of crises. The crisis of Judaism, however, has been always the same. It is the crisis of survival.

The prophets of crisis, those who have lived before its

[4] It should not be thought that our decision to single out Kaplan, Steinberg, Heschel, and Herberg from among the many talented and useful thinkers on the American Jewish scene was hasty or ill considered. Our decision to concentrate upon these is founded less upon our conviction of their excellence or endurance than upon their undeniable influence at the present time. They are not representative thinkers in the sense of being spokesmen for normative Judaism; they are representative in that other and more significant sense of having made articulate and public attitudes of mind which are currently to be found in American Judaism. Other thinkers could have been considered whose technical contributions are as vast or whose concentration on particular problems has been profoundly illuminating, but they have not enjoyed the extent of contact with and penetration of the popular Jewish mind which these thinkers have achieved. We should add (and it is a personal bias which shall become obvious) that there are a number of thinkers—Eugene Borowitz, Emil Fackenheim, Nahum N. Glatzer, Ben Halpern, Max Kadushin, Jakob J. Petuchowski, Steven S. Schwarzschild, David Silverman, and Jacob Taubes among others—from whose persons and writings we have learned as much as from those we shall consider here in greater detail. We attempt merely the calculation of the present. History makes the fuller and God the final judgment of worth and consequence.

face and defined the solutions by which erosion, absorption, and extinction were to be avoided, have been of two types. Either they have sought to ensure survival by moving deeper into the traditional strongholds of Judaism, or else they have moved out of Judaism, finding connections which bound them to their current environment. Both enable Judaism to endure: the former by locating the unexplored or forgotten reaches of the tradition, the latter by defining the relations which unite Judaism with that which is now open and hospitable. In both cases the motive to endure has been the concern that the Jewish people shall survive.

Survival is not a simple concept. Since there are degrees and varieties of survival, it must be determined—if an ideology of survival is to be meaningful or effective—what it is that one wishes to preserve. The problem of survival, once posed, is not answered by the simple assertion that one wishes to preserve all. To argue in this manner is to be unrealistic and perhaps disastrously naïve. Obviously if one could preserve all one would not be faced with the problem of survival. Survival is always selective. The determination of substance or emphasis to be retained or cast off, the techniques of moderation or adaptation to be employed form the practical program of any survivalist ideology.

Confronted by the problem of survival in stormy seas the clever captain will cast the weighty overboard. Unfortunately cultures cannot be made seaworthy by such expedients. Neither the extinction nor the survival of cultures is achieved by simple means: in lightening the burden or jettisoning the excess there is no assurance that a culture will be made more serviceable. It is often the case that in the process of discard the culture will have exposed itself to more devastating assault: the French knight was rendered more fleet and mobile by reducing the bulk of his armor, but the English bowman found at Agincourt that it was henceforth easier to penetrate his mail.

III. Judaism and Survival

There is no assurance that by rearranging the components of culture, revising its formulas, constructing new *sancta* to replace old, devising new liturgies, worshipping at more contemporary altars, the old culture will survive. The crucial, indeed, the only question is: To what end survival, if that which survives bears little resemblance to what was; if it becomes a new creature, trimmed to fly in all weathers, acclimated to all seasons? What shall become of a people's character, its authenticity, its historical continuity, its formative past, if the new shape which it assumes bears but a resemblance to its antiquity? Indeed it can survive, but there should be no self-deception: a culture, a civilization, and in the case of the Jewish people a religion, perish.

The ideologist of survival wishes neither radical separatism nor assimilation. He wishes rather that the people shall be enabled to take part in its foster civilization, to live among strangers and make of them friends, to share their cultures, blend their virtues, and fashion from their affinity a richer and more rewarding destiny for men. The slight flaw, and it is slight but crucial, is that such blending and intermixture cannot be equal. Cultures do not keep separate ledgers, scoring accounts on separate pages, crediting individual achievements to the right party, keeping the records clean and unconfused. Cultures interfuse, but numbers assure strength, and the weaker are absorbed, however peacefully and profitably, by the stronger. This is not to say that a century, possibly even centuries, might not elapse before the final absorption shall have transpired; but that it shall transpire there can be no doubt.

There is little question but that a theory which founds the survival of the weak and numerically insignificant upon the charity of the strong is folly. There is equally little question but that such survivalists also believe that the morally superior will survive. Their ironic predicament is that the ideologists of survival usually represent the weak whom they also consider to be morally superior.

However, moral superiority is not a judgment which the natural intelligence can form without bias and distortion. Its system of ethics, its cultural arrangements, its patterns of behavior, to the extent that they are founded upon natural hopes and expectations, are too subject to the shifting winds of political and social fortune to be reliable. They may indeed be modern; they may enjoy the satisfaction of temporary adjustment and harmony, but they are not enduring. Tied as they are to political fashions and social arrangements which are subject to the wasting of history and the change in men's hearts, they do not give promise of more than marginal survival. No religious community, surely no religious civilization, unless it be a civilization of syncretistic flabbiness, can hope to survive in such an inclement and changeable atmosphere.

Given our understanding of the nature of survival we cannot but conclude that the ideology of survival on which Mordecai Kaplan has founded the reconstruction of historical Judaism is one which cannot give hope or assurance to the future of Judaism. It is marked by every conceivable idiom of contemporary historicism, relativism, and behaviorism. In themselves historicism, relativism, and behaviorism have their place; they are vague doctrines, but not of necessity execrable. They demonstrate their impermanence when they are presented as the platform on which a millennial civilization is to rest its case for survival.

Mordecai Kaplan has been justly disenchanted of the promise of classical Reform and classical Orthodoxy as both have defined themselves upon the American scene.[1] Both versions of historical Judaism are precisely that—versions, representations, images refracted upon the broken mirror of modernity. Kaplan's criticism of Reform—

[1] See the chapters on Reform Judaism and what Kaplan termed in 1934 "The Neo-Orthodox Version of Judaism," in *Judaism as a Civilization* (New York, The Macmillan Company, 1934; The Reconstructionist Press, 1957), pp. 91–107; pp. 133–50.

its destructive truncation of historical Judaism into a mission without a people, an ideal world without a real one—is accurate.[2] As well Kaplan's criticism of what he terms "Neo-Orthodoxy" is to the point, for modern Orthodoxy has retained the Law and the commandments, but has subjected them to a de-theologizing which has in the main removed the concepts of *galut,* Messiah, the Kingdom of God, the world to come, and eternal life from its active theology.[3]

Why submit, however, Orthodox, Conservative, or Reform Judaism to such criticism? The doctrines of each movement, to the extent that they are neither normative nor enforceable, are so many reflections of the historical pressures out of which each grew and to which each reacts. Essentially Kaplan's concern derives from the fact that, acknowledging their responsiveness to history, he contends they have failed. What then is the mark of their failure? Their failure is not simply a failure of truth but a failure of following. No one of the movements on the American Jewish scene, regardless of emphasis or reinterpretation, has succeeded in capturing the affections and support of the majority of American Jews. Nearly half of the Jews of America are still outside of the synagogue; nevertheless they continue overwhelmingly to consider themselves as Jews. It is to these, for whom Ju-

[2] "Only in Wonderland can there be a cat which leaves its grin behind it. In the world of reality it is not feasible to try to have the grin without the cat. That experiment has been undertaken by Reformism in trying to have the Jewish cat without the living entity to which that religion belongs—without a living, functioning Jewish people." *Judaism as a Civilization,* p. 125. Substantially the same criticism, although modified to accord with the shifts in Reform Judaism during recent decades, has been made by Kaplan in his more recent essay, "Where Reform and Reconstructionism Part Company," *CCAR Journal,* April, 1960, pp. 3–10. Unfortunately the Kaplan criticism of the thirties was more to the point than its reiteration in 1960. Reform theology has changed, whereas Kaplan's emphasis upon the central role that Jewish ethnicity plays in Jewish survival appears even more ethnocentric and clannish than it did several decades ago.

[3] *Judaism as a Civilization,* pp. 151–59

daism in its classic or reforming versions is still inadequate, that Kaplan seeks to speak. They are Jews, whether in response to pressures which prevent them from ceasing to be Jews or in acquiescence to the misfortunes of destiny. Kaplan is realist enough to recognize that the unwillingness of the majority to relinquish their Jewishness is but a temporary forbearance of history. Without an articulation of positive ties and allegiances, without the formation of an ideology and a community, these Jews will eventually pass out of Judaism, each successive generation losing further the connections of memory until the last thread is broken.

It is the modern world, not the necessities of historical Judaism, which becomes the backdrop against which the plot of Jewish survival is to be unfolded. For Kaplan, the classic Jewish world—the world that commenced with the Bible and continued, without breach or interruption, until the early nineteenth century—has not only come to an end, but has been transcended by conditions and exigencies which it could neither anticipate nor prepare for.[4] Classic Judaism was tied to a supernaturalism which is,

[4] Although Kaplan has often argued, as one link in his defense of the reconstruction of *halachah,* that change and adaptation is an historical hallmark of Judaism, his radical polarization of what precedes the French Revolution and the Enlightenment from what comes after reveals a more alarming sense of discontinuity. Although he is correct in pointing to moderation and change in classic Judaism and the adaptability of medieval Jewish thought to the forms of thought defined by Greece and Islam, such adaptability took place in what is for Kaplan an essentially closed universe. The Jewish universe prior to the Enlightenment and the rise of the nation-state (which he also dates from the emergence of the laic state in post-1789 Europe) was a universe governed by the relation of nature to super-nature, of man to a wholly absolute God. The post-Enlightenment universe was one where supernaturalism was debunked and critical reason became the sole arbiter of truth. Obviously, then, the adaptability of Judaism in a closed universe is of a vastly different order from reconstruction in a universe adjudicated by the sovereignty of reason. They are incommensurable: to bring forth the one to demonstrate the historicity of change in Judaism and to justify the legitimacy of change in a vastly different intellectual climate is inaccurate.

in Kaplan's view, so patently false and inaccurate as to require thorough expungement. Supernaturalism, identified as it is in his thought with a naïve doctrine of revelation, theurgy, and superstition, is an anachronism. Science, natural, psychological, and historical, has destroyed the Biblical world on which Jewish supernaturalism was founded. The evolution of the Bible, the historical unfolding of Jewish law and custom, the sociopsychological foundations of religion have all served to undermine the world of Orthodoxy. In such a postsupernatural universe Judaism cannot survive, Kaplan argues, unless reconstructed. Jewish religion cannot, however, be discarded. Although at first glance it might appear that such a congerie of misconceptions as Judaism sustains should be repudiated, such a conclusion would be erroneous, if not disastrous. Religion is rather the underpinning of the people, its functioning ideology, its source of cohesion. Not God but the people becomes the mysterious source of life; salvation is from the people and all else—God, nature, and history— are so many variable functions of the self-saving of the community.

Religion, Kaplan has affirmed, is a social instrument by which man's instinctual atavism is contained and his capacity for nobility and self-transcendence enhanced.[5] It is essentially a device for acclimating the individual to his social role, supplying the conditions of control and direction which enable him to adjust his individualism to the requirements of society. Social religion is, in short, a healthy myth. It contrasts favorably with alternate mythologies—mythologies which encourage man to escape time and history to the presumably liberating aethers of eternity—because it returns man to his own condition, forcing him to acknowledge his involvement in the immediacies of life and the requirements of the community. Religion is focused, therefore, not upon the indi-

[5] *Judaism as a Civilization,* p. 332.

vidual but upon the group; the group becomes the bearer of salvation, the power of enforcement, the agency by whose guidance the individual is ordered into his proper role. The collective demands of primitive societies are forced upon the individual by the projection of an order of imaginary beings who serve "as patrons and guardians of man." The gods serve as the embodied image of the society, the elevated, transcending form by which the group expresses the obligations of the individual. Religion in this view (and Kaplan acknowledges his debt to Emile Durkheim and Bronislaw Malinowski) is essentially social: it is founded upon the community and the people.[6] The individual has merely the task of affirming, defining his identity with, and developing modes of perpetuating the self-enhancement which he enjoys through linking his personal destiny to the destiny of the people. The people "will always constitute one's chief source of salvation, and therefore one's chief medium of religion." [7]

The normative principles formulated by Durkheim and Malinowski serve to elaborate the psychological mechanisms operative in tribal societies. What makes the primitive society primitive is not the unsophistication of its experience of the divine but its inability to learn the lesson of its experience. Sophisticated religion is sophisticated precisely because it possesses a measure of discriminating judgment, a capacity to disentangle the authentic from the inauthentic, the single God from his plural manifestations. What marks the transition from natural to revealed religion is not, as Kaplan believes, a retrogression into primitivism but a progress toward a more free and independent divinity. For the primitive, the gods are not free. They are subject to the will of man. What, indeed, is magic other than the assumption that the proper human action can alter the conduct of the gods? Tribal re-

[6] *Judaism as a Civilization,* pp. 333–34; Mordecai M. Kaplan, *The Future of the American Jew* (New York, The Macmillan Company, 1948), p. 198.
[7] *Judaism as a Civilization,* p. 335.

ligion, religion founded upon the dominion of the group, is indeed primitive. It may, in its genetic simplicity, illuminate the backslidings of sophisticated religions, but it cannot serve complex civilizations as the model for emulation. Primitive religion is simply that—primitive and tribal; an idolatrous worship of the will and submission to the kingdom of fate. The gods are neither free nor capricious; they are the subject powers of the tribe. The tribe defines its *sancta*—its social *sancta*—as so many techniques of storing up the power of the gods, manipulating them, bringing them down into the heart of life to strike terror, establish the reign of fear, and ensure physical survival.

Kaplan is correct in criticizing those who, like Freud (whose *The Future of an Illusion* he cites), reduce the conception of God to its social constituents, who having located the superstitious psychology which underlies many theologies are satisfied to debunk all theology.[8] Kaplan objects to this unwarranted use of science. On the other hand Kaplan distinguishes between the proper science of religion and the insupportable theorizing of theologians and metaphysicians.[9] The metaphysician is held to be as much a builder of chimeras as science is a destroyer of illusion. The proper science of religion, presumably the science into which Durkheim inducted Kaplan, is that which sees God and his universe as functions of the individual's enrichment, the group's self-preservation, and the elevation of both to the service of holy ends. The knowledge of God and the confirmation of his existence and nature are so many idle speculations. They may serve, if at all, only to make more precise and articulate those useful conceptions which assist the molding of the group and the ensuring of its self-identity. They are, however, in themselves, speculations without utility.

To adopt what purports to be only a descriptive anthro-

[8] *Ibid.*, p. 309.

[9] *Ibid.*, pp. 308 f.

pology, a device of interpreting the life mechanisms of the religious society, as though it were regulative and legislating doctrine is the mystery of Kaplan's acceptance of Durkheim's views. The mystery is partially illuminated by knowledge of Kaplan's biography in his early years.[10] It is insufficient, however, to moderate our wonder by the recognition of Kaplan's—and not only Kaplan's but his generation's—shock at the discovery that Higher Criticism (whether scriptural, anthropological, archaeological, or psychological) had cast doubt upon the fundamental theology of the Bible. The crisis of Kaplan's thought, one must conclude, was a superficial crisis.[11] It was superficial if we assume that it consisted merely in the discovery that it was no longer possible to have a simple-minded view of Biblical faith; that it was no longer possible to imagine that God was an illustrious and enthroned graybeard; that science had demonstrated that God could no longer run riot with nature, stopping the sun in its path, cleaving seas, or speaking on mountains. It would appear, however, if one consults Kaplan's argument against "supernaturalism," that his objections really center upon a version of its claims which no theologian of the twentieth century has seriously supported. It is a supernaturalism of the nineteenth century, one which he is correct in despising for its intransigence and palpable stupidity.[12]

The only possible explanation of Kaplan's insistent

[10] Mordecai M. Kaplan, "The Way I Have Come," in Ira Eisenstein, and Eugene Kohn, eds., *Mordecai M. Kaplan: An Evaluation* (New York, Jewish Reconstructionist Foundation, 1952), pp. 283–321.

[11] "The Way I Have Come," pp. 289–95; see particularly p. 294.

[12] Why Kaplan has chosen to belabor a poor version of a possibly significant doctrine continues to elude us. It is, however, indicative of the ideologizing character of his thought, for once the pattern of his rhetoric has been defined and proved effective it is retained without alteration. From his earliest books, *Judaism as a Civilization* and *The Meaning of God in Modern Jewish Religion* (New York, Behrman House, Inc., 1937), to his more recent *Judaism Without Supernaturalism* (New York, Jewish Reconstructionist Foundation, 1958) the formulas of argument and attack have not altered.

mocking of a defunct version of supernaturalism as though it were a live religious option is that he is primarily concerned with shifting the weight of religious assent from the individual's *relation* to God to the community's *need* for Him. Kaplan has explicitly argued that the doctrine of salvation which followed from traditional supernaturalism tended to create the unreal separation of the individual from the community, the extrusion of such eccentric types as the ascetic and saint, and the projection of a view of salvation which followed from the individual's personal relation and obedience to God's will. The fact that this interpretation is a half-truth, a partial and incomplete reading of both Judaism and Christianity, is beside the point. What is of significance is that Kaplan is intent upon building a specific kind of case, a case for people-centered religion, for religion in which personal relation and faith become exceptional (and therefore useless) and folk religion becomes normative.

The theology of Mordecai Kaplan is unclear. Undoubtedly his theology is nonsupernatural; nevertheless he continues to use the term "transcendent" to describe the relation of the community to that which eludes it. The transcendence of God consists in the fact that he eludes the understanding of man—in this Kaplan is correct, and he has discerned, almost as an accidental by-product of his theological vagueness, one aspect of the God who, as revealing and concealing person, is transcendent to our intelligence. But transcendence is quickly seen to be but the obverse, the reflex to human ignorance and insufficiency. God is that nameless "Power" which inspirits man's self-unfolding. God is obviously all that is good in ourselves, in the community, and in history.[13]

[13] *Judaism Without Supernaturalism,* pp. 25, 30, 32, 52. It is a singularly spineless and uncourageous God who never opposes his creatures, who neither rebukes nor judges them, who is almost totally unconscious of evil (a happy condition for God but one which a human interpreter can ill afford to accredit). To the best of our knowledge there is little or no sustained discussion in Kaplan's writings of the problem of evil. He has criticized in *Judaism as a*

What emerges, in reflecting upon Kaplan's notion of God, is that He is anything the community, the folk, the civilization define Him to be. Since religion is the vitalizing source of civilization, and civilization is a phenomenon subject to change and adaptation, a civilization's concept of God will shift as its needs shift. God is refashioned in the image of man and history. The theurgic divinities of primitive religion, the supernatural God of classic Judaism, the imperialistic divinity of Roman Christianity were but expressions of the requirements of the folk, an expression of their needs. Given such a view it is inevitable that a different people and an altered civilization—one fashioned in a scientific age and submissive to the requirements of living in two civilizations—will have to construct a new God, a more serviceable agency of adaptation and fulfillment. To speak of the naturalism, humanism, pragmatism of Kaplan's theology is to take seriously what can be taken with no theological seriousness at all. Such intellectual labels, reflecting positions seriously developed by conscientious thinkers, do not stick; for Kaplan is indifferent as to whether his God is naturalist, humanist, or pragmatist.[14] The naturalism and pragmatism of Kaplan's theory of God and religion result not from any concentrated reflection upon the

---

Civilization the neglect of theodicy in the theology of Kohler and Montefiore, but the best he was able to offer was: "In other words, we are called upon to be martyrs for a religion which fails in its *raison d'être,* that of enabling us to adjust ourselves constructively to the evil in ourselves and in the world" (pp. 115 f.). His subsequent discussion of evil in *The Future of the American Jew,* pp. 231 ff., was equally indecisive.

[14] It is illuminating to read Henry Wieman's essay, "Kaplan's Idea of God," in Eisenstein and Kohn, *Mordecai M. Kaplan: An Evaluation,* pp. 193–210. Wieman quotes at length from Kaplan's statements on the nature and action of God and comes to the conclusion that he is not quite certain what Kaplan's doctrine really is. Is it pantheist? Is it naturalist? Is it process theology? What it really is never becomes clear or articulate. All of Wieman's gentle criticisms of Kaplan are respectful; but it is evident nevertheless in Wieman's discussion that Kaplan's notion of God cannot be adequately clarified or communicated.

meaning of these positions or upon the philosophic problems of God and religion which they are intended to illuminate. Kaplan backed up into naturalism; he does not appear to have formulated it as a philosophic position. After supernatural theology collapsed, the rationale and *praxis* of Orthodoxy was undermined, and Jews drifted into indifference. Clearly something radical was required if the Jewish people was to be saved.

The reconstruction of Judaism to which Mordecai Kaplan has given his life is no reconstruction of *Judaism,* but a reconstruction of the *Jewish people.* The people, not its faith, must live; for if the people live, some faith, any faith—as long as it reflects the conscience and history of the people—will do. The people, not the faith, must be rendered eternal; for if the people shall not live, to what purpose shall have been the history of the Jews? Why the martyrdom of Israel, why its sufferings and anguish, if the people shall be allowed to perish? The people will perish only through the stubborn inflexibility of its traditional leaders, who continue to see its religion as its defining center, and its secular leaders, who make the threat of anti-Semitism into a sufficient reason for social cohesion. Both are destructive positions because both are partial positions: the former makes a dimension of culture into the whole of culture, while the latter fashions continuity upon the foundations of *ressentiment* and alienation.

The position of Mordecai Kaplan is the shell of a great view: Judaism as a civilization. He alone of all contemporary Jewish thinkers, building upon the insights of Krochmal and Ahad Ha-Am, envisions an embracing culture. Only a culture which encompasses all—the community, the arts, literature, and religion—can endure, for only a complete culture can fulfill the multiple requirements of man.

The center of Jewish civilization is the Jewish people. This conclusion is inescapable. There is a sense, however, in which Kaplan has not only retained but embellished the mystique and uniqueness of the Jewish people against which, stated otherwise, he has struggled so profoundly. On the one hand Kaplan rejects the doctrine of the election of Israel, while on the other hand he centralizes and enhances the destiny of the natural people. The supernatural people perishes in the past of the Exile and a new people, a natural civilization, is born. The former, a divine necessity, is repudiated; the latter, a natural necessity, is enthroned. The modern Jewish people, whose ancestry is the Enlightenment and the rise of secular nationalism,[15] is a folk civilization whose mysterious coherence and self-identity is but the unwritten law of nature, the implicit destiny of peoples and cultures to retain their self-identity. For the mysterious choice of God, Kaplan has substituted the mystery of nature and history. In either case the Jewish people is "elected" to persevere.

The worth of any ideology is determined by its ability to shape action. Ideology does not represent itself as either revelation or philosophy; it is but a loose constellation of programmatic principles, flexible, changing, adjustable. As a mediate doctrine, intended to alter men's minds and influence their conduct, it is not to be subjected to philosophic scrutiny. Its principles are indifferent to the forays of the scrupulous intelligence, intent upon consistency, clarity, and precision. The ideologist shifts ground with ease: as one argument fails, another comes forth; as one program fails, another is defined.

It is legitimate to inquire whether the ideology of reconstruction, the program of Jewish civilization which Kaplan has defined, can achieve its end. We do not ask for the proof of numbers—great doctrine need not have adherents (although it ceases to be effective ideology if it cannot gain adherents); we do not ask for convincing evidence of impact or influence (for actually Kaplan's impact and influence have been enormous). There is only one question of importance that needs asking: Will Kap-

[15] Kaplan, *Judaism as a Civilization*, pp. 337 f.

lan's conception of Judaism as a civilization enable the Jewish people to survive?

The perseverance of a people is a function of history. The people endures; the civilization survives, if it retains its capacity to recall the instruction of its past and transmit the harvest of its present experience to the future. This, however, is to describe only the process of social reproduction. It is to say nothing of the quality of its experience, the meaning of its historical presence, or the significance of its destiny. History is unmindful of the proclamations of peoples. When peoples announce their meaning and significance they speak to each other; history never overhears their intentions. The ideologist always imagines that he addresses more than his own when he proclaims the destiny of an idea. If his idea is fashioned out of response to history—out of receiving and returning, for example, the echo of emancipation, enlightenment, and democratic toleration—history is still allowed the last word.

The adjustment of the Jew to the natural conditions of his environment divests him of the only weapon, his supernatural vocation, which allows him to survive what he must always survive—terrestrial history. The moment the civilization of the Jew is refashioned in order to accommodate his role in natural history the terms of his eclipse have been granted. The natural Jew as such has, we believe, no hope. There is no future to a civilization which must, at this moment in history, begin to equip itself with the habiliments of secular culture, to acquire arts and music which are indigenous, to define folk liturgies and folk pageants to duplicate and complement the subtler and more developed patterns of historical nations and peoples.

It is precisely the genius of the Jew that he is unnatural—not that he is maladjusted, but that he is unadjusted; not that he is reconstructed, but that he is unreconstructed. This is to face the fact that, whether one likes election and choice, mystery and uniqueness, it is impossible to make over the difficult destiny of the Jewish people into one which is historically more convenient. Since history is no respecter of pliability and convenience, there are no guarantees that the modes of adjustment which Mordecai Kaplan has defined—the system of double *sancta,* the definition of an American religion to underwrite the normality of Jewish religion, the doctrine of two natural civilizations (that of the Jew and that of the nation among which he lives)—will do more than hasten the destruction of the Jewish people.[16]

It is neither just nor charitable to conclude our discussion of Mordecai Kaplan without acknowledging his im-

[16] This position has been a continuing thread throughout Kaplan's thought. Cf. particularly, "Towards a Philosophy of Cultural Integration," in Lyman Bryson *et al.*, eds., *Approaches to Group Understanding* (New York, Harper & Brothers, 1947). Also, "Jewish Education for Democracy," *The Reconstructionist,* Vol. V, No. 15; "The Place of Religion in a Democracy," *Review of Religion,* Vol. XII; "The Religious Foundations of Democracy," *The Reconstructionist,* Vol. IX, No. 5. A most passionate echoing of Kaplan's position is contained in Ira Eisenstein, "Toward a Religion of Democracy in America," *The Reconstructionist,* Vol. XI, No. 1, pp. 55–61. Although it has been pointed out—increasingly of late—that there could be nothing more dangerous to both religion and democracy than the development of an "American religion," Dr. Eisenstein is sufficiently sanguine as to observe: "there is no inherent danger in creating a religion of democracy in America, since such a religion would be national in form, but universal in content, and hence not narrow and chauvinistic. . . ." Neither Kaplan's nor Eisenstein's confidence seems to me to take account of the possible emergence of an American Jacobinism which could impair not only the foundations of religion but the freedom of the democratic polity. Cf. Will Herberg, *Protestant-Catholic-Jew* (New York, Doubleday & Company, Inc., 1955), pp. 85–112; 270–89; A. Roy Eckardt, "The New Look of American Piety," *The Christian Century,* November 17, 1954; William Lee Miller, "Piety Along the Potomac," *The Reporter,* August 17, 1954; William Lee Miller, "Religion and the American Way of Life," *Religion and the Free Society* (New York, The Fund for the Republic, 1958), pp. 3–21. This is but a small sample of an expanding group of writers, including John Courtney Murray, S.J., Reinhold Niebuhr, Martin E. Marty, William Clancy, and the present writer, who have addressed themselves to a criticism of precisely the "soteric" unity of religion and the democratic way which Kaplan and the Reconstructionists seem to consider unassailably good doctrine.

mense contribution to contemporary Judaism.[17] It is not our intention to be unjust or lacking in charity. It is rather that for too long Mordecai Kaplan has been alone and unchallenged, the undisputed American ideologist of Jewish survival. We too, with him, passionately affirm the future of the Jew; but unlike him—and we shall later take pains to define our views more sharply—we believe that the future of Judaism as a civilization rests only upon a renewal of Israel's relation with God and consequent restimulation of the vocation of Jacob, which was to wrestle with God until He be found and to release Him only after having won from Him the promise of salvation.

IV. JUDAISM IN TRANSITION: MILTON STEINBERG

In every generation there are those few who do more than move with the tide of culture, who succeed in transcending its conditions and thereby altering them. Such individuals may anticipate new formations of culture, breaking with its historical past in order to chart new directions for its development. Or they may summarize in themselves so much that was best in their environment that they anticipate and instruct the future without consciously setting forth to shape it. They become leaders because they articulate so fully the standards which ennoble culture that they regenerate those standards, give them new currency, re-establish their contemporaneity. They may not create tradition or break new ground, but they till the fallow soil with such industry and devotion as to make the work of later planters easier. Such leaders live between the past and the future. They take their

[17] See the author's discussion of Kaplan, his introduction to Milton Steinberg, *Anatomy of Faith* (New York, Harcourt, Brace & World, Inc., 1960), pp. 37–39.

stand upon the mixed truth, the unfulfilled vision, the imperfect present; yet their stance is in a real sense more dangerous than that of even the true creators of the future, for they take the profounder risks. Their lot is to be uncertain of the new truth, but to know the inadequacy of the old; not to know the future, but to know the limitations of holding with the past; to be the possessors, as Henri Bergson has observed, not of the creating but of the denying intuition—the awareness of what cannot be, but an uncertainty of what is. Theirs is the dangerous role, for they take all the risks, and history profits by their oversights as well as by their prudent judgments. They reap none of the rewards, for they rarely live to see their own vivid consciousness of what is false and wrong transformed into what is true and right.

Milton Steinberg (1903–1950) was born into a transitional half-century of Jewish life and died before he had completed its full measure. As a transitional thinker in a transitional age, he suffered from the limitations of the era whose spirit he embodied; but as a transitional thinker he reflected accurately the plight which social attrition and religious unclarity had created for Judaism in America. There are those who will, no doubt, take issue with this preliminary judgment, claiming for Milton Steinberg greater glory than he would have thought he merited or than posterity has accorded him. His importance lies in the fact that his realistic awareness of the impasse of American Judaism, his desperate search for medicaments and remedies, his passionate commitment to current ideologies of survival, and his gradual, hesitant, but unmistakable return to more classic modes of theological and philosophic reflection anticipated the intellectual phases through which American Judaism has passed, and is continuing to pass in the twentieth century.[1]

[1] A more complete biography of Milton Steinberg is contained in our introduction to *Anatomy of Faith* (New York, Harcourt, Brace

Milton Steinberg came to Judaism as many Jews subsequently would come—through a vocation of the intellect. Neither in his generation nor in ours has it been easy to become a philosopher, to maintain the attitude of question and exploration, to keep open and unfinished the speculative work of the mind. Everything conspires to close the mind, to finish its work prematurely, to still its insistent dissatisfaction with current and fashionable solutions. It is eccentric to say, but close scrutiny of his life and work bears out our view, that Steinberg entered the rabbinate in order to maintain and extend a speculative passion which his experience of academic philosophy had constricted and dulled.[2] There is little question, however, that Steinberg's understanding of the nature of philosophy was unconventionally personal and engaged. Philosophy was, as he later said, the search for "a *weltanschauung*" which would invest human life with dignity and meaning. It was an inquiry into the grounds of human conduct, history, and destiny. As such, philosophy was always the ancilla of religion, the formal inquiry to which religion supplied articulate, particular, and necessary concreteness. Both philosophy and religion were indispensable means of human apprehension: the former to ask proper questions, the latter to describe the domain in which proper answers might be sought.

One mistakes the authentic power of his thought if one misjudges and overemphasizes the role which popular thinking and popular writing played in his career. Such works as *A Partisan Guide to the Jewish Problem, Basic*

& World, Inc., 1960), pp. 11–60. We have tried there to avoid critical judgment, reserving such for these pages. What is clear is that the essays contained in *Anatomy of Faith* suggest the essential lines of Steinberg's theological thinking. All of his other writings, we believe, are of lesser and passing importance, with the exception of his first book, *The Making of the Modern Jew* (Indianapolis, The Bobbs-Merrill Company, Inc., 1933), and his novel, *As a Driven Leaf* (Indianapolis, The Bobbs-Merrill Company, Inc., 1940).

[2] *Anatomy of Faith*, pp. 26 f.

Judaism, and the posthumous collection of his essays and sermons, *A Believing Jew,* suffer in quality of thought what they accomplish in directness of communication. This is not to say that the necessary price of communication is unclarity (or, as is often the case with popular writing, too much clarity), but undoubtedly it is simplicity. Simplicity is the prevailing mark of Steinberg's popular writing, but it is simplicity that proceeds from an honest and uncompromised conscience. Steinberg on the pulpit or in his popular writing—which was an extension of his pulpit—exhibits his concerns as ideologist, not his talents as critic of theology and constructive theologian.

Milton Steinberg was one of his generation in his admiration and support of Mordecai Kaplan and the Reconstructionist movement. He came to Reconstructionism, however, as he came to all of his conclusions, not through the press of events or the necessities of locating a modern home for a wandering Judaism, but through the requirements of defining a personal intellectual position. Unlike many of the seminarians who were his classmates at the Jewish Theological Seminary in the 1920s, Steinberg had not been reared in an uncompromisingly Orthodox home, where European Judaism ruled the hearth, indifferent to the winds of historical criticism which raged in the chimney flue. He did not come to Conservative Judaism as a refuge from Orthodoxy, as a resolution of the tension of alienation and nostalgia which beset many of his fellow students. He came, so his biography instructs us, because he was disenchanted with the inconclusive, negative, and often hectoring empiricism that characterized philosophy as he had pursued it under Morris Raphael Cohen at the City College of New York. He came, in effect, because he was troubled by questions which ostensibly philosophy could not answer.

Steinberg had arrived at an unshakable conclusion, a conclusion which he sought subsequently to articulate and develop, but which he succeeded only in reiterating (always with ingenuity and passion)—that reason could not function without faith. Most religious men take this principle for granted, assuming the philosophic issue is closed by a fiat of faith. The refusal to play the intellectual "game" any longer is mistaken by many believers as a sign of faith. Faith becomes an insurance policy against doubt. But for Steinberg, such anti-intellectualism was always a corruption of faith and a distortion of reason. The failure of empiricism to satisfy him lay in its inability to understand that man was a creature who was compelled to transcend himself. Although only in Steinberg's later writings, "The Theological Problems of the Hour" and "New Currents in Religious Thought," was he to make reference to man's transcending direction to God, it underlay his thought from the beginning. It was the essential given,[3] the fundamental datum from which the life of rational faith departs.

Man is initially a wonderer and an inquirer. His metaphysical concern, perhaps more than anything else, is that which defines his nature and marks off his intelligence from that of the animals. Man, like the animals, is sentient, discriminating, practical. Undoubtedly the common sense of man as well as the sophisticated intellectual judgment of man is superior to that of lower creatures; however, Steinberg was of the opinion that between man and beast there was a difference only of quality and degree. What distinguished man from the animal was that man's reason could not only carry itself to the end of the inquiry but pose the question for which reason could not provide the answer. This was man's metaphysical passion: his concern to locate himself in the universe, to de-

[3] "Toward the Rehabilitation of the Word 'Faith,'" *Anatomy of Faith*, pp. 64–79. This essay and that which accompanies it, "The Common Sense of Religious Faith," pp. 81–108, are both popular, indeed pedestrian, essays, but they serve to underscore that most insistent of Steinberg's convictions: It is more plausible, more reasonable, more in accord with the explicit character of nature to accept belief in a motive and creating God, than to seek to understand the universe without him.

fine his ultimate station and destiny, to reconcile his world with the being of Him who was its creator.

The Jew, no less than the Christian and the pagan, is a creature with a metaphysical passion. The metaphysical interest of the Jew is, however, not without a history. If the Jew asks questions in the twentieth century, these are Jewish questions to the extent that they are fashioned by the conditions which Jewish history has supplied and the forms which Jewish tradition has perpetuated. It is evident that if the metaphysical accent of Judaism is to survive, the Jewish community which sustains and defines that accent must first survive.

It was the necessity of perpetuating the community while awaiting the renewal of its metaphysical vocation that drew Steinberg to Reconstructionism.[4] One must willingly grant—indeed it is almost to ignore the facts to deny it—that until his later years, what we have described as the inner discourse of Steinberg's theology was well concealed. It was well concealed if one wishes to disregard his *The Making of the Modern Jew,* which, for all its scrupulous attention to historical events, begins with the "riddle" of Jewish existence and ends with the affirmation that its future is still enigmatic;[5] his *A Partisan Guide to the Jewish Problem,* which, although accepting the Reconstructionist definition of Jewish civilization, repeatedly observes that that which is characteristic of traditional formulas of definition—that Judaism is a "re-

[4] It is undoubtedly true that we run the risk of imparting more order and symmetry to Steinberg's thought than its formal development discloses. Although we do not admit to distortion or purposeful imbalance, we readily admit our interest in making sense out of the obvious split in his career: the public vocation of the preaching, teaching, and writing rabbi and the private vocation of the personal thinker, whose novel, *As a Driven Leaf,* whose disciplined and painstaking reading of technical philosophy and theology in the last years of his life, and whose late theological essays in *Anatomy of Faith* evidence a mind whose concerns were frankly speculative and metaphysical. The split is a real split, but it is one which we believe enjoyed an essential union.

[5] Steinberg, *The Making of the Modern Jew,* pp. 11–27; p. 317.

ligion" pure and simple—is nevertheless the most neglected aspect of the contemporary Jewish renaissance;[6] his novel, *As a Driven Leaf,* whose outstanding motif is the very un-Reconstructionist postulate that the deepest problem of human life is not the survival of the group but the survival of individual conscience and private intellectual and religious integrity; and lastly, the fact that the two posthumous volumes of his essays, *A Believing Jew* and *Anatomy of Faith,* abundantly illustrate that his own religious problems were primarily the problems of personal faith at war with both the simplistic solutions of historical traditionalism and the irrationalism implicit in pragmatism, intuitionism, and existentialism.

There is much with which one might cavil in our discussion. We need no critics to remind us of the public record. Steinberg was a thoroughgoing Reconstructionist —his synagogue was Reconstructionist in outlook, his

[6] Milton Steinberg, *A Partisan Guide to the Jewish Problem* (Indianapolis, The Bobbs-Merrill Company, Inc., 1945), p. 184. It is interesting that this most apologetic of works introduces its discussion of "A Creative Program" with the realistic advice to readers to skim the chapter and pass on to the more immediately pressing chapter on Zionism. It is this chapter, however, which—for all its fundamental approval of Reconstructionism—affirms the one reservation which would later become the foundation of Steinberg's criticism of Reconstructionist thought. On the one hand Steinberg asserts, presumably in agreement with Reconstructionism, that "religious faith, in the sense of a theistic world outlook, is in many regards the neglected aspect of the Jewish heritage" (p. 184); while on the other he holds that "wherever the traditional and the contemporary are at loggerheads, every effort ought to be made to resolve the conflict with minimal damage to the former" (p. 185). This note of reserve was intensified in Steinberg's essay on the Reconstructionist movement, in which he openly criticizes the latter's lack of theological and philosophic substance ("The Test of Time," in *A Believing Jew* (New York, Harcourt, Brace & World, Inc., 1951), pp. 174–76) and in his letter to Dr. Kaplan declining the latter's invitation to participate in the preparation of a Reconstructionist High Holy Day prayerbook (*Anatomy of Faith,* p. 48, note 5) and, finally, in his discussions of Kaplan's theology in his essays, "The Theological Problems of the Hour" and "New Currents in Religious Thought" (*Anatomy of Faith,* pp. 181–84, 246–49).

personal allegiance was to Mordecai Kaplan, and his party affiliation was to the Reconstructionist Foundation. All this is admitted; but such admission only serves to underscore what we have suggested earlier: there is both a cleavage and a lamentable confusion in modern Judaism between ideology and theology. As a transitional figure, as one who expressed in the best fashion the worst in Jewish ideology and moved in his closing years to the development of what was best in Jewish theology, Steinberg is an index of his generation. He reflected the ideology of Jewish survival, accepting it, not out of any conviction regarding the sociology of religion, but because he was convinced that Judaism had something to say which was imperishable and true, a trust and salvation to the Jews, and a prophetic reproof and instruction to the Gentiles.

It is our persuasion that one must discount much of the public career of Milton Steinberg—like him we are too passionately intellectual, too ratiocinative, to consider his public works sufficient evidence of the subtlety of his mind.

The moral action is always public and definite; moral judgment is more private, hesitant, and qualified. Action allows us none of the outs and hedges which the complexity of human events demands. What action cannot properly display is the ambiguity and uncertainty which assail the mind. Milton Steinberg evidences this tension of intellect and action: his lectures, his sermons, his popular writings, are firm and clear; his intellectual judgments, represented in his treatment of the person of Elisha ben Abuyah in *As a Driven Leaf* and refined in numerous essays in *A Believing Jew* and *Anatomy of Faith,* are textured by his knowledge that God, man, and the world are vastly more opaque than modern Judaism is accustomed to acknowledge.

Steinberg emerged from one tradition to judge it with instruments fashioned by others which he could not accept. He was trapped by the knowledge that the avowed optimism, perfectionism, and confidence expressed by

American Judaism could withstand neither the assault of historical events nor the criticism of more pessimistic traditions which drew evidence for their pessimism and despair from the very matter of human history. Steinberg lived therefore between two pairs of traditions: the Greek and the Jewish; the Christian European and the Jewish American. The former pair defined the philosophic antipodes between which his thought moved; the latter expressed the extremes from which the historical situation of the modern Jew was to be viewed.

The ambiguity of Steinberg's thought is a reflection of the unsureness of our age, not a characterization of the quality of his mind. His mind was all too clear, all too definite, all too explicit. This was its strength and this was its weakness. For his mode of intellection was not the dialectic of modern theologians, but the *sic et non* of an older tradition of theological speculation, albeit defined without the latter's rigor and precision. His partialities were, however, the partialities of his age—the partialities of a reasonable faith (all too often confused with Jewish naturalism), of an optimistic, self-perfecting doctrine of man (all too often confused with the dispensation of American democracy), and a conviction regarding the power of history to pile up a high score of virtue (all too often confused with the progress of a technically ingenious West). Steinberg held with these views. His philosophic scientism, his horror of unreason, his reluctance to accredit the heart with as much constructive insight as the head, his faith in America, his optimistic view of man and history, form the background to the unsettling experience of the years from the early 1930s to the end of his life. To the affirmations of a modernized Judaism—an acclimated Judaism which had parted with the supernatural affinities of classic theologies and had historicized and explicated the mystery of the Jew—there came the external challenge of Greek speculation, which raised a different order of question to the postulations of Biblical and rabbinic theology and Christian European theology.

It injected a note of anxiety, despair, and crisis into the muddled securities of American Judaism.

The challenge of Greece was formulated early in Steinberg's development.[7] Although his view of Greece was furiously Hebraic, it was unsettled by the presence of Greek intellectual serenity. The Greek was a keeper of slaves, an aristocrat, intolerant of poverty, unsympathetic to the "barbarian." The Greek was securely anti-equalitarian and, to Steinberg's view, essentially undemocratic. To the moral deficiencies of the Greek Steinberg opposed the vividness of the Biblical sense of justice, equity, and mercy. And yet, for all the transgressions of the classical world, Steinberg was responsive to the Greek passion for comprehensive and rational truth. To the Biblical logic of the heart, the Greek posed the persistent problem of demonstration and rational clarification. The example of Euclidean geometry—that model of rational order and demonstration—recurs throughout Steinberg's work.[8] What was Euclid to Steinberg? Surely not the greatest of Greek philosophers, but something more immediately significant, for Euclid expressed the axioms of thought with

[7] Early in Steinberg's career in the rabbinate he wrote a short and masterful essay, "Judaism and Hellenism," which concludes as follows: "But if these cultures could not . . . be forced into a syncretism, it was extremely important for man's future that they be maintained independently. The values for which the Jews fought were fully as necessary for mankind as those which the Greeks sought to impose upon them. The long service which the Hebraic genius has rendered to humanity in the past and the possibility of an ultimate synthesis in the future between the Hellenistic and Hebraic spirits are due to the courage of a band of Judaean insurrectionists who fought not only for freedom and faith but also for values indispensable for man's salvation." Milton Steinberg, "Judaism and Hellenism," in Emily Solis-Cohen, Jr., ed., *Hanukkah: The Feast of Lights* (Philadelphia, Jewish Publication Society of America, 1937), p. 16.

[8] The denouement of his novel, *As a Driven Leaf*, centers upon a geometric demonstration in which proof collapses because its axioms are founded, not upon experience, but upon a suprarational faith. (*As a Driven Leaf*, pp. 460–68; also pp. 364–70). There are numerous references throughout Steinberg's sermons and essays to Euclidean order and the non-Euclidean geometries of Riemann and Lobachevsky (cf. *Anatomy of Faith*, pp. 66, 74, 102, 160, 217).

architectural simplicity, directness, and practical relevance. The simplicity of the geometric method of demonstration, undercutting the rationalisms of the West from antiquity to modern times, suggested all that was most telling in the philosopher's way to the truth: nothing essentially unreasonable could be demonstrated; only the demonstrable could be true; hence nothing unreasonable could be true.

The shock to Steinberg—and it was a shock to which he often referred—was that Euclidean geometry was overturned. Non-Euclidean systems of geometry, notably those of Riemann and Lobachevsky, founded upon principles that did not conform to the symmetrical rationality of Euclidean assumptions, were developed in the nineteenth century. This signified to Steinberg the undermining not merely of an inherited philosophy but of a world-view founded upon the rationality of the universe. The universe was no longer quite so rational. Presumably it was no longer quite so orderly or demonstrable. Admittedly Steinberg's perspective on the philosophic enterprise was partial and incomplete. The shock of contemporary unreason—and Steinberg brought together under this rubric not only non-Euclidean geometries and the new physics but Bergsonian intuition, Kierkegaardian subjectivity, and American pragmatism and naturalism —was severe, because philosophy was intended by him to supply to religion what religion could not demonstrate for itself: the order of the universe. The order of nature suggested the reasonableness of faith. Philosophy became, therefore, less the dauntless pursuit of intellectual clarity than the confirmation of moral truth. This is well evidenced by the dilemma of Steinberg's hero Elisha ben Abuyah,[9] whose defection from Greek philosophy he in-

[9] Elisha ben Abuyah, an obscure and shadowy heretic, was an historical figure, remnants of whose life survive in the records of the Palestinian and Babylonian Talmud. It is upon a free reconstruction of the facts of his life that Steinberg based *As a Driven Leaf*.

terprets less as a search for truth *in itself* than as a search for truths which would justify the goodness of man and the providence of God. Moral certainty, not intellectual certainty, was the end of philosophy. The Jew defined the subject matter and dynamics of the virtuous life, but it was to the Greek that one turned for method and order.

The governed universe which the marriage of Greek philosophy and Biblical faith had produced has been distorted by the facile philosophizing of popular American Jewish theologies. The reasonable God, the plausible God, the so-called "God-idea" (a barbarism popular in American Jewish writing) is intended to be the God of the "thinking Jew." This God—an arbitrary cluster of prideful energies, desires, and ideas to which therapeutic sanctity is imparted—is not the God of the Greeks nor the God of the Hebrews. It is a modern God from whom the God of Plato and Aristotle and the God of the Bible are equally distant.

The God of Milton Steinberg was a philosopher's God. It was difficult to pray to such a God, but he was at least a God whom one might take seriously. Steinberg entertained the criticism directed against absolutist conceptions of God which confused the *one* with the *simple,* accepting here the complaint of Alfred North Whitehead and Charles Hartshorne, who wonder at a God whose perfection consists in the exclusion of new experience and whose simplicity is purchased at the expense of richness and involvement.[10] Steinberg was influenced as well by the exposition of the role of chance and the "surd" as Peirce and Brightman had defined them in their efforts to come to terms with the problem of irrationality and evil.[11] Moreover, among contemporary Jewish thinkers Steinberg's interest in modern currents of philosophic theology was unique. No other contemporary Jewish thinker had examined with comparable care and concern the rele-

[10] *Anatomy of Faith,* pp. 177–79; 179–81; 270–71.
[11] *Ibid.,* pp. 177–81; 234–36; 272–74.

vance of contemporary metaphysical theory to the problem of Jewish theism. He alone among his contemporaries sustained a concern for the relevance of reasoned inquiry to the task of faith.[12]

Philosophy is not disjunct from faith; God is not separated from the moral predicament of man. As philosophy serves to illumine and strengthen right belief, the God whom philosophy defines as idea lives in his relations to man and history. Inevitably, therefore, as the Greek and Hebrew sustain the tension of reason and faith, so the Christian European addresses the historical predicament of the American Jew.

The Jew has, above all, an obligation to be a realist. He can ill afford the enjoyment of an unexamined environment—such indifference would be at best ignorant, at worst suicidal. If indeed the religious atmosphere which surrounds him alters, it is well that he reflect upon its shifts and modulations. It will instruct him regarding not only the present which he must endure, but the future whose lineaments it is prudent to discern in advance.

Milton Steinberg was such a realist, and Christian theology was the instructor of his realism. Christian theology, and by this Steinberg intended primarily Protestant theology,[13] formulated the response to which the decade

[12] The hyperbole will be perhaps forgiven, for indeed there was one exception on the American scene: Jacob Agus. In his *Modern Philosophies of Judaism* (New York, Behrman House, Inc., 1941) Dr. Agus had elaborated, with considerably more rigor and attention to philosophic argument, the philosophic and theological relevance to contemporary Judaism of Hermann Cohen, Franz Rosenzweig, Martin Buber, and Mordecai Kaplan. Although his work antedates Steinberg's theological essays by nearly a decade, *Modern Philosophies of Judaism* is characterized by a cooler and more detached assessment of his subjects than was usual for Steinberg.

[13] Steinberg's understanding, familiarity, and patience with Roman Catholic theology was lamentably short. There being, Steinberg states, no neoscholasticism among Jews, it is unnecessary to take account of what he regards as mere neoscholasticism among Catholics. This is an accurate judgment upon much Catholic philosophy in the twentieth century, but it is less than accurate in estimating the achievement of Jacques Maritain, Jean Daniélou, Josef Pieper,

of Hitler had been the challenge. Hitler had succeeded for Steinberg, as he had for other contemporary Jewish thinkers, in undermining the optimism upon which he had founded his estimation of contemporary man and history. American Jewish theology in the forties, as yet unfamiliar with the thought of Franz Rosenzweig and resolutely indifferent to the writings of Martin Buber, had nowhere to turn for the exegesis of the times. Protestant theology afforded the tools of such an exegesis. It was only natural, therefore, that Steinberg should have asked of Protestant theology: "What has this to teach us?" [14]

When the analysis is done and the thought of Kierkegaard, Barth, Brunner, Niebuhr, and Tillich has been stated and appraised,[15] it becomes clear that what they had succeeded in communicating to Steinberg was little more than a moderation and tempering of his already well-articulated philosophic preferences. They had introduced into his thinking a note of ambiguity, a hesitancy, an unsureness, a referent against which to check his own proclivities; for where Steinberg had unconditional faith in reason, confidence in human perfectability, sureness of the ultimate achievement of a natural Kingdom of God, the pessimism and sense of sin which defined Protestant theology supplied a chastening corrective.

Steinberg's theological thinking during the closing year of his life defined a promise which death denied. His own mandate to the Rabbinical Assembly Convention of 1949 that there be, quoting Will Herberg, "a renewal of Jewish theology" [16] was itself an innovating augury, for no one, since the formative days of Reform and Conservative Judaism, much less a theologian affili-

---

Urs von Balthasar, Romano Guardini, and several other inventive and imaginative Catholic theologians. Cf. *Anatomy of Faith,* p. 158.

[14] *Ibid.,* p. 131. [15] *Idem.*

[16] *Ibid.,* p. 208. In order to implement a theological renaissance, Steinberg met with Will Herberg, Albert Salomon, the present writer, and others in 1949 to consider the establishment of a serious, party-free journal of Jewish theology.

ated with a traditional branch of Judaism, had called for a renaissance of Jewish theology.

Steinberg's call for a renewal of Jewish theology affords us the clue to his enduring importance. He was not a creative thinker. He formulated no theology, defined no new direction, developed no movement. Yet he was perhaps the most astute barometer of the intellectual disability of American Judaism which the transitional era of the thirties and forties had produced. He was uncompromisingly committed to Judaism, but he was painfully aware that it had somehow lost touch, that it was no longer, as Jehuda Halevi had suggested, the heart of Western culture which registered, as does a sensitive seismograph, the shifting impulses and attitudes of Western man. It had lost touch because, on the one hand, in its pursuit of survival it ran the risk of turning religion into a gelatinous preservative, and because, on the other hand, it was frightened of engaging the Christian West in argument. He was quite content—and in this he illustrates his fundamental demurral from Christianity—to affirm that what in Judaism is called its intellectual naïveté "is really a maturity that has risen above easy skepticisms, childish delight in riddles for their own sake, self-abasing protestations of an ignorance greater than it has in fact. It has the daring to admit that while man can know little, very little, about God and himself, he can and does know something." [17] What is recognizable as authentically Jewish in this observation—its acceptance of the possibility of man's pleasing God—is also the other side of Steinberg's faith: his conviction that reason alone, whatever the need of a transcending risk of faith, is the only tool on which we can possibly rely.

The living fusion of the Greek and the Jewish, implicit and unargued as it was, was the legacy of Steinberg to the generation that succeeded him. If one were to risk

[17] *Ibid.*, p. 213.

an anticipation of our conclusion, it would be pertinent—drawing from the living thought of Milton Steinberg—to suggest that any authentic Jewish theology must combine the wise innocence of the Jew, the intellectual rigor of the Greek, and the irresoluble ambiguity of the modern Christian to be at all adequate to the modern Jew who is all three—Greek, Christian, and Jew.

V. THE RHETORIC OF FAITH: ABRAHAM JOSHUA HESCHEL

Rhetoric, a practical discipline of great antiquity, has fallen into disfavor in our day. It has become synonymous with disingenuousness and trickery, a species of vulgar appeal to which only politicians resort and the unsophisticated succumb. But rhetoric, now come on hard days, has a distinguished, an illustrious past.

Aristotle, complimenting the power of rhetoric, defines it to be nothing less than "the counterpart of dialectic," a device of displaying truths in such a fashion as to persuade men to alter their conduct and pursue a course of noble and right action. Well aware that rhetoric is often confused with sophistry, Aristotle is unambiguous in affirming that what differentiates the sophist from the rhetorician is not the intellectual faculties or the techniques of argument which both employ, but the ends toward which they seek to conduct men. Where the sophist, by definition, distorts and shadows the truth, persuading that the image is the object, the appearance the reality, the rhetorician, because of the morality of his end, possesses a constructive art. He may employ his art correctly, in which case he not only is a passive servant of truth and justice but enables others to actively pursue them; or he may employ it poorly, in which case his hearers depart his presence as ignorant and uninformed as they were before.[1]

It is the universality of rhetoric, its applicability to the communication of all arts and sciences, which is in part responsible for its decline. Since it has no proper subject matter, no limited field of specialty, it may be used to persuade us of anything at all. Unlike dialectic, the art of logical inquiry, rhetoric persuades. The sound rhetorician assesses his audience, considers their prejudices and predilections, judges the degree of trust and confidence which they repose in him, and fashions those arguments which will attractively display the truths to which he wishes to gain their assent.

The rhetorician most acutely exhibits his talents when he functions as a moralist—for what greater purpose could he serve than to instruct others in the nature, character, and end of the moral life? He can trivialize his art to serve vulgar causes, as do the advertiser and promoter, or he can fulfill the potency of his calling by turning man to the pursuit of the good life or even to the service of God.

Clearly, if we invest the tradition of classic philosophy with more than uncomprehending respect, we must acknowledge that the art of rhetoric, far from being a technique of obfuscation and confusion, is a powerful instrument of manifesting truth. It is to this older and more respectable usage that we refer when we speak of Abraham Joshua Heschel, undoubtedly the most significant thinker which traditional Judaism has given to contemporary America, as a rhetorical theologian. His rhetoric is both the strength and the undoing of his theology.

One argues in those ages where the mind is receptive to argument; it is obviously folly to argue, however, if one believes one's age to be unresponsive to argument. Such

[1] Aristotle, *Rhetoric,* trans. by W. Rhys Roberts, in *The Basic Works of Aristotle,* ed. by Richard P. McKeon (New York, Random House, Inc., 1941), 1354a–1355b.

an age must be addressed by other means. In either case, whether one thinks in order to *demonstrate* or thinks in order to *persuade,* the presupposition of all communication is that a privately furnished universe is thrown open to public inspection, that others may be persuaded to refurbish their conceptions accordingly or be so swayed by the richness and subtlety of its interior as to remodel on faith.

The twentieth century is a faithless century. However one chooses to address it, one's choice is precarious. Argument is suspect and rhetoric is dismissed as a mere show of eloquence. The universe to which philosophy pays court shrinks to the point where a few courtiers, speaking in clipped, precise, but prosaic language, remain to wait upon a starving king. Fiefs gone, traditions broken, tithes unpaid, how shall philosophic truth reign in such a kingdom? And faith, that turning of the soul to God of which theologians spoke, how shall it be restored? Can it be defended meaningfully: can its former handmaidens, now courtesans in another, but impoverished, court, be brought home to serve it once more? Can the means of philosophy—reason, exposition, dialectic—be returned to the quest for their eternal source? It is this dilemma which renews the contest of faith and reason—those twin kingdoms, once conjugal, now divorced.

Abraham Joshua Heschel is a thinker of our times. He is a bearer of the dilemma of our times and in his thought the war of reason and faith is fought, battles are joined, and victories are won. What remains to be estimated is whether his victories are purchased at the price of maintaining the disunion of reason and faith, philosophy and theology, dialectic and rhetoric. It may well be that in a faithless age the pious are justified in forgoing the patient wonder of philosophy, if faith—which proceeds unmediated to the source of wonder—can be renewed. Philosophy, an apparent luxury of the intellect, might well be put aside, preserved intact and frozen, until the advent of those halcyon times when the speculative impulse of man may be renewed. But this would be to make philosophy the diversion of our quiet hours, dispensable in crisis. It is as well to conceal the weapon of rhetoric in the sheath of argument; to project a caricature of philosophy; to imagine that the destruction of philosophic pretensions vanquishes true philosophy.

If faith is only to be reborn out of the ashes of philosophy, we risk giving life to a crippled phoenix. Such faith, phoenixlike, may soar with youthful vitality, but in the end, cut off as it is from the finitude of its proper humanity, it too will perish. There is to our view no faith, no wonder, no amazement, however radical and extreme, which can survive unless founded upon the immediacies of man's everyday existence. Indeed, both faith and philosophy ultimately surpass the contingency of our world; but where faith leaps, moving, as in an instant, quickly and beyond our world, philosophy rises slowly. In the end, only philosophy and faith conjoined can ensure that the marveling of the one—in which philosophy begins—and the "radical amazement" of the other—in which faith arises—will comport to man's nature and God's design.

All experience points beyond itself. "The magnificent and the common"—all that we encounter on the way of life insinuates its transcendent origin and destiny. Nothing—no person, no object, no event—is self-explanatory. This is not to say that the analytic intellect cannot devise definitions which are sufficient and adequate; but such adequacy and sufficiency as its definitions enjoy are limited to the superficial reality. Such intellect really misses the point. It fails presumably to take note of that which all life discloses—namely, the insufficiency of the solitary. Nothing is alone; all points to all; each moment, however unique, is bound up "in the bonds of life"; every event moves out from a single center and the infinite centers of unique events ultimately coalesce and are united in that single, wondrous center which is God.[2]

The coalescence of reality, the transitiveness and self-transcendence of all things, can be sensed. It cannot be expressed. Language may circle reality, making gestures and feints of entry into the inner being of the world, but language cannot enter. Only intuition—mute and inarticulate—can really touch and record the "ineffable." The "ineffable"—multifarious, rich, and elusive as is Heschel's use of the term—would seem to be a "quality" of events; [3] sometimes, as well, it appears to be substantive reality; [4] but most consistently, over and beyond all stratagems of language, the ineffable is that medium, that aether, that atmosphere through which man senses "the true meaning, source and end of being." [5] The ineffable is the divine presence which veils God, but covers all things.

The ineffable is a given dimension of reality. It is always there to be caught, sensed, felt, intuited. It can also be missed and avoided. Some enter life with the wonder of the ineffable upon them; some, prisoners of their world, happen upon the ineffable—in a chance moment of incaution and unguarded embrace of the world, they discover and are freed; some never know, and to them it cannot be taught. Although the sense of the ineffable cannot be taught, it can be evoked. What some manifest and articulate, lies quiet and at rest in others. Those who speak can be taught to speak more wisely;

[2] The image we have employed to suggest the structure of Heschel's primary insight, that of the "center" and the coalescence of centers in God, is drawn from Maurice Friedman's description of Heschel's thought as being like that of "concentric circles that are produced when a stone is thrown into a pool. . . ." Maurice Friedman, "Abraham Joshua Heschel: Toward a Philosophy of Judaism," *Conservative Judaism,* Winter, 1956, p. 10.

[3] Abraham Joshua Heschel, *Man Is Not Alone* (New York, Farrar, Straus & Cudahy, Inc., 1951), p. 5.

[4] "The ineffable in us communes with the ineffable beyond us." *Ibid.,* p. 131.

[5] *Ibid.,* p. 5.

those who speak not at all can be brought to speech. *Man Is Not Alone,* Heschel's first nonexegetic theological work, was an attempt to evoke man's awareness of the ineffable.[6]

The ineffable is given with man's experience of the world. It is not open to the description of science or the conceptualization of philosophy. Science and philosophy, though they may enlarge and enrich man's sense of the ineffable, cannot in themselves discover it. By definition intellectual argument cannot discern what is, by definition, the unknown.[7] The ineffable is prior in the order of nature, though our awareness of it may be posterior in the order of knowledge. The articulate and manifest forms of the world are founded upon that hidden, inarticulate, and concealed source of reality which is the mystery of the unknown.

The unknown is the beginning of wisdom. This is not to say, with evident self-contradiction (although Heschel is not averse to pronouncing evident and clear-cut self-contradictions under the popular form of paradox), that the known begins with the unknown. It is rather to say that all real knowledge of the world depends upon the reality of the ineffable, or as the Bible might have it, that all knowledge begins with "the awe of God."

Even here, in the opening argument of *Man Is Not Alone* and *God in Search of Man,*[8] a characteristic transformation begins. The forms of traditional philosophic cognition are discarded in favor of their Biblical antecedents. Heschel, to be sure, is well aware that Plato believed that "philosophy begins in wonder." [9] He is at

[6] *Die Prophetic* (Cracow, The Polish Academy of Sciences, 1936), one of Heschel's most important works, may be considered an exegetic, if not a hermeneutic, study.

[7] *Ibid.*, p. 7.

[8] *Man Is Not Alone,* which was subtitled "A Philosophy of Religion," was followed by "A Philosophy of Judaism" (Abraham Joshua Heschel, *God in Search of Man* [New York, Farrar, Straus & Cudahy, Inc., 1955]).

[9] Heschel quotes Plato's affirmation in the *Theatetus,* 155D, but it is very unclear in the gloss that follows his quotation whether he

pains nevertheless to demonstrate that the "wonder" of Plato, to judge by the subsequent history of philosophy, results in a species of doubt which inhibits man's fresh encounter with the world, deadens his sense of the unknown, and issues finally in that "radical despair" which is the predicament of modern man. Presumably philosophy is a dead end.

The fact of the ineffable reflects our relation to the unnamed ground of the universe. It is not a mere synonym for the unknown,[10] but is suggestive rather of the limitations of man's ability to express the certainties which his heart knows. The fact that the sublime cannot be named and described ought not lead us to think that the sublime is a subjective experience, devoid of cognitive significance. It is, on the contrary, a "certainty without knowledge; it is real without being expressible." [11]

The peculiar difficulties posed by founding a complex exposition of general and Jewish religion upon an intuition which is ultimately beyond explicit statement are enormous. The sense of the ineffable, the radical amazement and wonder which attend it, can only be evoked by a rich mosaic of aphorism, illustration, psychological analysis, and existential argument. The fundamental reality of the ineffable can be described, but it is the description of seeing to the blind. Its meaningfulness is

---

really believes Plato's "wonder" is so different from his own, or whether he in fact means what he says when he contends that Plato's wonder is a species of doubt which "ends in radical despair." *Man Is Not Alone*, p. 13.

[10] *Ibid.*, p. 22.

[11] *Idem.;* also p. 20 *passim.* Heschel's phrase "a certainty without knowledge" is perplexing. It is an example of purposeful obscurity. Certainty presumes the presence of some form of knowledge. The knowledge may not be discursive or even translatable from non-discursive into rational discourse, but it is knowledge, whatever its privacy and incommunicability. We cannot believe that one who experiences the ineffable and is certain of that to which the ineffable points is unknowing. Since we do not consider Heschel a mystic the complexities of the famous *The Cloud of Unknowing* do not help.

contingent upon the trust that description will be so vivid as to make clear and intense what is not seen, and the hope that the unseeing may yet have the capacity for vision if placed in proper relation to the source of light.

The ineffable is not, Heschel believes, a private reality. It is open and accessible to all. It cannot, however, be approached and recognized by every means. There are certain avenues of apprehension which are unavailing: the way of science, if by science is meant that precise inquiry which follows from the assumption that there is no meaningful mystery which cannot be scientifically described; and the way of philosophy, if by philosophy is meant that which Hegel described at the beginning of *The Phenomenology of the Mind* as the effort to enable philosophy to be transformed from the "love of wisdom" into real knowledge. Goethe has already dispatched the pretensions of such scientism and such philosophy with his ironic observation that "these gentry think they lord it over God, Soul, and World, though no one can comprehend what it all means." [12]

Heschel is clearly dissatisfied with philosophy. He is sufficiently passionate in his dissatisfaction as to be reluctant to draw distinctions, to acknowledge the abyss which separates philosophy, as the Greeks understood its nature, from the attitudes of Western scientific empiricism; medieval philosophy from the idealisms of German philosophy; Kant from Hegel. To be sure, he favors some philosophers over others: Plato and Kant over Aristotle and Hegel. But even his preferences are not founded upon explicit scrutiny of principles or method, but upon moral predispositions which he discerns to be present in the former and absent in the latter. The favored philosophers, Plato and Kant, were at least sensitized to Heschel's fundamental categories: Plato acknowledged the role of wonder and marvel in the philosophic enter-

[12] From Goethe's letter to Zelter, October 27, 1827. Quoted from Josef Pieper, *Leisure the Basis of Culture* (New York, Pantheon Books, 1952), p. 144.

prise and Kant affirmed the "sense of wonder and transcendence."[13] Aristotle and Hegel, though discernibly different, are disqualified for the reason that Aristotle's God is self-sufficient and independent of the world and Hegel's God drives through history in relentless pursuit of egoistical self-completion.

Heschel's prejudices against philosophy are not unfounded. Philosophy and science have often succumbed to an idolatrous worship of reason. The spirit which is directed, in Heschel's view, toward that truth which transcends reason[14] has been disqualified. Philosophy and science threaten religion by undercutting its claim, by affirming that they can demonstrate while religion can only conjecture; by insisting that the claims of religion, unless validated by reason, are unacceptable; by denying, in effect, the limits which reason must set to its own competency. Heschel's inquiry is designed therefore to disentangle philosophy from faith, to set off what he describes as the "Greek" (meaning, presumably, speculative philosophy) from the "Biblical" (meaning, presumably, faith founded upon the experience of and commitment to the Mystery who is God).[15]

Heschel polarizes philosophy, science, and reason and the Biblical. The former cluster of attitudes and doctrines reflects all that bespeaks the self-arrogating *hybris* of man, his assumption of self-sufficiency and completeness. The latter casts man into a universe of existential risk and involvement. The former yields, at best, a species of knowledge which is by definition confined to the limits of the human intellect. The latter yields, at least, a certainty that man is not alone, that God lives and has need of him.

The Hebrew Bible discloses the history of God's concern for man. It is not, as disengaged criticism would have it, a document of man's efforts to record, texture, and sophisticate his apprehension of God. "The Bible is primarily not man's vision of God but God's vision of

[13] *God in Search of Man*, p. 51. [14] *Ibid.*, p. 19.
[15] *Ibid.*, p. 23, note 8.

man. The Bible is not man's theology, but God's anthropology, dealing with man and what He asks of him rather than with the nature of God." [16] The Bible ceases to be the training ground of theologians: Philo's analogical readings of Scripture, Maimonides' exegesis of Biblical anthropomorphisms, Spinoza's investigation of Biblical unreason are all beside the point. What matters is not the consistency of revelation, but the fact of revelation; not the logic of the narrative—its order, coherence, probability—but the fact that God has need to disclose his person in time and history.

The God of Scripture is not the God of the philosophers. This would seem apparent. The philosophers presumably concern themselves with God in order that their vision of reality may be complete and ordered to unity. God completes the architectural symmetry of the intellectual system. The God of the Bible is rather different. He is not a construct of the system, an intellectual requirement without which unity, causality, perfection would become meaningless concepts. Heschel rightly affirms that all such attributions are irrelevant to Biblical thinking.[17]

The philosopher experiences the events of the world, reflects upon their appearance, and interprets their significance. The world is an object of philosophizing. The end of the philosopher is to restate his experience of the world in such a way as to make its rationality coherent with its reality. The world is passive before the philosopher's intellect. The world is not, however, passive before God. God is not man's object, but his subject; man is not God's object, but His manifest presence in the world. God, world, and man are interfused. "God is not all in all. He is in all beings but He is *not* all beings." [18] God is given with our world: to think of him is to experience him, to acknowledge his life is already to accept his life into ours, to apprehend his reality is to place our-

[16] *Man Is Not Alone,* p. 129.
[17] *Ibid.,* pp. 100–109.
[18] *Ibid.,* p. 148.

selves before him and to accede to his dominion.[19] This is but to say—and Heschel says it often and variously—that the only way to enter the orbit of faith is *to enter it*, the only way to apprehend God is *to apprehend him.* This seeming tautology—and it is a persistent and aggravating tautology—underscores the fact that Heschel is essentially disinterested in argument. The argument is won long before the conclusion is reached. So often in Heschel's work the argument begins with all seriousness and candor only to gather speed, accelerate, dropping premises along the way, until it culminates in a rhapsodic evocation of the conclusion. The reason for this eccentricity of style is not hard to locate. Essentially Heschel is bored with argument. What need is there for argument in the presence of the pious and of him who lives before the ineffable?

Similarly one does not argue with the nature of Scripture. The Bible is *prima facie* evidence of its own divinity. There is no need of the philosopher if one has the prophet. The patient intellection of the philosopher is necessary if one is not assaulted by the world, if the world is mute, inarticulate, obdurate. The philosopher must scratch hard at the surface of reality to disturb its impassivity. The prophet is manifestly superior to the philosopher, for the philosopher seeks at the end what the prophet knows at the beginning.

The prophet, it would appear, is the Jewish counterpart to the philosopher. But where the philosopher occupies himself with quiddity and essence, the prophet concerns himself with consequences and effects. He assumes the essence, being content to report an image of divinity which takes existence, nature, and presence for granted.[20]

The prophet exemplifies what Heschel has described as "situational thinking" by contrast with the philosopher's

[19] *Ibid.*, pp. 126–29.
[20] Abraham Joshua Heschel, *Between God and Man,* ed. by Fritz A. Rothschild (New York, Harper & Brothers, 1959), pp. 116–24.

"conceptual thinking." [21] This distinction, as many of Heschel's favorite distinctions, ought not to be scrutinized too rigorously. Heschel's distinctions are too fragile. They possess rhetorical power, but they are not intellectually resilient. Clearly the prophet is different from the philosopher. Something happens to the prophet which cannot happen to the sound philosopher—namely, his reason is overwhelmed by an experience, whose nature and source his awe of the numinous restrains him from investigating. This is all well and good; but to say that the difference between "situational thinking" and "conceptual thinking" is that the former "involves an inner experience," [22] while the latter is "an act of reasoning" is simply not true. It is to be doubted whether Augustine, Pascal, Kierkegaard, Nietzsche, or the existentialists (atheist and believing alike) would agree that they do not think out of the concrete situation of man and history; on the other hand, they would most certainly deny either that they are oblivious to the "act of reasoning" or that they are prophets. The prophets, moreover, whose words "are never detached from the concrete, historic situation," who always refer their message "to an actual situation," are certainly users of reason.[23] The distinction is too neat. As with all neat distinctions, it is useful as a device for sharpening persuasion, concentrating passion, and convincing the believer that it is best if he have no intimate commerce with the intellect; but whatever

[21] *God in Search of Man,* pp. 5 f. [22] *Idem.*

[23] Heschel comes embarrassingly close to a Biblical fundamentalism in his implicit denial that the prophets did not make use of "the act of reasoning." The moral reasoning of the prophets is incomparable; surely their close investigation of the nature and consequences of sin is not so simply designated as "situational thinking" to be disjoined from reason. Is it not rather that the prophet denies that reason is autonomous, independent, and underived? The prophet reasons, but the impulse to reason is elsewhere than in the inquisitiveness of the free intellect. It is to be sought, as Maimonides suggested, in the *intellectus agens* which has its source in God. But then, if this is so, can philosophic theology really be set outside the purview of Biblical and prophetic thinking?

its use in intensifying the faith of the committed,[24] it cannot aid in turning the mind of the unbeliever toward the possibility of faith.

More convincing than his innumerable attempts to distinguish philosophic and prophetic thinking is Heschel's moving and profound interpretation of the prophetic experience. Heschel speaks here, not as a Biblical thinker arguing with a tradition whose character and destiny he neither fully grasps nor with whose pathos he sympathizes, but as a Biblical man. The Biblical man cannot be argued nor defended. He is not an opponent of philosophy; he is not an arguer. He simply *is*—his experience, his world, his faith are given with his being in the world.

The Biblical man, the prophet, the situational thinkers of all time illustrate what Heschel considers "an ontological presupposition." [25] This somewhat portentous phrase is nothing more than an acknowledgment that the experience of God presupposes the reality of God; that God is never demonstrable; that his existence and presence are predicated by man's wonder and involvement in the mystery of the world. The "certainty of the realness of God" recalls a phase of man's life where certainty is given with experience, where truth is correlative to the depth, intensity, and inexpressible mystery of experience.[26] Heschel relies finally upon an argument which ends in the silence to which Maimonides recommends that we repair when the immensity of the truth known

[24] *God in Search of Man*, p. 5; p. 204.
[25] Whether this presupposition is "preconceptual and presymbolic," as Heschel claims, is debatable. Heschel is so evidently concerned with evacuating from the religious experience all contact with common modes of rational and philosophic discourse that he makes use of phrases such as "preconceptual and presymbolic," which are at best suggestive, at worst meaningless. One's impatience with Heschel's often freighted language ought not to blind one to the fact that Heschel is trying to ground the religious experience in those recesses of human consciousness and intellect where proof, confirmation, and truth follow from the immediate and direct apprehension of God. Cf. *God in Search of Man*, pp. 114–24.
[26] *Ibid.*, p. 121.

exceeds the distortionary, incomplete, and pallid capacity of language.[27] The "ontological presupposition" is of course the defeat of reason; if reason is incapacitated, if language fails, if arguments wither, then surely certainty is to be accompanied by silence. It is questionable, however, whether the natural certainty of man, unaided as it is by revelation, is ever possible without reason. There is a rather considerable body of Jewish and non-Jewish thought which would recommend silence only after reason had secured all that was possible to reason. This is only to say that, quite possibly, the prophet does not oppose the philosopher nor for that matter precede the philosopher, but rather that the prophet builds upon the foundations established by reason.

The prophet undoubtedly begins with the experience of the "living God." The experience of the God who lives presupposes that divine life is involved in the life of man. Were it not so, it would be meaningless to speak of the "living God." God lives precisely because he is concerned with man, because man and God are reciprocally related.[28] The Bible speaks of God's search for man, his repetitive "Where art thou?" The "Where art thou?" of God elicits man's consciousness that he is "exposed to His presence," to an "awareness of . . . being called upon."[29] Since faith is man's response to the concern of God, it is proper for Biblical religion to be defined as "God's question and man's answer."[30]

Unless man marvels and wonders, turns his face to the ineffable, surrenders himself to the suggestive mystery of experience, he cannot comprehend "the impact with which the realness of God is pursuing man."[31] To be without that natural wonder which discloses the reality

[27] *Ibid.*, pp. 121–22.
[28] *Ibid.*, p. 128. "The supreme fact in the eyes of the prophets is the presence of God's concern for man and the absence of man's concern for God."
[29] *Ibid.*, p. 137.
[30] *Idem.* "There is a grain of the prophet in the recesses of every human existence." *Ibid.*, p. 255.
[31] *Ibid.*, p. 175.

of God is to remain closed to that supernatural wonder which is God's revelation in Scripture. Scripture testifies less to an idea or possibility than to a claim—a claim, one should add, *upon us, but not upon its contemporaries.* The prophets did not *claim* to speak the will of God. They *spoke* and allowed history to judge. "Claim" is already compounded of hesitation and doubt. It is now a claim because the living testimony of history which was available in the centuries from Moses to Malachi is now, together with revelation itself, subject to the doubt of unbelievers and the unsubstantiated faith of believers. Today the prophetic claim to speak is indeed a claim upon faith, a claim upon that in all of us which is like to the prophets, namely our capacity to experience the living God beyond the ineffable and the mystery.[32]

The experience of prophecy, which Heschel rightly distinguishes from mysticism,[33] is a reflection of God's

[32] *Ibid.*, p. 176 *passim.* We have restated Heschel's argument concerning the "claim" of revelation only because we accept his teaching so wholeheartedly we would have wished it stated here strongly. There is a difference between the hearer who hears the Word of God and disobeys and the hearer who hears only the record of the Word of God and disobeys. The prophetic claim upon Israel in the days of God's public revelation is of an order of unqualified claim. To refuse to hear then, to fashion instead a Golden Calf, or wander off in submission to Baalim and Ashtaroth, is of a piece with what Kierkegaard has called, in *The Concept of Dread* ([Princeton, N. J., Princeton University Press, 1944], p. 110), the "shut-upness" of unbelief. Faith can only interpret the backslidings of Israel as the "dread of the good," a commitment to finitude which is almost demonic, precisely because revelation had already educated man to the knowledge of that infinity of which he was capable. But today, twenty centuries or more later, our condition is different. We have not heard with our own ears. We have heard only through the ears of history which records and transcribes. We do not trust history; we do not trust transcriptions. We are closed to revelation—not for having heard, but for not having heard. The burden of faith is greater upon us than upon our forefathers, because we must believe without hearing. This is why, as shall be noted later, we cannot finally accept Heschel's forensic theology. Post-Biblical man cannot be shamed into belief. We deserve more compassion—if we do not deserve it from God, we insist upon it from theologians.

[33] *God in Search of Man*, p. 198.

concern for man, of "God's turning toward man." Whereas mysticism centers upon the single man's preoccupation with experiencing divinity, prophecy depends upon the disclosure of God to man.[34] Prophecy, the medium of revelation, is consummated in that moment in which God reaches man.[35] The prophetic event represents, therefore, the nexus of man and God, the focus of that reciprocal relation which signifies that the seeking of God and the seeking of man are ended in the finding of each other.[36]

To speak, as Heschel repeatedly speaks, of the Bible as God's anthropology, suggests that God's intimacy and association with man and history is of a different order from that usually described by more formalistic theologies. Quite definitely the God of the philosophers and the God of the prophets differ.[37] They differ primarily because the God of the prophets is a God of temporal involvement. Since it is not for man to surmise the peculiar means by which an infinite God enters time, to determine the sense in which "suffering" and "longing," "grief" and "consternation" enter the divine life, it is sufficient that he accredit the prophetic record of God's pathos. The divine pathos to which the prophets testify is "from the point of view of God, the *pathos* of sympathy and that of rejection." [38] Of course Heschel begs the theological question by denying that pathos is *essential* to God's nature. The divine pathos is without "substantial reality." It is rather a functional variable of God's will, a consequence of his precarious relations with man and history. Heschel's effort to explain why pathos is not an attribute of God's nature is unavailing—to have made pathos an essential dimension of the divine life would not, as he suggests, have rendered God immutable and unresponsive to further trial. The question still remains,

[34] *Idem.*
[35] *Ibid.*, p. 199.
[36] *Idem.*
[37] *Ibid.*, p. 213.
[38] *Between God and Man*, p. 118. This anthropopathetic interpretation of prophecy is the essential theme of *Die Prophetie.*

and Heschel has not answered it, whether pathos is an essential or an accidental attribute of God. If it is essential, grief and suffering are introduced into God's life; if it is accidental, it is liable to the complaints of traditional theologians who would consider the imputation of the transitory and impermanent to God to be a self-contradiction. If it is neither—neither essential nor accidental—it is simply a mode of speech, an anthropomorphism by which man seeks to establish God's complicity in human destiny.[39]

Notwithstanding theological unclarity Heschel emerges with a striking affirmation that states, more concisely and brilliantly than he has stated elsewhere, his conviction regarding the meaning of the divine pathos:

> The divine *pathos* is the unity of the eternal and the temporal, of the rational and the irrational, of the metaphysical and the historical. It is the real basis of the relation between God and man, of the correlation of Creator and creation, of the

[39] At the same time that Heschel affirms that pathos has no substantial reality, he still avers "that God can actually suffer." (*Between God and Man*, p. 120.) This exemplifies what has bothered us frequently in our reading of Heschel: namely, Heschel is aware of all the problems, all the dilemmas, all the mysteries inherent in theology, but has not yet elected the resolute way. He is still too much the disciple of the Jewish Philosopher, Maimonides, whose strictures against anthropomorphism prevent him from imputing to God's essence the meaningful and instructive experience of anything which might, in the view of human finitude, compromise divine perfection. Both Alfred North Whitehead and Charles Hartshorne have done much to indicate that perfection is not compromised by richness of experience; that there is no reason why simplicity is any more to be desired in the divine nature than complexity and involvement. At the same time Heschel is profoundly aware that the Biblical testimony to divine tears and repentance, sorrow and compassion, cannot be put aside, for the Biblical authors ascribed these experiences to God *really*, and not merely as an inaccurate metaphor. Symbolic ascription has the value of pointing to being, even if it is unable to name it precisely. Heschel's way out of the dilemma may be religiously satisfactory, but it is theologically unconvincing.

> dialogue between the Holy One of Israel and His people.[40]

Clearly it ceases to be important whether pathos is essential or accidental. What is important is that pathos is a mirror through which God refracts the tragedy of history and through which man refracts the disappointment of God in man. It is but a step from the prophet's record of divine pathos to the articulation of the life of service. The man who has learned to live in the faith of the prophets cannot but say, as Heschel has said, that "if God is not everything, He is nothing." The sanctification of time and history, the transformation of the profane, the bringing down of holiness into time, issue inescapably in the life of commandment and observance which describe the practice of traditional Judaism. From awe and amazement issues faith; out of faith arises the vindication of divine self-disclosure; revelation is given the intuition of divine pathos; and, with the acquaintance of God's suffering, there arises the passion to serve, thank, and glorify.[41]

For too long philosophy and faith have been separated in Judaism. Philosophy has been surrendered to unbelief and faith has either retreated into the dull and repetitious recital of formula or been content to confirm its disenchantment with philosophy by reviving the ancient opposition of Scripture and reason. This is lamentable—not so much because philosophy suffers by the absence of faith as because faith suffers by the loss of contact with that common world of sensation and experience in

[40] *Between God and Man*, p. 120.

[41] Heschel's most pure and perfect books, *The Earth Is the Lord: The Inner World of the Jew in East Europe* (New York, Henry Schuman, 1950) and *The Sabbath: Its Meaning for Modern Man* (New York, Farrar, Straus & Cudahy, Inc., 1951), are invocations of the life of faith. They are high rhetoric, for they do not argue—they exhibit and evoke; they do not present the illusion of system or demonstration—they are rich, sentient, lyrical statements of the Jewish hallowing of creation.

which men live and through which they pursue their destinies to God. Faith, cut off from its foundation in the finitude of man, is easily deluded. Its rhetoric parts company from the facts; the disabilities of time and history are underrated; the pathos seems to be all on God's side; there is a deficient sympathy and compassion for those who are trapped in their unknowing and disbelief.[42]

It would appear, if we accredit the underlying assumption of Heschel's writing, that unbelief is sheer dishonesty. "There can be no honest denial of the existence of God. There can only be faith or the honest confession of inability to believe—or arrogance. Man could maintain inability to believe or suspend his judgment, if he were not driven by the pressure of existence into a situation in which he must decide between yes and no; in which he must decide what or whom to worship. He is driven toward some sort of affirmation. In whatever decision he makes he implicitly accepts either the realness of God or the absurdity of denying him." [43]

Faithlessness—that is, the demonic refusal of Biblical man before the revealed God and the authentic uncertainty of post-Biblical man before the divine claimant—may assume two forms. There is the disbelief so common in modern literature: the disbelief of Nietzsche; the disbelief of Dostoevsky's Kirillov or Stavrogin; the disbelief of Sartre. Disbelief is the response of man to a world no longer inhabited by the living God. To such a world

[42] Emil Fackenheim's observation that Heschel "lacks understanding for the tragedy of unbelief" seems to us eminently to the point. Emil Fackenheim, "Man Is Not Alone" (review), *Judaism,* Vol. I, No. 1 (January, 1952), p. 86. Jakob J. Petuchowski makes much the same point when he observes, with the pathos of finitude: "Can the 'God of the philosophers' be so cavalierly dismissed from the mind of the twentieth-century Jew? How, indeed, can Heschel hope to communicate his insights to those of us who are benighted enough to tarry in the realms of 'conceptual thinking' if he shuns conceptual thought altogether?" ("Faith as the Leap of Action: The Theology of Abraham Joshua Heschel," *Commentary,* May, 1958, p. 396.)

[43] *God in Search of Man,* p. 119.

Nietzsche replies that God is dead; Kirillov propounds the suicidal triumph of man over God; and Sartre affirms that "He is dead, He spoke to us and now is silent." Such disbelief issues from belief. The disbeliever affirms that God no longer counts, that He is ineffective, meaningless, trivial. The cruelty and suffering of history, the solitude and despair of individuality, the anguish of the lonely ego cannot be mitigated by this burned-out God. Disbelief is real and tragic.

Unbelief is rather different and far less terrifying. The unbeliever is simply not interested—God is an amusing or grand hypothesis, but little more. The fact of historical belief is a curiosity to unbelief or else a mere possibility among innumerable possibilities. There are few modern examples of unbelief—not even Bertrand Russell, whose *Free Man's Worship* is often cited by enthusiastic believers as an example of modern unbelief, qualifies, for Russell is still concerned and the problem of divinity is a real problem to him however much he may be outraged by some of the more preposterous—to his view—forms which it has taken. Unbelief is not the doctrine of significant minds, for serious thinkers know the history of belief and the grounds on which it was affirmed sufficiently well to disbelieve. They do not put away belief with boredom and disinterest. No! For the thinker there is belief or disbelief. Unbelief—the condition of being unaware—is the situation of those who do not think deeply at all.

Who then is dishonest or arrogant in his denial? He may exist, but surely we need not belabor him. To fashion as Heschel has done a rhetoric of belief to shame disbelief into faith or harass unbelief into the open is neither meaningful nor effective. The believing may be strengthened in their certitude, but the faithless are not turned nor the faithful deepened. Rather the opposite is the case. The faithless are confirmed in disbelief and the faithful become arrogant.

There must be another way.

In an early volume of Heschel, his rich and absorbing account of the life and thought of Maimonides, Heschel describes the closing years of Maimonides' life. The work projected for those years—his intention of writing a book on the Agadic literature, his desire to translate his works from Arabic into Hebrew, to complete his commentary on the Babylonian and Jerusalem Talmud, to write a source book to the *Yad*—are all put aside. Instead, as Heschel notes:

> . . . he renounced all these things and went on healing the sick. . . . This is Maimonides' last metamorphosis from contemplation to practice, from the perception to the imitation of God. God is no longer the object of knowledge. He becomes the example one is to follow. His works, living creatures, whom He guides in His providence, take the place of the abstract concepts which constitute the spiritual act in the intellectual perception of God. Observation of concrete events and absorption in them is substituted for the abstract view. The thinker no longer troubles himself to deny God any attribute, but "to be like God in his actions." [44]

Let it be granted that the last years of Maimonides were spent, not in the contemplation of God, but in the imitation of Him. This is but to say that the intellect, nourished and abundant, was so joined to its divine source as to destroy all distinction between contemplation and practice, thought and act. Maimonides had achieved what Heschel, in fact, suggests he believed himself to have achieved: that union of God and man which is prophecy.[45]

[44] Abraham Joshua Heschel, "The Last Years of Maimonides," *National Jewish Monthly*, June, 1955, p. 7; *Maimonides* (Berlin, Erich Reiss Verlag, 1935), p. 274–75.

[45] Cf. "Did Maimonides Strive for Prophetic Inspiration?" *Louis Ginzberg Jubilee Volume* (in Hebrew) (New York, The American Academy for Jewish Research, 1945, pp. 159–88), p. 22, 30. In this

It is proper that the intellect issue ultimately in that transcendent union which some call "the mystic union," but which Judaism calls "prophecy." Prophecy is, as Heschel has defined it, that correlation of God and man, that reciprocal play of concern and response, divine pathos and human longing, which eliminates all disunion and separation. There is no need to discriminate philosophy and religion, reason and faith, contemplation and act, when all men are prophets. Surely that is the goal of Israel—that all Jews be prophets—but it is rather rushing the history of redemption to speak as though we "prisoners of hope" had come to our fulfillment.

Our situation is more modest and for that reason more precarious, indeed tragic. Not only are we distant from prophecy, we are distant from that approach of faith which turns our contemplation to God that we might one day forgo contemplation for imitation. We are so distant from Maimonides as to be incomparable to him. We are also so distant from Heschel as to be incomparable to him. Heschel has written for us all, unlike Maimonides who wrote ostensibly only for Joseph Ibn Aknin and a small, select coterie of initiates. We are confronted by the whole prophetic truth and counseled to remove the robes of thought, our concealing vestments of argument and circumspection, and imitate the pious who know and are informed.

It is not alone because of our intransigence and disbelief that we cannot do this. We cannot do this because, if we are to come to the goal of Maimonides, we must, like

---

essay Heschel examines Maimonides' doctrine of prophecy and, although he does not state that Maimonides actually affirmed that he enjoyed the spirit of prophecy, there are enough indications to suggest that what modesty prevented Maimonides from openly acknowledging, he in fact believed. There is, in confirmation of this view, Heschel's direct statement: "For him (Maimonides) every act of thought is a receipt of revelation, the uninterrupted emanation of the divine enters into thought but also into every happening in the world, wherever matter is acquiring form." ("The Last Years of Maimonides," p. 275.)

him, come by his way. If we too are to "imitate God" we must first, like Maimonides who contemplated before he abandoned contemplation, who philosophized before he prophesied, contemplate and philosophize.

There is an older philosophizing than that which Heschel opposes. It is not the philosophizing which would put aside wonder and marvel in favor of radical doubt and disbelief. It is the philosophizing of which Diotima spoke in the *Symposium:* "Who then, Diotima, I [Socrates] asked, who then philosophizes, if neither the wise nor the foolish philosophize? And to that she answered: It must surely be clear, even to a child, that it is those who are between the two, in the middle." [46] The wise do not philosophize, for the gods, who are wise, already know.[47] Nor do the ignorant philosophize, for ignorance is self-satisfied. Only "the middle," that truly human sphere, yields philosophy. "The truly human thing is neither to conceive or comprehend (like God), nor to harden and dry up; neither to shut oneself up in the supposedly clear and enlightened everyday world, nor to resign oneself to remaining ignorant; not to lose the childlike suppleness of hope, the freedom of movement that belongs to those who hope." [48]

Such a view of philosophy is, it would appear, similar to the view of prophecy. Philosophy is unlike science. It ought not to be lumped with science. Though philosophy reasons and science reasons, though philosophy scrutinizes and science scrutinizes, their sharing of inquiry does not involve the sharing of wonder. The questions of science are, in principle, answerable. There is little point in the scientist's pursuing questions which *cannot* be answered, for which no evidence can be accumulated, no experience defined, no facts delimited and described. But precisely where science ranges the universe of the possible and demonstrable, it is the courage of philosophy that

[46] Plato, *Symposium,* 204 f.
[47] *Idem.* "No God is a philosopher or seeker after wisdom."
[48] Pieper, *Leisure the Basis of Culture,* p. 139.

it takes up the cause of the impossible and unanswerable. It does this because philosophy begins with the assumption of wonder and humility. Not only has philosophy not "claimed to be a superior form of knowledge but, on the contrary, a form of humility, and restrained, and conscious of this restraint in relation to knowledge." [49]

The philosophy of which we speak, like prophecy, begins in wonder. It departs from the prosaic and routine, moving beyond the givenness of experience, in search of the ground of experience. It is discontented by the commonplace and bored by the characteristically bourgeois acceptance of the tangible and comprehensible. Philosophy has its origins in the conviction that there is a more complicated truth than that which is apparent and sufficient to trusting common sense. Like prophecy, philosophy thrives on hope that wisdom is possessed somewhere and that by patient hearing, faithful attentiveness, and uncompromised purity of intention a portion of it may become the legacy of men. The difference, to be sure, between prophet and philosopher is that the prophet is granted his endowment of wisdom, whereas the philosopher must work arduously. This is only to say that God chooses his prophets, whereas philosophers must go forth to find their God.

Who are we then—in this generation or in the last or in the future—prophets or philosophers, given by God or in search of him? There is little question but that we are philosophers, not prophets. Be it said immediately, however, we are philosophers with wonder. We are not, as we noted earlier, among those who would have philosophy converted from "the love of wisdom" into real knowledge. Real knowledge, as Hegel understood it, has passed beyond the questioning stance of classic philosophizing to the assertion of an egoism which is indifferent not only to the constantly shifting horizon of experience but to all

[49] *Ibid.*, p. 141. Pieper's essay "The Philosophical Act" has been a source of constant stimulation and excitement to us.

those refinements of the classic dialectic which the unresolved mysteries of existence demand. The philosophizing which we recommend ends with prophecy, but it cannot begin there. It begins only with the acknowledgment of the known and the unknown, and from there—from these simple recognitions of connection and interrelation between the understood and the problematic—moves to the discovery of the world, of man, and of God.

Philosophy commences with no assumption other than that of the question—or as the young mathematician of the *Theatetus* enthusiastically observes: "By all the Gods, Socrates, I really cannot stop marveling at the significance of these things," to which Socrates replies, with his characteristically freighted irony, "Yes, that is the very frame of mind that constitutes the philosopher, that and nothing else is the beginning of philosophy." [50] But question leads to question, and wonder rises above wonder, and depths are discovered beneath depths; and finally the ineffable—that medium of wonder—is pierced and a new understanding achieved. The philosopher here joins with the theologian and both begin the pilgrimage of prophecy.

It is therefore inadequate to commend the prophet to modern man, to juxtapose prophet to philosopher, to identify philosophy and science, to establish, on the foundation of incomplete contrasts and analyses, the truth and wisdom of Biblical religion. The vindication of Biblical religion can surely be accomplished by rhetorical exhibition—by intensity of passion, by roseate eloquence, by descriptions of piety and the pious life. This leaves the already pious moved, diverts and fascinates the unbeliever, but fails to penetrate the forms of disbelief, those distorted, incomplete, and idolatrous masks of authentic belief.

It is the strength and weakness of rhetoric that undermine the persuasiveness of Heschel's thought. Were his

[50] Plato, *Theatetus*, 155.

rhetoric sure and classic it would be founded upon sure and classic argument: that is to say, his rhetoric would be but the art of securing popular confirmation of his theology. It would not be, as it is, a substitute for theology. Like that of Aristotle, his rhetoric would be the visible and manifest consequence of his metaphysics and ethics, the expression by argument, homily, example, and display of those virtues of the mind and soul which are commended to the care of men.

The renaissance of belief has been awaited now for several centuries. Ardent and profound belief is dead and conventional belief and practice dull and weary both believer and nonbeliever. We have waited long for a new moment. Perhaps that moment is now. It cannot be risked, however, that in an excess of steaming conviction, impatient and passionate, the waters of belief be scattered at random, renewing the willing but drowning the unprepared. This is the danger of theology pursued by rhetoric, rather than in the patient way of sages who would have us move by confident action and patient philosophizing to that moment of prescience at which the Biblical witness of prophecy may be ours once more.

VI. "NOT ONLY" A JEWISH THINKER: WILL HERBERG

The uniqueness of Will Herberg, that which endows his thought with particular richness and relevance, derives from the unrelenting seriousness with which he has understood the vocation of the Jewish thinker to consist in being *not only* a Jewish thinker. It is precisely this quality of "not only" which defines the enigmatic and ambiguous role which Herberg has played in contemporary Jewish thought. He is not traditional enough to be acceptable to the Orthodox; not survivalist enough to be countenanced by Zionist or Reconstructionist; not distant and critical enough to instruct the secular Jewish intellectuals.[1] His views of law and revelation share enough with Buber and Rosenzweig to make his Orthodoxy questionable; his sense of survival, so sharply theological, cares little for the rituals of cohesion by which radical versions of Judaism seek to perpetuate the Jewish people; his neo-Orthodox impatience with the pretensions of reason, his apparent disinterest in literature and the arts, his thorough and unregretting repudiation of his Marxist past, exclude him from the limbo in which nonreligious Jewish intellectuals continue to make their society.

The theology of Will Herberg baffles precisely because

[1] It had been our intention to include in this volume an essay on the important, but indirect, role played in modern Judaism by the so-called "secular" Jewish intellectuals. This proved to be impossible here—the problem is too vast and too fascinating to be limited to a brief essay. It should be observed, however, that of all the contemporary Jewish theologians, Will Herberg comes closest to having connection with the world of the nonreligious Jewish intellectuals. If we are correct in understanding the Jewish intellectual to be he who is—however marginally related to Jewish religion—textured throughout by the uncertainties, nostalgias, pains and pleasures of a dead world of Jewish securities and symbolic meanings, Herberg is not a Jewish intellectual. There is nothing in him that recalls the early intellectual awakening which Isaac Rosenfeld, Paul Goodman, Delmore Schwartz, Alfred Kazin, and Saul Bellow have, in their own ways, so beautifully documented in fiction, essay, and autobiography. It is improper to mention Herberg along with them. Herberg is an impatient thinker, not an artist. His world is not fashioned out of enshrined memory whose intricate skein of feeling and sensibility proved evanescent on contact with the solid genius and businesslike realism of Western culture. The "writer" intellectuals to whom we have referred are more truly Jewish intellectuals than Herberg—that is, late children of the American *haskalah*. Herberg is not of them, although ostensibly more passionately involved in Judaism than they; they remain more Jewish than he, for where he emerges as a Jewish thinker fresh from the war of Jerusalem with the West, their thought is so resolutely of the West, that all of Jerusalem that remains is the immemorial burden of flesh, memory, and a "suffering become too deep to share" (Irving A. Sanes and Harvey Swados, "Certain Jewish Writers: Notes on Their Stereotypes," *The Menorah Journal*, Spring, 1949, p. 197).

it is consonant with no past, no legacy of opinion, no doctrine of commitment or disenchantment. It is a personal theology become public; a private discovery, fashioned from disparate sources and experiences, which makes insistent demands upon all. It is a personal theology, moreover, whose sources are spelled out, whose derivations are explicit; it is uneccentric, not in the sense that it is conventional Jewish theology, but in the sense that it is the currently conventional doctrine of both Christians and Jews who have come to doubt the relevance and serviceability of their own immediate theological past. Herberg mystifies because he is so clear and unconditional. He is perhaps thought a strangely unprofessional polymath for having assimilated all the jarring, disconcerting anxieties of the age and formed them into an argument of uncompromising and resolute affirmation. Herberg is a kind of intellectual's evangelist; he is converting us always, because he is always converting himself, rooting out from his own position those suspicions of paganism and infidelity which marked his old paganism, his residual unconverted self. He is most important precisely because he has crystallized in his own position the whole history of Christian and Jew—the pagan who would wish to be transformed by Jesus Christ and the Jew who is, by nature and history, already transformed. It is not improper, therefore, to see the thought of Will Herberg as an unending personal dialectic, a state of enduring war with the sin of confident unknowing which is paganism.

By 1947 Will Herberg had effected the transition from Marxism to Judaism. He, perhaps alone, from among the thousands of Jews who had departed the American communist movement, not only left Marxism behind but rediscovered in Judaism its effective counterpoise.[2]

[2] No doubt others leaving communism rediscovered Judaism, but only Herberg—to the best of our knowledge—became a Jewish theologian.

Marxism had been to Herberg, not simply a movement assuring participation and involvement in the history of our times, but a comprehensive and thorough system, embracing a metaphysics (or rather the debunking of metaphysics), an ethics (or more precisely a scientific exposé of moral imperatives), and a religion and eschatology (or more accurately an obligation to work on behalf of an inevitable historical parousia).[3] The breaking-point for Herberg was not, as it was for many Marxists, the inability of Marxism to conform to the expectations of an unpolitical liberalism, or disenchantment with the uncompromising and amoral pursuit of power which defined the operation of the Communist Party in the United States during the thirties and forties. Herberg was never a political legman. He was then and he has remained an intellectual. Marxism defined an imperturbable and resolute dialectic of history; an underside of providence, as comprehensive, precise, and redemptive as providence itself. The test of Marxism was whether it worked; however, its workability was not to be tested by its undoubted expansion and success, but by the conformance of its principle to its practice. Marxism was ostensibly dedicated to the extension of freedom, the liberation of the individual from a depriving system. And yet, as Herberg testifies, the course of history controverted the claim of theory: the Russian Revolution was corrupted by the same terrorism and totalitarian unfreedom which it commenced by opposing; Hitler triumphed and Russia joined with Hitler; "sacrificial dedication to the welfare of humanity had given way to narrow, ruthless, self-defeating power politics." [4]

The ideals—vague and inchoate—which supplied the occasion for Herberg's entrance into the radical movement had not altered when he ceased to be a Marxist in the late thirties. The "great ideals of freedom and social

[3] Will Herberg, "From Marxism to Judaism," *Commentary*, January, 1947, p. 25.
[4] *Ibid.*, p. 26.

justice"[5] were not rejected; the matter of history was still open to the work of men; the ambiguity of human action—the deficiency of man's intellect and the defect of his will—were not yet defined in his thought. The balance, that unity of pessimism and hope, which clear faith and adequate theology demand was still to be located. What had collapsed had really collapsed. The ideals persisted; however, they were now suspended without support and grounding. With the destruction of Marxism much more than a movement had been destroyed. An ethic which could not transcend "the relativities of power and class interest" was no ethic. A metaphysics which perjured the legitimacy of metaphysics, which made of reality an arational commingling of irresistible powers and energies, could not supply the theoretical foundations for conduct, much less an adequate interpretation of the whole of reality. Naturalism—the halfway house of philosophic Marxists—went as well, for however man may be situated in nature it is by his reason, his spirit, his imagination that he "undeniably transcends it."

> This Marxist religion itself, it now became clear to me, was in part illusion, and in part idolatry; in part a delusive utopianism promising heaven on earth in our time, and in part a totalitarian worship of collective man; in part a naïve faith in the finality of economics, material production; in part a sentimental optimism as to the goodness of human nature, and in part a hard-boiled, amoral cult of power at any price. There could be no question to my mind that as religion, Marxism had proved itself bankrupt.[6]

In describing his rites of passage, Herberg correctly affirms—and it is to his credit that he does so without blushing—the consolations of religion. It is indeed possible to speak of the "secure spiritual groundwork"[7] which

[5] *Idem.*
[6] *Idem.*
[7] *Ibid.*, p. 27.

religion affords an effective social radicalism, for in the same measure as socialism would be provided with "a philosophy and a dynamic far superior to the shallow materialism that had led it so woefully astray," [8] theology might be vitalized by contact with the obduracy of man and the ambiguity of history. The consolations of religion, like the consolations of philosophy of which Boethius wrote more than fourteen hundred years ago, involve a double stance; in the same measure as philosophy consoles the uprooted mind by enabling it to apprehend that superior Wisdom which is in God, so religion consoles by enabling the believer to return again into the company of men and to regenerate his trust in them.

The disaster which attends the passing of the Marxist intellectual is not so much the evaporation of involvement, the inevitable disappearance of the politically engaged, but the consequent assumption that with the failure of Marxism the curtain of darkness has descended, the last cause has been lost, and the modern situation become irredeemably hopeless. The antitheological stance of the post-Marxist intellectual is, as has been pointed out, covertly theological, for it affirms one half of the theological dialectic: the evil of history, man's suicidal *hybris,* his willful, and presumably unavoidable, betrayal of meaning.[9] The Marxist *manqué,* one might assume, is not wholly genuine. If he is indeed a seeker of truth; if he has once held truth to be found in a movement of historical redemption, and that redemption has failed and its "sacraments" of salvation been repudiated, is he then free to contemplate the ruins? Does his task become, with self-justification, that of collecting and arranging the shards of broken events, of mourning the passing of that great era of passion and engagement (even though it proved false and delusive) ? Does he not

[8] *Idem.*

[9] Philip Rieff, "The Theology of Politics: Reflections on Totalitarianism as the Burden of Our Time," *Journal of Religion,* April, 1952, p. 120.

have, as he once had, the continuing task of seeking truth—but this time of seeking a more realistic truth, a truth more adequate to the self-corrupting potency of man and history?

The more realistic truth is theological, Will Herberg affirms. And theological truth, for any Jew, is essentially Biblical. The Biblical description of the nature of man and history is, however, distinctly untheological. How shall one, it may be argued (and this is the plaint of representative Judaism as well as antitheological critics of Judaism and Christianity) fashion out of the Bible a theology? The paradox is only superficial. It is never affirmed that the Bible is theology; it is suggested rather that theology is man's ordered reflection upon the matter of the Bible. The Bible is substance, with but the lineaments of form. Its matter is *heilsgeschichte,* the successive events of holy history which define the span of creation, revelation, and redemption. Theology is not the Bible, but it cannot exist without the Bible. It is the earnest working of man to achieve a measure of understanding of God, of the significance of his action, and of the relevance of his Word.

The temptation of representative Judaism—and it is against this temptation that Will Herberg has fought—is to assume that Judaism is fully enacted when its ordinance is observed. Judaism is thus reduced to religious experience.[10] Though the experience may be broad and comprehensive, involving not only subjective participation in the life of faith but fulfillment of the objective commandments, what is essentially accredited is an "action-faith." The quality of belief is assessed by the quantity of action. The danger of such an attitude of faith is that it insulates the believer from both the fresh address of God and the challenge of man and history. The Torah becomes a "shield and buckler," an instru-

[10] Will Herberg, "Discussion of Milton Steinberg's 'The Theological Issues of the Hour,'" *Proceedings of the Rabbinical Assembly of America,* June, 1949, p. 409.

mentality of shoring up faith against the world, rather than the opening out of faith to the unbelief of the world and the dislocating movement of divine freedom.

Theology comes to liberate the believer. When it devolves into subtle and intricate speculations, theology becomes the tyranny of fine distinctions. Such theology is always dead or dying. Biblical theology, if it is authentic thinking about the events of sacred history, cannot die, for it is by definition thinking about the word and action of God. It dies only when the thinker ceases to think of God and becomes enamoured with the eccentricity of his own formulations. Such theology ends as idolatry—and the marks of idolatry are always evident.

The Jewish prejudice against theology is consequent upon the assumption that theology becomes dogma, that thought necessarily becomes system.[11] The transformation of theology into dogma and system cannot occur in Judaism, for Judaism is already circumscribed by a dogma which prevents "dogma" and by a system that evades "system." The dogma of Judaism is that the speech of God is to be acknowledged as the Word of God; the system of Judaism is the establishment of the grammar of that speech. The dogma is given by the Bible and the system is given by the Law. Both dogma and system are founded upon the sanctity of the Word and the sacred linguistics of exegesis. They are the living experience to which all theology (conceived of as *thinking about* the Word and its grammar) is posterior.

Jewish theology, rightly understood, is existential and Jewish theology is of necessity centered upon "the *all-importance of history.*" [12]

Man's existential interest—it matters little whether it be religious or unbelieving—issues from his longing for

[11] Will Herberg, "Has Judaism Still Power To Speak?" *Commentary,* May, 1949, p. 455.
[12] Will Herberg, "Historicism as Touchstone," *The Christian Century,* March 16, 1960, p. 311. Italics Herberg's.

the transcendent. The characteristic departure of classical rationalisms, those which we identify with the tradition of Greece, is the assumption that all things possess an intelligible nature in terms of which their opacity or clarity in the hierarchy of nature and reason is defined. "What distinguishes the Bible from Greek philosophy," Leo Strauss has affirmed, "is the fact that Greek philosophy is based on the premise that there is such a thing as nature or natures, a notion which has no equivalent in biblical thought." [13] The rational universe, that universe in which, as Buber has noted, man feels comfortable and at home,[14] is not without its sense of the transcendent, although to the extent that it is present it is "subsidiary." [15] It is not, as it becomes in Biblical thought, the sense of the elusive, the mysterious, and the sublime. The sense of transcendence which we may discern in those thinkers who make up the nominal camp of existentialists—all reviling the nomenclature, and appalled by their fashionable popularity and public attention—is this: experience contains an emptiness and insufficiency. The immediate routine of life is shot through with incompletion, deception, and absurdity. The diagnosis runs differently for each, but the universe of private life reveals for each a gaping abyss through which both the Nothing and the Something are apprehended. This abyss—affirmed by both the religious and the unbelieving existentialist—is the condition of transcendence. The dissatisfaction may terminate in consummate emptiness, a Nothing made substantive and real (Heidegger) or it may open out to a Transcendent whose name is not known or

[13] Leo Strauss, *Progress or Return?* Three brilliant but unpublished lectures at the University of Chicago, cited by Will Herberg in his important essay, "Athens and Jerusalem: Confrontation and Dialogue," *Drew Gateway*, Vol. XXVIII, No. 3 (Spring, 1958), p. 180.
[14] Martin Buber, *What Is Man?* (New York, The Macmillan Company, 1947), pp. 126 f.
[15] Herberg, "Athens and Jerusalem: Confrontation and Dialogue," p. 180.

has been forgotten (Hoelderlin and Jaspers), or a Person whose name is known but who can no longer be named. The variations are considerable. In all events the common mark is the insufficiency of finite experience. Experience is no longer self-explanatory. Neither of the ways of Greece suffices: neither that which affirms divinity within nature (the moral coefficient of its rationality) nor that which affirms the rational order and continuity of nature (the logical coefficient of its being according to nature). The objective order has apparently transgressed the borders of pantheism—divinity supervening and penetrating all—or the borders of materialism—divinity being identified with the irresistible logic of finite history and nature. From both corruptions existential thinking flies. It opens itself out to the Nameless who was, but is no longer; who lived, but is now dead; who if he lives on is abscondite, hidden, and unavailing. Or else it opens itself to the One who bears a Name which is the Living God.

The movement of existential thinking is essentially Biblical, even where its impetus derives from the permutations by which the vision of the Hebrews has reached us through the words of Augustine or Pascal, Hegel or Schelling, Kierkegaard or Stirner, Rosenzweig or Rosenstock-Huessy, Heidegger or Sartre, Tillich or Buber. Where existentialism is atheist, Herberg argues, it is as unconvincing as are the other "false" faiths of our time, for despite its superficial resemblance to the religious existentialism of Kierkegaard or Buber, "the forlornness and despair of existence are strangely transmuted into a kind of self-satisfied, rather cozy, defiance of the universe." [16] Dostoevsky's grand vision of the apotheosis of Kirillov, the mysterious daemon of *The Possessed,* culminates finally in Sartre's affirmation that "man is the being whose project is to be God" or "man is

[16] Will Herberg, *Judaism and Modern Man* (New York, Farrar, Straus & Cudahy, Inc., 1951), p. 31.

fundamentally the desire to be God." [17] The entrapment of man, to Herberg's view, follows inevitably from the dissolution of meaning which attends the naturalist reduction of man to nature and the existentialist assimilation of nature to the sway of human freedom. However man may attempt to escape the Absolute, he cannot finally do without the Absolute, for only in the movement of transcendence can he diagnose the deficiency of his constricted, relative, and finite world. The movement of transcendence, like Heschel's sense of the ineffable, reaches out to the infinite and discovers the unknown. Where it does not discover the unknown, the abyss of meaninglessness deepens. Relativity gone, finitude grasped, nature dissolved, the unbeliever is cast back upon his freedom—his vanquished and proud freedom which can seek to be God, but can never become God. The atheist existentialist can apprehend the predicament of man, but only the believing existentialist can be saved from his predicament. The so-called "leap of faith"—a concept magnificently misunderstood by Jewish defenders of a naïve rationalism—is not, as Herberg has made abundantly clear, a leap of despair, "but rather a leap in triumph over despair. It is a leap made not in order to search blindly for an unknown God somewhere on the other side; it is a leap that is made because God has *already* been found." [18]

Existential thinking is the prolegomenon to Biblical theology. It is precisely what it says: thinking about one's own existence. It is not objective thinking, except insofar as one seeks to know oneself through apprehension of the life of others (no guarantee of objectivity). Existential thinking depends upon the correlation of the

[17] Jean-Paul Sartre, *Being and Nothingness,* trans. by Hazel E. Barnes (New York, Philosophical Library, Inc., 1956), p. 566; *L'être et le néant* (Paris, Gallimard, 1943), p. 655. A different translation of this passage is cited by Herberg, *Judaism and Modern Man,* p. 31.

[18] Herberg, *Judaism and Modern Man,* p. 39.

world to one's own situation. The world is apprehended as the living subject of one's seeking or as the locus in which one's answer is to be found. The world is enormously personal; for this reason existential thinking is always involved in the *consequence* of its seeking and answering. What is sought gives meaning or confirms meaninglessness; what is found is either the Nothing that absolutizes nothingness or the God whose person confers meaning.

Clearly there was existential thinking long before there were existentialists. What we speak of as existential thinking is but our effort to give formal structure to that which defies structure, which goes out over and beyond the ordering demand of reason. Existential thinking is the beginning of Biblical theology. Only against the background of man's awareness of his finitude can the passion of Biblical man to know God be comprehended.

Inescapably when modern man comes to the Bible (and it seems to us that Herberg is sensitive to this dilemma) he brings to it problems which are uniquely his own. He cannot approach it with the detachment of scholarship; were he to do so he would function with greater accuracy and precision, but he would have first to put aside both his existential perplexity and the necessary questions of theology. The Bible is open to the extent that God addresses man through the Bible, but the manner of man's position before the Bible determines from the beginning whether the Bible will speak or remain silent. The Jew comes to the Bible out of his predicament—and his immediate predicament, it ought not to be forgotten, is often different from the predicament of tradition. It may well be the task of normative theology to establish the correlations between the existential perplexities of the tradition and those of modern man, but such correlation cannot be assumed. All that is given is the relation of man and the Bible. Once that relation is established in faith, as soon as the man of today acknowledges that the

Living God of the Bible is his God, the correlation of tradition and contemporary life can begin.[19]

Herberg's argument throughout *Judaism and Modern Man* is founded upon Paul Tillich's method of correlation:

> Continuous thinking about the possibility of uniting the religious power of so-called neo-orthodox theology with the duty of every theology to address itself to a "method of correlation"—that is, between existential questions and theological answers. The human situation as interpreted in existential philosophy and the (depth) psychology and sociology related to it, posits the question; the divine revelation, as interpreted in the symbols of classical theology, gives the answer.[20]

The method of correlation (similar, it should be noted, to the earlier discussed method of Hermann Cohen) is particularly suitable to the precarious condition of modern theology. Theology can no longer be both traditional and meaningful without a radical inquiry into the existential situation to which theological truth responds. The Bible is already the living example of correlation—the incompleteness of man and history and the completeness of God and his Word. Yet for modern man to locate himself in the dialogue of Scripture requires that he first identify his questions with those of Biblical man and acknowledge the enduring contemporaneity of God's answers. The role of the Bible and rabbinic thought in

[19] Emil Fackenheim, "Judaism and Modern Man" (review), *Judaism,* April, 1952, pp. 173 f. "It is impossible to approach tradition in search of truth and *not* be selective; and since modern man approaches tradition with problems which are his, and not necessarily those of tradition, his selection will of necessity distort in part. Only an objective scholarly approach could escape this difficulty; but such an approach would not be theological, since it would remain neutral as to the religious truth of tradition."

[20] "Discussion of Milton Steinberg's 'Theological Problems of the Hour,'" p. 426; Paul Tillich, "Beyond Religious Socialism," *The Christian Century,* June 15, 1949.

Herberg's thinking is therefore both central and selective at the same time. Herberg emerges as both a Biblical thinker and a modern thinker; a Jewish thinker, but a Jewish thinker in a predominantly non-Jewish, indeed, a nonbelieving world. The concern with authenticity is therefore prior to the concern with fidelity to tradition. And, paradoxical as it may appear, the theology which results will be more accurate to the scope and power of tradition if it is first accurate to the demands of general history. This is true of the Bible as it is true of the history of Judaism—the tradition has been most creative when it addressed the universal condition of man as man, rather than the conditional fortunes of the Jewish people. Only in one sense is the Bible the possession of the Jews—in the sense in which it is the book of Jewish origins; to the extent, however, that it is the book "of the generations of man" it is the source of all creation, revelation, and redemption.

At the same time, however, it must be recognized that Will Herberg cannot be a satisfactory Jewish thinker. This is an impossibility. Herberg's history is *heilsgeschichte*—that is, the history of providence—but not the history of the Jews. This centralization of an overriding concern for the *whole* of history and culture is enormously important. It has allowed him to broaden the terms of the discussion, to enter into communication with Christians more freely (but not necessarily more profoundly) than more traditional Jewish thinkers, to address himself to the common dilemmas of religion in America, to use theological insight in the analysis of political and social problems. These are the strengths of his breadth. He is not as anguished, however, by the high price he has paid for such universality. He is not dismayed, as are his Jewish admirers, by the loss of the particularity and concreteness of the Jewish people and Jewish history which his general cultural concerns have required. The danger of Herberg's thought is the danger of any excessive striving, for in the attempt to encompass and resolve the common predicament of Christian and Jew (and Herberg has done more than any other modern Jewish thinker to justify that questionable phenomenon "the Judeo-Christian" tradition) he tends to fall into two traps: either his thought delights in the dialectical inquiry for its own sake, pitting Jewish insufficiency against Christian strength or Christian insufficiency against Jewish corrective, or else he transcends both, losing the real particularity which is the history of each.

The dialectic of universal and particular history which moves through the Bible is what gives to it both its trans-temporal grandeur and its contemporaneity. It does not chronicle the destiny of Israel alone, but the destiny of man. It does not reveal the God of Israel alone, but the Lord of all creation. The destiny of Israel and the God of Israel become paradigmatic of all history and all providence, for through an understanding of God's intercourse with Israel do we come to understand God's concern for what is most human and imperfect in all creation and what of history is in most need of redemption.

It is for these reasons, we believe, that Herberg was so preoccupied in *Judaism and Modern Man* with establishing the confusions of modern history and ideology as the prelude to the unfolding of successive correlations. His method there—and it is repeated in his major essays [21]—is first to establish the insufficiency of current modes of philosophic and ideological thinking. Each prevailing doctrine of the West—naturalism, positivism, scientific materialism—and each ideology of the West—scientism, humanism, Marxism—is searched out for its essential flaw. In each case the flaw is dialectically defined over against the primary conviction of the Bible: that, before God, all else is but relatively true and trustworthy. All

[21] Will Herberg, "Jewish Existence and Survival: A Theological View," *Judaism,* Vol. I, No. 1 (January, 1952), pp. 19–26; "Has Judaism Still Power To Speak?"; "Discussion of Milton Steinberg's 'The Theological Problems of the Hour' "; "Judaism and Christianity: Their Unity and Difference," *The Journal of Bible and Religion,* April, 1953, pp. 67–78.

the incomplete and limited doctrines of man pretend to more than they possess or can deliver. Of necessity they are idolatrous—idolatry being defined as "the absolutization of the relative" [22]—for they enthrone a partial truth as though it were the whole of truth, endow a conditional virtue with perfection, in short, make of the finite and limited an absolute. Disposing of the idolatries of man, Herberg then confronts modern man—divested and shorn of his unavailing securities. The process of criticism is one compounded of the existential question and the theological answer. Both are used as devices of analysis: the existential question to locate man's longing for truth, the theological answer to disclose the falsity of any answer which is not the divine answer.

Having passed beyond the deceptions of modern man the task of theology is to re-establish the relevance of Biblical faith. The Bible becomes the source of a divine anthropology—the predicament of man is one which can be meaningfully apprehended only in a universe in which a living, personal, transcendent, and absolute God has dominion. The task of theology is then to reconstruct the world in the image of God, to define the interconnections and community by which despair vanishes before grace, alienation before love, sin before salvation. The ontological deficiencies of creation (which have their Scriptural parallels in the myth of the fall of Adam and the flooding of creation) are set before the redeeming perfections of God (which also have their Scriptural parallels in numberless examples of divine concern and loving care). In sum, man is set before God, and the Word of God—which is always spoken—may now be heard.

Biblical theology, we have suggested, is the source of Jewish theology, but it is not by itself Jewish theology. Existential thinking is the prelude to the Bible and the Bible is the substance of Jewish theology. Both are the necessary elements from which authentic Jewish the-

[22] *Judaism and Modern Man,* p. 94.

ology derives; however, they do not by themselves constitute Jewish theology. This is only to say that they do not exhaust theology. Without them there could not be theology—that is, without the man of faith infinitely concerned with his salvation and without the Biblical paradigm of salvation, there could be no theology. But both existential concern and Biblical response are insufficient unless the echoes of each be communicated through the medium of history. The tremors of faith and grace are transmitted through the substance of history. Faith may establish the contemporaneity of Biblical promise, but without history faith becomes a flight from the present obligation of man to God. Biblical promise may offer the gifts of grace to faith, but without history it lacks living confirmation.

The progress of Herberg's theological thinking is marked by the emergence of the primacy of history. Earlier in his thinking theology was restricted to the task of clarifying the Bible in the light of tradition. Although it is not necessary that he modify his contention that a "living [Jewish] theology can be built upon Scripture and the materials of Jewish religious tradition," [23] he has in his most recent writing [24] overcome his suspicion of the historical medium out of which living theology emerges and upon which living theology works. The infectious relativity of events no longer suffices to debar the historical medium from primacy. For all its being the receptacle of sin, history is also the bearer of salvation. The debasement of history has been, Herberg is quick to affirm, one of the significant errors of contemporary religion. He is correct in recognizing that the failure of Protestantism to organize its opposition to Nazi totalitarianism stemmed from its inability to transcend a merely situational evaluation of social and political evil; he is equally accurate in observing that the inability of

[23] "Discussion of Milton Steinberg's 'The Theological Problems of the Hour,' " p. 410.
[24] "Historicism as Touchstone."

Judaism to formulate a coherent theology of our times results from its having inflated a crisis of ethnic survival into a self-justifying principle of disengagement from history. The analogy is structurally plausible: what the neutrality of divine judgment as respects the nations and their politics has been to the theology of Karl Barth, the absolutization of survival has been to the Jew. Both have been means by which to escape the total demand of history, to ask the fundamental question: How does my faith enable me to survive not *in spite of* history but *in* and *through* history.

It is no easy task. But it is no less the fundamental task.

Will Herberg has not been a novel theologian. This is only to say that he explicates his sources, makes clear his indebtedness and obligation to those who have instructed his vision. But then we should be suspicious of that theologian who would have but novelty—and a tenacious investment in novelty—to recommend him. The novelty does not lie in the inventiveness of formulation, in the brilliance of language, but—at this moment—in the insistence upon the discovery of older truths and the assessment of their serviceability. In this Herberg has been without peer in contemporary Judaism. He has not been, however, without detractors—those who would with dull and nagging petulance require him to pass through the labyrinthine underground of Jewish study before he is accredited to speak as a Jew; or those who, with shocking unfamiliarity with the character of modern Christian thinking, anathematize anyone who is intellectually curious enough to examine it before rejecting it. Herberg has, to be sure, his imbalances: in his passion to polarize the function of reason and the *hybris* of the will he frequently confuses "sin" (an excess or corruption of the will) with "limit" (a metaphysical correlative of our finitude); he hypostasizes, in the Christian idiom, the "Biblical man" as though indeed an essential "Biblical man" could be distilled from the existential squall of passion and contradiction which the Bible exposes; he has, in his earlier work (although he has since modified it) given unduly short shrift to the critical function of philosophy in the refinement of faith; having formed many of his judgments of the nature of faith from the prior influence of a prevailing Christian reading of the interplay of faith, grace, sin, and salvation he has given undue importance to confirmative, but incidental, judgments of Scripture and the rabbis; and, last but not least, his thought has until recent days been marked by so emphatic and unbending a theological "realism" as to betray the very play of dialectic (what we should prefer to call the "ironic" dimension of history) which is so central to his theology and to ours.

These deficiencies others would magnify. We would not, for we find ourself more closely identified with his thought than distant from it. He gives us something which most American Jewish theology in this century has lacked: a conviction of its relevance to all of human history, rather than to the special needs and preoccupations of the Jew. This is not to say that his theology has been sufficiently evolved as to be adequate to the Jew. He would be the first to affirm its inadequacy, for what he once demanded as fundamental to the emergence of a Jewish theology for our times he has himself not performed.[25] Surely no single thinker, be he less than Mai-

[25] "The problems that press for solution are many and important. I need mention only a few of the more urgent: (1) a theology of *halachah*—not a codification or modification of the Law but an effort to define its nature and authority in terms of basic theology; (2) a theological account of our liturgical year. . . . ; (3) a theological interpretation of the inner relation between Judaism and Christianity, following up Franz Rosenzweig's brilliant insights; (4) a theological analysis of anti-Semitism, in which the results of recent depth-psychology can prove most suggestive; (5) a theological evaluation of the contemporary crisis of Israel and mankind in an attempt to discern the deeper meaning of the upheavals and disasters of our time; and finally (6) a realistic theology of society. . . ." ("Discussion of Milton Steinberg's 'The Theological Problems of the Hour,' " p. 427.)

monides, could meet the challenge as Herberg has defined it. But *he* has defined it and he has defined it in such a way as to compel the Jew to answer him if he refuse it or to take it up if he cannot.

The theologian can make the way clear for the prophet; he can prepare the atmosphere, dispel confusion, delimit the alternatives. The theologian cannot compel us to take up the task. That we must leave to the eventualities of history and the declaration of its prophetic interpreters. At this moment there are no prophets; history is making itself ready for a denouement; and the theologians are clarifying the alternatives. For that at least we may put cavils aside and be grateful.

VII. THE IMPOSSIBILITY OF JEWISH THEOLOGY: OBSERVATIONS ON A DEFECT OF VOCATION

Recent decades in America have seen the ambivalence of the Jewish people towards its vocation pushed to the forefront. The quest for self-definition has assumed a position of primacy. The quest, however, has been pursued in directions which signify the abandonment of all of the classic orientations which gave individuality and uniqueness to the Jewish mind. The issue of self-definition is no longer that of coming to terms with the condition of Jewish history and the unique role which that condition has defined. The pursuit of self-definition consists presently in the achievement of the happy compromise: individuality amid homogeneity, ethnic distinctiveness amid the denial of significant difference, nationalist self-expression masked by the duties of charity and philanthropy. Judaism has all but disappeared, while Jewishness—the whole array of atavisms and sentimentalities which a secure minority can now afford—is well indulged. It is irrelevant to belabor the obvious. Serious students of

Jewish life, although they often lack compassion and a tolerance for the pathos of our confusion, have been quite just in their description of the shallowness and mediocrity of Jewish life in America—indeed of life in America, Jewish or otherwise. This latter qualification also has its poignancy: that we are so little distinguishable that the same sharp eye of criticism turns up nothing unique in the Jewish "mediocrity"—that it is all of a piece with that monumental edifice of mediocrity which is middle-class American culture and American life.

There cannot be, we believe, any significant development of Jewish theology unless the vocation of the Jewish people, that which encumbers it with supernatural charge and obligation, is reaffirmed. As we indicated in our discussion of Mordecai Kaplan and Milton Steinberg, survival can be ensured, the physical people can endure, but the vocation of the people may perish. Heschel and Herberg, with differing emphases, are profoundly aware that it is the quality of supernatural vocation which gives substance and magnitude to the task of Jewish theology. The role of theology, whether that theology be founded upon the radical empiricism of the Bible or on the realistic estimation of post-Biblical history, is directed toward a community. It has no authority without a community.

Theology is both abstract and conceptual, but its context—its emergence at a specific moment in history—is eminently concrete. Theology may be forbiddingly rational, but the history of theology, upon which new theology is founded, is as all things human a compound of reason and the affections, of passion seeking a justification. The peculiar hostility of some centuries of Jewish thought to theology arises out of acceptance of a version of theological method which is neither essential to theology as such, nor characteristic of any and all theologies. Within Christendom there are different methods of theological thinking: abstract and logically rigid systems; rich and affective configurations of insight and ordering judgment; mystic, rationalist, intuitionist theologies.

Theology is not all scholastic in Christianity, Islam, or Judaism. But all theologies *are* founded upon fundamental agreement: agreement respecting those few indispensable, crucial principles which are the *realia* of faith, without which there can be no community of the faithful. These fundamental principles are "dogmas": they are that without which religious thought cannot begin.[1]

It is clear that there is agreement in contemporary American Judaism upon one fact *sine qua non:* the necessity of the existence of the Jewish people, a corollary, it should be noted, of the evident fact that the Jewish people has refused, in the face of innumerable opportunities, to die. The fact of the Jewish people is by consensus the beginning of modern Jewish thought. Historically it is the one reality which has endured as the center of Jewish life. It is that which binds together Orthodox and Reform, the believer and the secularist, the Hebraist and the Yiddishist, the committed and the alienated. The existence of the Jewish people, not alone a point of consent among Jews, is that upon which the non-Jewish world agrees as well. Historical fatalists affirm that history allows no exit to the Jew; theologians affirm that God allows no exit to the Jew. What the former removes from the volition of the Jew to the necessities of history, God enforces upon the will of the Jew in transcendence of history.

The natural Jew, the Jew of history, the Jew of affections and needs, lusts and torments of conscience, cannot be escaped. The natural Jew is a *fact,* but no longer a dogma. He is a reality, but not an object of trust and

[1] Solomon Schechter, "The Dogmas of Judaism," *Studies in Judaism,* First Series (Philadelphia, Jewish Publication Society of America, 1945), pp. 147–81. Several of the author's essays dealing with the nature and structure of Jewish theology might be useful: "On Scriptural Exegesis," *Cross Currents,* Vol. V, No. 1 (Winter, 1955); also his review of Eugene Kohn's *Religion and Humanity,* in *Judaism,* Vol. III, No. 3 (Summer, 1954). Cf. also David Silverman, "Current Theological Trends: A Survey and Analysis," *Proceedings of the Rabbinical Assembly of America,* 1960, pp. 71–100.

faith. The Reconstructionist Jew would refashion the conditions of faith so that the natural Jew might survive as Jew amid the nations of the world. The Reform and Conservative Jew would reassess the social effects of Jewish faith so that faith might flourish while interfering as little as possible with the natural condition of the Jew—that he lives among the nations of the world, and is unavoidably involved in that neutral arena of society where the secular life of the nations is carried on. The Orthodox temporize and rationalize, but hold fast, modifying the extremity of doctrine (without removing the duty of observance) so that at least the mind may be equable and at ease, however observance remains at odds with that of one's non-Jewish neighbor. All in all, the undue modern emphasis on the simple factuality of the Jewish people has undercut the vocation of the people. All adjustments and rationalizations are designed to ensure that the natural Jew will survive, even though the supernatural Jew may perish.

What concerns us, however, is that the supernatural Jew shall survive. Christianity shares with us the mystery of our presence. Though it compromises its own history when it destroys us, it treasures the mystery of our presence and marvels at the constancy of our "disbelief." This is only to say that the non-Jew conserves the dogma of our supernatural vocation; while we—its legatees and bearers—would sacrifice dogma for fact, vocation for our natural condition.

Theology, of necessity, addresses the supernatural vocation of the Jew. When the Jewish vocation is abandoned, not theology but religious sociology takes over. The question of Jewish survival becomes an issue of strategems, opinion polls, and community surveys. The artifacts of survival and cohesion take over from thought and feeling the center of Jewish existence. The ideologists of survival turn their attentions to perfecting the social instruments of the community, its modes of communication and habits of behavior. The rhetoricians of the older and abandoned order become disdainful and olympian in their demands upon our spiritually wayward people. The few who remain clear and serious seek to redefine the objective content of Jewish belief, asking again and again the decisive questions of the modern Jew: Can he believe? What does he understand his belief to be? What obligations does his belief confer?

The rediscovery of the supernatural vocation of the Jew is the turning-point of modern Jewish history. That vocation was rediscovered in the German Jewish renaissance of the nineteenth and early twentieth centuries, but Armageddon overtook and destroyed it. A new beginning must be made. The renewal of the Jewish vocation is that beginning, for the Jewish people is not a fact of history but an article of faith.

4

The Vocation of the Jewish Mind

I. CATHOLIC ISRAEL

Undoubtedly Solomon Schechter—that luminous and profound Anglo-American Jewish theologian [1]—intended to adumbrate with his famous phrase "Catholic Israel" something of the essence of Judaism. The only passage in Schechter's writings which treats at any length of "Catholic Israel" makes clear that its catholicity consists in its consensus. What counters or distorts consensus—the rigorism of a tenacious fundamentalism, the authoritarianism of schools and movements, the rising sacerdotalism of the rabbinate—conceals the catholicity of Israel. Schechter underscores this observation with characteristic vigor and precision:

[1] Actually Schechter was born in 1849 in the small Rumanian town of Foscani, but his arrival in England in 1882, where he was to make his home until he came to the United States to become president of the Jewish Theological Seminary of America in 1902, justifies the propriety of describing him as an Anglo-American Jewish theologian. See Norman Bentwich, *Solomon Schechter* (Philadelphia, Jewish Publication Society of America, 1938).

> This living body . . . is not represented by any section of the nation, or any corporate priesthood or rabbihood, but by the collective conscience of Catholic Israel as embodied in the Universal Synagogue. The Synagogue, with its continuous cry after God for more than twenty-three centuries, with its unremittent activity in teaching and developing the word of God, the only true witness to the past, and forming in all ages the sublimest expression of Israel's religious life, must also retain its authority as the sole true guide for the present and the future. . . . Another consequence of this conception of Tradition is that it is neither Scripture nor primitive Judaism, but general custom, which forms the real rule of practice. . . . The norm as well as the sanction of Judaism is the practice actually in vogue. Its consecration is the consecration of general use—or, in other words, of Catholic Israel.[2]

Schechter's understanding of Catholic Israel suggests something of the nature of authentic Jewish theology. The conscience of Israel is informed by canons of tradition and practice, which are indifferent to the reticulated and complex constructions of rational religion. This is not to say that Catholic Israel is of necessity unreasoning Israel. It is merely to suggest that catholicity consists in that more delicate fabric which historical consciousness and the instructed conscience devise.

Historical consciousness receives the continuous narrative of tradition which comprehends an "uninterrupted

[2] Solomon Schechter, *Studies in Judaism,* First Series (Philadelphia, Jewish Publication Society of America, 1945), pp. xi–xxv; particularly p. xix. See also *Studies in Judaism,* Third Series (Philadelphia, Jewish Publication Society of America, 1924), p. 10; *Some Aspects of Rabbinic Theology* (New York, The Macmillan Company, 1909), p. viii. It should be noted that Schechter's notion of Catholic Israel has its origin in medieval doctrine—Christian, Moslem, and Jewish. The Jewish notion of *haskamat haklal* (general agreement) is Schechter's immediate precedent.

succession of prophets, Psalmists, Scribes, Assideans, Rabbis, Patriarchs, Interpreters, Elucidators, Eminences, and Teachers, with its glorious record of Saints, martyrs, sages, philosophers, scholars, and mystics";[3] it is of the essence of Catholic Israel, for it marks the Jew as a creature of history and the bearer of the instruction of an historical God. Consciousness, however, defines only the superficies of catholicity; it suggests only the outer limits which are compassed by tradition. What transforms consciousness from recipient into bearer, from passive receptacle into creator, is that what passes through the filter of consciousness informs conscience. As conscience is the especial faculty of the religious man, so historical consciousness is the instructor of conscience. There is no catholicity unless consciousness is open to the whole of tradition and conscience is susceptible to the demands and obligations of tradition. The catholicity of Judaism is a union in which history and anticipation are joined in conscience. Each Jew decides for himself; out of his assent to tradition the constantly renewed catholicity of Judaism is affirmed.

Catholic Israel manifests the living substance of the Jewish people. But Catholic Israel, as both concept and reality, does not go far enough. Rich and suggestive as it is, Schechter's understanding of catholicity is limited. To the obvious retort that his conception of catholicity and universality, Catholic Israel and Universal Synagogue, is but an adaptation of glorious, but palpably inappropriate, formulations of Roman Catholic theology, Schechter was monumentally indifferent. Schechter could hardly be accused of "Christianizing" Judaism. Schechter's understanding of Catholic Israel is defective because his conception of historical Judaism as its source results in a restriction of its catholicity to the private task of self-definition. Catholic Israel emerges as a retrospective judgment upon the history of the Jews. It serves as a device of argument against dissidents and assimila-

[3] Schechter, *Studies in Judaism,* First Series, p. xviii.

tionists, extreme reformers and narrow-minded fanatics; but it does not aid us—in Schechter's definition—to locate ourselves in that vaster universe of human culture to which Catholic Israel must lay claim. Catholic Israel is much more a weapon in a war against destruction by attrition and desuetude than it is a conception—metaphysical, mystical, eschatological—which might suggest something of the eternal nature of Judaism and the vocation of the Jew.

We wish to transform the catholicity of Israel from a *deduction from a specific history* into a *category of all history,* from a rallying standard of factional and sectarian movements within Judaism to a reality with which Judaism may confront the world.

To accomplish such a transformation, to redefine Catholic Israel in such a way as to maintain what Schechter achieved but to extend its claim to the whole of human culture, requires that our catholicity be founded upon more than the narrative of history and the voluntary affections of conscience. Schechter was painfully aware of the one problem which his view could not compel: as he defined Catholic Israel, history could *educate* consciousness and *form* conscience, but it could *command* neither. Catholic Israel has no apodictic force. It is that fitful, unpredictable, indeed, on occasion, capricious response of the Jewish people to its collective history and obligation. Jewish catholicity too often degenerates into the vulgar response of mere collectivity—kinship feeling and camaraderie.

Catholic Israel issues from and returns to the attitude of the tradition and the individual Jew toward the God who called them forth. Israel is catholic in the sense that the truth of Judaism has relevance and bearing upon the destiny of mankind and in that it is the obligation of the Jew—not for himself alone, but for mankind—to preserve, transmit, and communicate that truth. Catholic Israel is therefore both comprehensive and universal. It cannot be either without being both. Its catholicity is founded upon truth believed, possessed, and transmitted. Those truths are not saving truths; they have neither sacramental power nor sufficiency, for their efficacy lies only in their ability to transform conscience and inspirit acts. The sinner is not saved by faith, but neither is he saved by ignorance. He may believe correctly but be damned for the indifference and insufficiency of his acts, or he may behave rightly by accident or through self-interest and be damned as well. There can be little right action without purity of heart and spirit; there can be little purity of heart and spirit unless both be formed by the beliefs and hopes of tradition.

The beliefs and hopes of tradition are exhibited by the action of Judaism, by observance and practice, by prayer and works. It matters little how much the consensus of tradition (that is, its definition of appropriate acts and habits of action) may suffice the inner life of the Jew, for if it contributes little to that communication between Jew and pagan, Jew and Christian, Jew and Moslem, Jew and Oriental, which defines the relations of the Jew to world culture, its catholicity is reduced from an historical reality to a self-delusive phantasm. It is one thing to conceive of catholicity as an expression of the spirit, as a manifestation of the organic unity of Jewish life; it is quite another when this same spirit and this same unity confront an alien time and an inhospitable history, when the Jew must live in the presence of the Gentile. The Jew can no longer afford the luxury of isolated sanctity, cut off and disinclined to share the history and time of his environment.

Indeed, part of the crisis of the modern Jew is that the catholicity of Judaism was restricted for so long to the consensus of acts and observances, to the language of inner life and destiny, that it lived without connection with the world that surrounded it.

The essential problem which underlies all our concerns is the evident withering of the Jewish vocation and the vanishing supernatural consciousness of the Jew. As we stated in the Introduction, we are disinclined to ask whether it is better that the Jewish vocation pass and the supernatural Jew disappear. We regard both as beyond our discretion to confirm or disprove. The destiny of the Jew and the historical function of Judaism cannot be regarded as issues of religious controversy. They are objects of faith and silence. They are not urged upon the disbeliever; but they are affirmed for the believer. They are doctrines which give substance to the concept of Catholic Israel, for they define the sense in which our catholicity is related to the culture of the West. Were our catholicity restricted, as it has been, to an incapsulated unity of the spirit, we could not hope to speak before the West. Ours would continue to be a silent witness, a mute presence in the world, exhibiting the sanctity of "an uninterrupted succession" of prophets and priests, scholars and saints, but incapable of shaping the stream of history in whose currents we move and by whose tides and undertows we are now threatened.

We do not imagine that we have presented in the foregoing pages a conventional history of modern Jewish thought. Few if any of the normal canons of intellectual history have been observed. Ours has been less the task of definition than that of presentation. It would be foolhardy to attempt a formulation of the nature and characteristics of the Jewish mind. What such a procedure might have accomplished would have been offset by the unavoidable tendentiousness, abstraction, and historical condensation involved. Rather it has been our concern to indicate that the Jewish mind has been in constant interaction with other cultures than its own. To speak of the Jewish mind without reference to its surrounding environment would be to create a hypostatic fiction, an essence of little use to those who are genuinely preoccupied with Jewish life and destiny. The pursuit of definition as such is only useful to those who are indifferent to the reality defined—it enables them to file a history of experience, to classify and categorize, as in some intellectual lepidoptery, the various, multicolored, but now dead events of the past.

History is only dead when the living discard it. Moreover, history can only be written when the living succeed in distinguishing—at least to some extent—their own present from the past under view. We have been unable to do this, as the Jewish past is very much our present and future. We can only speak of the history of the Jewish mind as a living inheritance, for the situation of the modern Jewish mind differs only in degree from that of Jehuda Halevi or Maimonides. The general character and environment of our problem is the same. We can, perhaps, no longer profit from their specific solutions—we cannot really reconcile Scripture with Aristotle and the *Kalam* or interpret Judaism to the neo-Platonist, Sunnite orthodox, or triune Christian—but we can examine with great profit why in some ages the Jewish philosopher instructed the masses and why in others he was totally repudiated; why in some ages rabbis were the mystics, poets, preachers, and philosophers and why in ours few rabbis are numbered among our major thinkers; why in some ages Judaism was a universal religion, sensitive to the claim which it made upon all history, and why in ours that claim is all but buried beneath the pride of patriotism and the secure comfort of assimilation; why, in effect, in some ages Judaism lived—even though the people suffered—and in others Judaism waned.

In short there is nothing in the historical display of the modern Jewish mind that is worth recalling other than as a reminder and instructor to this moment. Although we could well recall thinkers and their systems, innovators and their innovations, we should be recalling not the history of the Jewish mind but the concrete achievement of individual Jewish minds. We are not interested, however, in Jewish minds apart from their participation in the whole of Jewish history; moreover, we are not interested in the whole of Jewish history—as but a department of the history of religions or the history of Christian and Islamic civilization or the history of sovereign national cultures—except insofar as that history informs us the better of providential history, of that which makes the Jewish people a chosen people.

It is necessary, therefore, if we are to profit from what has come before, to summarize its consequences. We propose to draw together the lines of argument which have defined our narrative and to inquire whether they are in fact relevant to the present. The considerations which have recurred throughout shall be treated here explicitly, no longer as points of suggestion and argumentative relief, but as explicit ideas which are thought to characterize the Jewish past and have significance for the Jewish present and future. Those specifically Jewish realities—Exile, Dispersion, prophetic judgment, messianic trust, and such like—are articulated in the context of history, theology, culture, and messianism. These four subject matters of Jewish thought are intimately related; moreover, we can speak very little of any one without animadverting to the others. They form a unity which suggests something of the vocation and destiny of Judaism and the Jewish people.

History is the substance of Jewish theology, and culture is the substance of Jewish messianism. Culture is a partial consummation of history; messianism is the trust and consummation of theology. But as the lines and markers of our intellectual disciplines converge, texturing and interpreting each other, they point to that reality which is bound and limit to our own, out of which ours takes its origin and through which ours is fulfilled.

There is little use in theory except as it orders life. If theory does not result in life—richer and more prescient life—it is but a tiresome exercise. We are less concerned, therefore, with *proving* that our theory is right than with stating it in such a way as to adumbrate something present in our lives. This is not to say that chimerical theory is to be excused merely because it has proved to be an instructive chimera. Not at all! It cannot assist life if it is a fiction; however, any "fiction" which informs life with greater richness and seriousness is, to that extent, no fiction but reality! The truth may be inadequately stated; it may be insufficiently rigorous to the demanding; it may only indicate by indirection that about which it speaks; it may be only symbolic truth; but it is still truth and for that we can be thankful.

II. REFLECTIONS UPON A METAPHYSICS OF HISTORY

The image of Exile has, like the cord of Theseus, passed through each chamber of the historic Jewish mind, imparting unity and continuity to disparate and seemingly unrelated moments of creation and despair.

The Exile has been not only a rationalization of historical events, an effort to elevate disaster into national triumph, a neurasthenic sublimation of pain and defeat; it has been a source of permanent meaning. To be sure, the naturalization of the Exile, accompanying as it did the naturalization of the Jew—his rejection of supernatural vocation and destiny and his conventional, frequently unresisting, acceptance of the hostility of the non-Jewish world—has made of Exile and physical diaspora an opprobrious reality for both Zionists, who revile the Exile, and Diaspora Jews, who would willingly exchange it for adjustment.

It is not our purpose, however, to prolong the war with Jewish nationalism or with Jewish assimilationism. That war is really over. It raged passionately in the last century and was continued in the present, but it is now over. The rhetoric of Zionist repudiation of the Exile lingers on, a reminder of this dead but eloquent war. It is a dead war because Zionism is now triumphant and yet millions of Jews are unwilling either to go up to the Land or to be assimilated. The situation of the modern Jew is substantially as it was before. There is limbo, an indeterminate stasis, where nothing appears changed, other than the fact that the present situation is clearer, more sharply etched, false and inadequate alternatives having been removed by the outcome of historic events.

It would appear that however much the controversies of the nineteenth century have been silenced by decisive historical fortune, the perpetual crisis of Jewish survival continues. Jewish survival is nevertheless an historical problem. It is a problem formed out of the pull and drag of events. It is a natural problem in the most immediate and meaningful of senses, for the issue of Jewish survival, so seen, is an issue of population and numbers. To be sure, Jewish survival is qualitative as well, since one would not be willing to settle for Jews in name only. But let us be equally clear that we will not be asked to settle for Jews in name only, if Jews indeed survive. It is hardly thinkable that the Jewish communities of the Dispersion could survive if every Jew intermarried, if there was no interest in raising one's children as Jews, if those powerful "symbols" of identification—Sabbath, the High Holy Days, the Kaddish of praise and mourning—were all discarded. Since we are not a race, marked off by ineffaceable physical characteristics, we cannot rest confident that race will enable us to survive; nor are we simply an ethnic community whose cultural artifacts are so agreeable, harmless, and undivisive that they can be perpetuated as links of sentimental continuity. No racial or ethnic unity—unless so minimally defined as to be all but worthless—helps us to survive. We are destined to disappear if our existence depends solely upon the slow action of history. The ethnic ties fray and rot, the cultural artifacts are abandoned, and our religion, cut off and separated from the whole of our life, becomes a formal piety—itself a fashion of history to be abandoned when the climate of opinion heralds the time of abandonment.

It is exceptionally difficult to articulate the lines of Jewish intellectual history from the beginnings of the Hellenistic world to the present day. The stages of Jewish history do not conform to the stages of Western history. Its middle ages were not followed by a renaissance, a reformation, an enlightenment, and an age of scientific rationalism and political ideology. Such historical periods have at best contingent validity. They reflect, not merely man's assessment of himself in the moment of his renaissance or enlightenment, but more intensely, the retrospective appraisal of later ages, seeking either to praise or blame, to epitomize and condense, to adjudge, define, and transmit their characteristics and accomplishments to later ages. Historical generalization apostrophizes an age, setting forth its emphases and directions; but it cannot report with accuracy the daily life which textured and gave relief to what men actually thought and felt. Systems of historical tagging, at best mnemonic devices, are useless to the historian, particularly to the historian of Christianity or Judaism! To lay the history of Judaism over the history of the West in the hope that it will fit is vain exertion and profitless history. It assumes that the intellectual history of Judaism and the development of European thought pass through identical stages. It assumes moreover that the history of Israel is similar to the history of the nations of the world. The first assumption is rendered implausible by the fact that the conditions of European history were relevant to the life of the Jew only recently and then only when his Judaism had radically changed or disappeared. Marx and Freud, whatever their Jewish syndromes, reacted to conditions which the West defined, not to presuppositions which the religion and culture of Israel imposed. Jewish culture cannot be said to exist *wherever* one finds Jews (though to be sure we may learn much about how the Jew considers himself in separation from Judaism by reflecting upon the Jewish genius sundered from his Judaism). Jewish culture can be said to exist only where one finds the Jew whose Judaism is the energizing center of his life and activity. It is equally implausible for the Jew to consider his own history to be like that of the nations. The scientific historian (who has problems enough of his own) may be unable to tolerate such a metaphysical bias; but the historian of Judaism cannot interpret many of the most shocking and scandalous assumptions of the Jewish religious mind unless he acknowledges that the Jew considered his own history to be the central event of a divine drama—a drama of covenant, sin, and purgation; a drama of divine dispersion and promised ingathering; a drama in which natural history was raised up to God and relocated within the order of providential causation.

If natural history does not supply the medium of Jewish survival, it is to sacred history that we must turn. If ours is not a history according to nature, then it must be considered as history according to God. Having affirmed this, we should nevertheless beware the sundering of all connection, indeed all intimacy and interaction, between natural and supernatural history. To determine our history according to God is not to repudiate our history according to nature. It is merely to suggest that history according to nature—separated from God—and time—independent of eternity—are insufficient. History cut off from its transcendent source and arbitration becomes either historicist phenomenalism, where all of life becomes history without the Archimedean point of judgment, or else a passionless and formal recurrence of events with which past history has already prepared and bored us.

History and the metaphysics of history are indispensable to the Jew. We need not expand upon the Greek indifference to history and the Hebraic preoccupation with history. History was meaningless to the Greek for the reason that concrete and immediate events were essentially meaningless; it was possible, as Ernst Troeltsch suggested, for the Greek to adumbrate a science of history precisely because the laws of fate (*vide* causality) were rigid, but it could not ask the question of meaning because such would be a metaphysical question inappropriate to nature and its animated presentation in history.[1] The Greek only began "providential" history when he had succeeded, paradoxically, in escaping it. He could discern meaning in his historical life, as did the Stoics, only when he had removed himself from history and affirmed his detachment and disengagement from it. But to be detached from history, to become as an object of nature, is to become unaware of time. Without the apprehension of time there can be no meaning in history. The Hebrew on the contrary could not escape time—every event that mediated divinity in time was sanctified and preserved in the historical memory.

History does not occur until selective judgments are pronounced upon the discrete events of the past. There is no history other than to him who remembers. In some sense, therefore, history is a myth of memory. The history of historians, no less than the history of metaphysicians of history, is a myth—the former more reticulated by evidence, proofs, and confirmation, the latter more dangerously patterned by ideologies and theses. The history of historians, quite as profoundly as the history of metaphysicans of history, attempts to do more than recount faithfully the phenomenal display of connected events. Both wish to elicit their own meaning, to explain why this particular past invades their present. The contemporary historian cannot prevent himself from

[1] Clearly this is a partial statement of the Greek view of history. If we were to undertake a more thorough treatment many refinements would emerge. It is true, however, that for Greek philosophy history was but an instructor of the natural fatality of events. History demonstrated only the limits of human power. It set the limit to expectation. It could not open the prospect of a transcendence acceptable to the gods, because man, nature, and the gods were all in competition and the gods invariably won. The Stoics were wise to counsel calm, serenity, and indifference.

relating the past to our present, for he is of our present and addresses us—and not as did a slightly mad German scholar of this century, who preferred to discourse to the busts of Roman emperors who ringed his study rather than to his students. The historian is always locating in the past his own fixities, his own truths, and his own eternity, for as R. G. Collingwood observed, the historian, even the historian without metaphysical interests, is only interested in self-understanding. The metaphysician of history is but a more bizarre and unavoidably pretentious synthesis of the working historian; for where the scientific historian wishes to identify a portion of the whole, to describe the hazy limits of a single moment within the flow of history, the metaphysicians of history—Augustine, Hegel, Marx—wish to locate nothing less than the meaning of all history.

The philosophy of history is, therefore, the greatest myth-making. It stands in the great tradition which begins in early Christian times with the sacramental transformation of late Jewish and Apostolic eschatology and proceeds through a neutralization and finally, in the nineteenth century, a secularization of the doctrine of the end of history. The philosophy of history is as well an asking of the most crucial of human questions: What is that whole which comprehends time and eternity, death and life, being and the perfection of being? To be preoccupied with history as such is to confront an essentially religious problem: the relation of history to God and the meaning of God in history.

Man is not a bystander of history who records the weathering of the past and observes the maturation of the future. If such be a view of history, it is one which cannot help but destroy all that is meaningful in it. Indeed, it is possible to speak of ages and times in which man was so serenely integrated into nature that time and history vanished, that history became a distortion of purity, and contemplation the most significant form of human activity. Inescapably our own concentration upon historical reality—that the past is our own past and the future our own future and memory the eternal link which defines the substance of history—is the consequence of disquiet. What the Greek called *hybris,* the sin of excessive and arrogant pride, can be read as little more than the presumption of some men that they were capable of effecting their destiny rather than submitting to their fate. As such, *hybris* was the presumption of the historical. Such presumption was not a sin to the Hebrew, but a requirement. It was a requirement because the Hebrew believed himself, his community, and his universe to have a beginning and a consummation.

Man can only have a destiny if he has a beginning which originates outside of time and an end which will transcend it. Time, we believe, is but an epoch in eternity. The false infinity of time, as Hegel describes a history without origin and fulfillment, is never broken unless time is construed as an outcropping of eternity. So viewed, history is not a succession of events in time and historical knowledge is not simply the recognition of pattern or the delight in novelty. Historical reality becomes an occasion for the spirit and the historical memory enacts the drama of eternity. In our view—and we acknowledge much in it which is painfully obscure and difficult to explain—the essential nature of God is freedom. The freedom of God is not to be understood as being the unruly and capricious option of the tyrant. The unlimited freedom of God is what gives meaning to the Biblical understanding of divine pathos and divine potency. The completeness of God is to be understood as the completeness of potency—all is possible to God, but all is not actualized. Indeed, there could be *nothing* but potency in the divine nature were eternity God's only habitation. The outpouring of God into time—in creation, revelation, and redemption—is the process of actualization. This is not to say that man is the actualization of divinity; it is only to say that man is that creature through whose life the endless richness and variety of divine possibility is realized. Time is the medium and history the substance of divine actualization.

We can only suggest—as Lurianic mysticism has done, as Jacob Boehme has done, as Nicholas Berdyaev has done—what we understand to be the incredible drama of God's life. Process within God is providence for man; unceasing actualization in God is destiny for man. We can do little more, at this moment in our thinking, than propose that our age and our aeon are but moments in eternity; that what we know as history is but an epoch in God's "history"; that our beginning and our end mean not the beginning and end of the only revelation and the only truth, but the beginning and end of the only truth which has been vouchsafed to us. Our history may not have been the first and our history may not be the last, but it is *our* history and therefore the only one with which we can be concerned.

It is foolish to speak of human destiny unless we speak of creation and consummation. This is the religious postulate of any metaphysics of history. Destiny "can exist," Berdyaev has written, "only if man is the child of God and not of the world." [2] Freedom of potency in the divine nature is freedom to good and evil in history. Only as potency is life, and eternal potency is eternal life, can we speak of God as good. Only the advent of death and corruption possesses the reality of evil. It is unimportant that the realized nature of God is as self-evident as his potency. What counts is that we *believe* the fixities of his eternal nature, but *live* in the face of his potency; that we are committed to his perfection, but pass our life in the shadow of *his* passion to consummation. We can know little or nothing of what God is in himself; we can only know what it is that God has made us and to what destiny we are appointed in the service of his freedom.

In the image of God's freedom we were created; but from God's realized perfection we are departed. This is

[2] Nicholas Berdyaev, *The Meaning of History*, trans. by George Reavey (London, Geoffrey Bles, 1936), p. 77.

the schism in our nature which is not present in God's. There could be no movement in our world if the freedom of God and the goodness of God were allowed to determine us. The interval which separates the beginning from the end is the interval of history in which faith makes the dead live, in which memory redeems the past and trust invests the future with novelty and hope.

Were history perfection it would be impossible to speak of incompletion, meaninglessness, waste, or distortion. History would contain its own fulfillment, its ends would be immanent in its unfolding; its process would be essentially good, even if it were obliged to press on through inadequacy to greater adequacy, through partial truth to consummate truth. Whether or not one's view of history is that of Vico or Condorcet (making reason the arbiter of progress) or Comte and Saint-Simon (viewing science and technology as the instruments of a continually self-perfecting man), the result is the same: history becomes a unity encompassing its own ends. For optimistic interpreters of history, history passes through evil to good. Good overwhelms evil as surely as reason overcomes superstition, science improves society, and technology enhances the comfort of man. In such views evil is not the foundation but the impediment of history.

It is our contention, however, that *within* history there is no meaning other than the self-illumination which the historian derives from the discernment of pattern and rhythm. Grand meaning does not exist, because grand meaning presupposes purpose and an end which uncreated and eternal history cannot allow. History becomes meaningful only when it is seen to commence and to conclude; and even though its commencement may be remote and unavailable to confirmation and its end but an image of an indefinite future, what passes between both points must be the inconclusive struggle of man to overcome the demonic. To consider the reality of evil as the foundation of history is never to say that history is evil *as such;* it is only to say that evil makes history significant, for in the evil which is possible to man our freedom and our finitude, our community with God and our estrangement from him are authenticated. We are not God's myth, but his creation; he created good and evil, said Isaiah, and we are both.

A metaphysics of history depends, therefore, for its significance upon the freedom to do evil—indeed, the reality of evil is the foundation of history.

It is in the presence of evil that we address ourselves again to the vocation and destiny of the Jews. Exile—that long and unbridged chasm which separates the Jew from his fulfillment—is a spiritual reality. To be sure, it is also a reality well founded upon the history and conduct of the nations. It is a spiritual reality of enormous importance, because it accords perfectly with that particular "freedom to evil" which is appropriate to the Jew. What the sin of Adam was to every man, the Exile of the Holy Spirit, the Exile of the community of Israel, the Exile of the faithful remnant of Zion, is to the Jew. The special destiny of the Jew is to witness to the evil which man does, not alone to the individual, but to providence. The election of Israel—that remarkable instance of God's unceasing pursuit of consummation—is degraded by the Exile of Israel; the good action of God is offset by the freedom to do evil which is at the root of history.

The Exile of Israel is, in the order of spiritual history, the first moment and the advent of the true Messiah is the last. God creates, man falls; God elects, the community sins; God disperses, the nations ravish. There is no center to history, no mid-point. There are innumerable centers, partial adumbrations; but the final word is indeed a final word. There can be no penultimate finalities, such as Jesus Christ. In the order of history Jesus is one among many centers, but if he be called Christ, the Messiah, he can be called such only by those who knew not the nature of history and discovered it through him. Jesus may be Christ for the Greek, but not for the Jew. Through Him the pagan discovered what had been known to the Jews: that God is present in history, that providence riddles time with possibility, and that no moment is ever the last until the final moment has come.

The rediscovery of sacred history is the first stage in the rejuvenescence of the Jewish theology. It was known to Scripture, known to the rabbis, known throughout the Middle Ages, known indeed until the dawn of modern history; but it was lost when history was disconnected from faith and the consummation of history was abandoned through the withering of trust.

III. THEOLOGY AS THE SCIENCE OF SACRED HISTORY

Theology need not be a pretentious discipline; it need not usurp the sciences, dismiss natural philosophy, nor overturn logic. It is a modest discipline founded, to be sure, upon an immodest history. Once theologians ruled the sciences and held court in universities, whereas presently they are hidden away in drafty seminaries and muster disciples from the thin readership of lugubrious journals. The unhappy condition of theology has undoubtedly made theologians snappish and defensive, but we can ill afford to forget that whereas theologians are human their object of concern remains God.

Theology is not concerned with any God. This is only to say that there is no general theology (leaving aside, for purposes of this discussion, the special history of natural theology or theology founded upon the decretals of unaided reason). There is only a theology which works upon the materials of faith. Again, not any and all faiths; but rather one's own true and chosen faith. There is Moslem theology and Christian theology; there is Jewish theology.

Jewish theology is directed to the explication of the

matter of Jewish faith. As we have indicated in the discussion just concluded, the matter of Jewish faith emerges from the juncture of God and history. The knowledge of God which we possess is knowledge consequent upon his action, whether it be his oblique conversations with the Patriarchs; his precise and disciplined discomfiting of Pharaoh; his marvelous manifestation in the flight from Egypt; his formal self-proclamation at Sinai; his innumerable rehearsals with the prophets of destiny and disaster; his alternately technical and passionate counsel to the sages. In all this history, in the transmitted word, in the myths of memory, in the written legacy, God is manifested. He is never manifest in generality. He is always a specific, concrete, and immediate presence to the Jew. He may be transcendent and distant, separated from us by the thin thread of eternity and the inadequacy of human words, but he is always a God of history, who is present in history to those who seek him.

The Jewish theologian must deal with a God of history; moreover he must deal with a God whose relation to history is not indefinite and uncertain, for the history through which God is disclosed is the theologian's *own* history—in seeking to understand God, the Jewish theologian, of necessity, seeks to understand himself. Insofar as the matter of Jewish theology is the history of God's presence to the Jew, theology becomes not a discipline of obscurity and abstraction, a spinning-out of formal answers to questions which nobody bothers any longer to ask, but a living discipline.

To the extent that theology is directed toward the God of history it becomes the link of the Jew to *all* history. The temptation of some Jewish theologians is to preserve the history of the Jews from contact and involvement with general history. The interpretation of Jewish history as sacred history, operating within its own time, its own logic of events, its own meaning, is deceptive. There is either real history or no history at all. The notion of Jewish history as independent of world history is a chimera. Its relation to general history may be paradigmatic—a distillate and pure exemplification of possibilities implicit in general history, but it is nevertheless real history, authentically united with the course of all history. The radical independence of Jewish history is an intellectual construction, a device whereby it is thought Judaism is rendered safe and protected from the challenge of alien doctrine; but, there can be no mistake: such construction is but a suspension of understanding, a refusal to acknowledge the inescapable fact of connection.

Secular history exists only in the absence of the transforming canon of faith. It is neutral and indifferent to providence, as long as the reality of providence is not interpolated into the action of events. Providence does not destroy normal causality or compromise scientific historiography—it merely adds to them the metaphysical optimism of which Joseph spoke when he addressed his malevolent and contrite brothers in the Land of the Pharaohs: "You meant evil against me, but God meant it for good." (Gen. 50:20; also 45:1–8) Joseph, the first Jewish metaphysician of history, understood that the fortunes of the Jews and the nations were bound together, that the neutral event shaped by the devisings of natural passions and interests could not compass the innumerable possibilities and perspectives which it contained. The single event—like all events—overwhelms the perspective of partial views. No man can perceive all the possibilities of an event. Its innumerable facets cannot be incorporated into the attitude either of the participant or of the historian who comes later. Faith assumes, however, that these possibilities are present to God, that his viewpoint is total and comprehensive, that his historical perspective is the perfect colligation of possibility and the understanding of what has actually come to pass.

There are those who will complain that this version of theology is vastly insufficient, that we have made the metaphysics of history into the sufficient subject matter of theology. Perhaps this is a legitimate criticism, but it should be noted in our favor that what we have forgone in rational theology—an inquiry into the nature of God and his formal relations to the universe—we have made up in revealed theology.[1] Otherwise spoken, we have declined to view theology either as a formal inquiry into the nature of God—which is too broad and uncompromisingly abstract—or as the narrow inquiry into the foundation of Jewish law and practice. Theology is neither the effort to apply the techniques of the sciences to the demonstration of God's existence (a hopeless enterprise) nor the attempt to apply findings of ethics, anthropology, or psychology to the rationalization of the commandments. Theology is rather the science of sacred history. It sets itself but one task: to apprehend and interpret the presence of God in time and history.

It is particularly appropriate that Jewish theology be understood as the knowledge (*scientia*) of sacred history. The disappearance of the theological center divests Judaism of both its special particularity and its catholic claim. Jewish history, removed from the antiphon of God and Israel, is little more than secular national history. The "theology" of the secular history of the Jews is sociology. Severed from the destiny and election of the Jews, Jewish history is but the consequence of the Jewish "problem." As the science of sacred history, however, theology

[1] We would be inclined to argue that Maimonides' *Sefer Ha-Mada* or the first two parts of his *Guide for the Perplexed* fall within the provenance of rational theology. Maimonides did not need the revelation of Scripture to define the nature of God. Reason, working upon the foundations of natural philosophy, might adduce sufficient proofs of God's existence and adequate interpretation of his nature. Only when Maimonides decided in favor of *creatio ex nihilo* (rather than the Aristotelian eternity of matter) was Scripture favored. All this on Maimonides' own statement, that where reason is not contradicted by Scripture, the formal elaborations of reason are to be preferred. Maimonides becomes, in our view, a proper Jewish theologian when he turns to the nature of prophecy, for here he is confronting a phenomenon of history in which the God who is beyond reason is present.

is founded upon an immediate reality—the community—and its consensual agreement upon doctrine (the tradition, *masorah*). The past and future interactions of community and doctrine are the sacred (spiritual) history of the Jews; but the definition of the grammar and the speech by which sacred history is apprehended and transmitted are the tasks of theology.

Theology need not become system; what counts is not that theology should complete its deliberations and build its own monument, but that it should leave open to sacred history the possibility of new creation and new revelation. Since the God of theology is the God of revealed history, there can be no final determinations: there can be at best the models of the past which adumbrate the future, but God's freedom to disclose himself is not limited by what he has already disclosed. A theology which would concern itself merely with conserving the past destroys what is most precious in the theological enterprise—namely, that the already spoken Word of God contains within it the insinuations of the yet unspoken Word, that the past is really the portent of the future. The promise is given but the promise is not yet fulfilled; unless the fulfillment of the promise be possible, no promise was given; unless there be redemption, there was no creation.

Finally, Jewish theology may be seen as the sieve and winnower of history. It cannot hope to become the master of all history, since its perspective is not God's. At best it must operate within the compass set by its limitations: that it is the theological thinking of a given faith, committed to the riches and the incompleteness of its own experience; moreover that it surveys the expanse of its inherited past from the narrow catwalk of its present moment. It is in this sense that theology is both the product of culture and the illuminator of culture.

If Judaism is to realize its catholic nature it must rediscover its relation to culture—not merely Jewish culture, but the culture of any time and any society of which it is both creature and creator.

IV. MESSIANISM AND THE CONSUMMATION OF CULTURE

Actually there can be no constructive thinking respecting history apart from culture. Since history is always the history of a people, it is reasonable that the historical event—a political movement, a style of art, a technological innovation, a scientific discovery—should be prepared by the ambience of culture. It is only possible to speak, therefore, with generality of the contours of culture, but not to fix them with finality, for culture is the latency of history, the actuality given and the possibilities implicit but unrealized.

The relation of Judaism and the Jewish people to the realities of culture has always been intimate and intense. Judaism was not matured independently of the formative and tributary cultures of the West. Judaism lived in profound and unbroken connection with the world that surrounded it, whether Near Eastern paganism, Hellenistic syncretism, Roman internationalism, pan-Islamism, or European Christianity. The Jewish people could not be sufficient to itself; its natural life was founded upon reaction and intermingling with the nations of the world. Were this condition *fact* alone it would only enable us to develop an argument based upon the historical involvement of Judaism with the West, and to define natural imperatives for the renewal of Jewish participation in the culture of the West. However, it is possible—as we have done throughout this study—to do more than adduce the compulsions of history as justification. It is not simply that Judaism can do no other than relate itself—for reasons of historical necessity, the urgencies of survival, or the requirements of ethnic pride—to the cultural life of the nations; it is rather that Judaism, theologically understood, cannot properly stand aloof from the world.

The vitality of Jewish culture is to be measured by the intensity with which it undertakes *galut* (Exile) as a cultural demand; indeed, as the living of its messianic vocation.

God witnesses the suffering of Israel, yet it is only to the natural eye of man that this suffering is suffering without purpose. The suffering is not ordained, nor, we believe, does God will our destruction. But if we are set among the nations who see themselves redeemed—whether through a God-Man or, as in the East, from the shambles of time—we are to them a mystery and a reproof. The role of Judaism, therefore, is not to create culture *as such,* but to be the critic of culture—to make culture the partial consummation of history and the anticipation of the Kingdom of God.

Culture is, we are increasingly aware, a precarious and indefinable phenomenon. As often as not culture is not discerned until it is past, until the new culture is born and the past may be accounted good or evil, productive or wasteful. The intellectual may call the culture of the moment popular and vulgar (and therefore inauthentic) and the historian who succeeds him in time may call it authentic (however popular and vulgar). The popular culture of Florence in the days of the Medicis was possibly no more exalted than the popular culture of contemporary America or England, but it is rather hard at this moment to set the prodigies and achievements of contemporary culture side by side with the culture of fifteenth-century Italy. It is our impatience to historicize that makes so many of our ventures into cultural appraisal risky; and yet such impatience is justified by the fact that our time and our history are not leisurely, that our age is covered with the veil of apocalypse and finality, and that many people—the best people of the West—are trying to locate the source of conservation and endurance.

The role of Judaism in the cultural enterprise is not different in kind from that of any other religion, although its role may be somewhat less precise and somewhat more oblique and tendentious. Any high culture—one that involves the amalgamation and fusion of well-articulated spheres of independent life and authority—results from the synthesis of different cultural traditions. It is not, as in primitive societies, the articulation of a unified whole, reflecting the penetration of primary myth into every aspect of life. In primitive society, the myth is so overwhelming as to transmute all activity into the bearer and fulfillment of the myth. The economy, the social organization, the family are all specific extrusions of myth, every aspect of life testifying to the psychic and spiritual claims of the regnant mythology. In the evolution of civilizations multiple cultural traditions are blended—not without pain to both the victor and the captive culture—independent spheres of authority are evolved, and individual and self-contained worlds of thought are refined and sustained. Where the culture succeeds, containing its diversity, the historic function of religion has been to conserve the vision toward which that unity is directed. Such societies are few and they have all declined, for the price of unity fashioned from the synthesis of discrete and individual centers of authority is that the vision is conventionalized by its conserving institutions and the rebellion of the diverse principalities of the mind and society which it once contained. The Kingdom of God on earth is always shattered when the vision is institutionalized; for the finite cannot routinize the infinite without tricking those whom it subjects, and the subjected finally rebel against the pretension of the conserving authority. It was the destiny of the medieval Church to pass and of the Holy Roman Empire to dissolve; it was the destiny of medieval Islam to decline in the face of the routinization of prophecy.

In our day the task of religion in culture is not to conserve the vision but to dislocate those who pretend to institutionalize *less* than the vision. In a disintegrating culture the task of religion is prophetic.

The paradox of God in time is always witnessed most acutely in the cultural consequences of the religious vision, for religion corrupts God when it would commit him now and forever to a single institution in time and yet it loses God when there is no institution at all through whom he speaks. This paradox drives us again to the unique vocation of Israel—neither committed nor aloof, neither rooted nor alien, neither of this world nor of any other. The Jew may stand astride time and eternity. Of needs he must! In the age of synthesis the cultural obligation of the Jew is to learn from culture that it may strengthen his prophecy, and in an age of prophecy to recapture tradition that the false prophet may not arise. So said, Judaism is the bearer of true prophets in ages of idolatrous self-sufficiency and the destroyer of false prophets in ages of dislocation.

The present obligation of religion to culture differs somewhat from its past, for the alternatives are no longer that religion either reigns or disintegrates. There is no religion; there is only religious sentiment. The real powers of our time are beyond the appeal of religion. This is, as Rosenzweig has said, the age of the Johannine gospel, which is beyond church and nation. There is no culture, as we have previously defined it; there are but the diverse authorities of society and the mind. There is profession; there is family; there are neighborhood and community; there are state, nation, and world—but there is little connection or communication between them. The spheres of authority are mute and inarticulate and, in the neutrality of the "between-sphere," the emptiness may be seen. There is neither vision nor the loss of vision; there is only ambiguity and the abyss.

The present task of the religious is neither to sustain nor to prophesy, but to begin again, to make new. It is here that Judaism is once more of the greatest importance, for Judaism has been committed neither to sustaining this world nor to prophesying the imminency of the next. Ours is the position of the "between" because we do not believe that redemption has come.

If Israel is "chosen," it is chosen for a distinguished

task—to outlast the world and its temporizing solutions, to be borne up to the end of time as His alone, to strain and winnow the pride of the world, to demonstrate that the burden of this incomplete time and this imperfect history is indeed insupportable, whereas all the ideologies of this world would render them bearable, indeed good and sufficient. This is unavoidably an aristocratic mission.

The messianic view of culture is not as the Rabbi of Prague said at the moment of the coming of the pretender savior, Sabbatai Zevi: We do not believe, for the world is not yet changed. The Rabbi of Prague was an insufficient messianist and a too committed mystic. But messianism is not mysticism; it is rather historical realism. It is the urging of undespairing realism toward this world. The transformation of the world is not demonstrated by the righting of wrongs, the justification of injustice; it is only partially this, for the transformation of the world consists in more than that the wolf and the lamb shall lie down together or that war shall cease from the world. This is the social image of salvation which is true enough as far as it goes. The change in the world that comes in the wake of the Messiah is not only social change, for social change requires but the restructuring of relations, the reordering of patterns. Social change assumes that the ultimate structure of the world, its being, is essentially perfect, but that its accidental historical arrangements are awry.

God does not work social change, attend diplomatic conferences, listen to political invocations, or bother with grace at charity banquets. He does not improve good will; rather he works on a universe in which society and man participate. Society does not reject God. The individual must first turn Him out of his life. It is the insufficiency of man that he should be unable to follow after God. A man may follow after his beloved, or seek after beauty, but to follow after God is a task of infinite difficulty. This is a condition of our world—and to such a world the Messiah comes not as reformer.[1] The Jew is the "between-man," between time and eternity, between the sadness of the world and the joy of redemption. He neither believes that in this time and history has the Kingdom of God been foretasted nor does he know when it is that God appoints this time and history for redemption.[2] For this reason the Jew is not bound to the stabilities of the world: he can create in ages when others would destroy and destroy in ages where others create—for he is the leaven of history. And this, we would think, is the messianic relation of the Jew to culture.

V. EPILOGUE: THE RENEWAL OF THE JEWISH VOCATION

A natural history of the Jewish mind is impossible. The Jewish mind, as a natural and empirical phenomenon, is an absurdity. It consists in but the pale images of theological models—prophetism and messianism trans-

[1] Indeed, the acute and critical disease from which Jewish messianic thinking suffers is that it has not perceived the enormous relevance which Rudolf Bultmann's demythologizing of Christianity has for Judaism. Jewish messianic thinking is beclouded by ethnic mythologies—the national restoration of Zion, the political rejuvenation of Israel, the punishing of the persecutors of the Jews, the miraculous return of all Jews to the Holy Land. Only if these limiting mythological conceptions are abandoned is it possible to discern what prophetic and rabbinic messianism really stands for—namely, the completion of one order of time and history and the inauguration of another. The regnancy of Israel is but a mythological symbol of a metaphysical transformation; for if the spiritual kingdom of the world is built again, that kingdom shall be the kingdom of the Jewish spirit.

[2] See a variety of the author's essays dealing with various aspects of the problem of messianism and the Jewish attitude toward Christian affirmation: "The Encounter of Judaism and Christendom," *Cross Currents*, Vol. I, No. 3 (Spring, 1951), pp. 91–95; "Messianism and the Jew," *Commonweal*, Vol. LXII, No. 15 (1955), pp. 367–69; "Moses, Mystery, and Jesus," *The Jewish Frontier*, Vol. XXIII,

formed into social and political ideologies, Exile recast as social alienation, the loneliness and spiritual discomfort of Biblical man translated into the self-estrangement of modern man. For the natural Jew all that remains of the supernatural community is a treasury of inspiriting maxims and heroic legends, divested not only of their mythological content but of their divinity as well. Judaism has been quietly and unconsciously demythologizing its tradition for centuries; but the purgation of myth has not been accompanied by a sharper, more compelling awareness of the personal truth and meaning of its history (much demythologizing, but little kerygma).

The Jewish mind is demythologized, but the natural Jew has lost, in the process, all contact with and approach to his supernatural life. For centuries the supernatural Jew struggled to survive, and though he perished in the flesh, he did survive. Faith in the promise of the past and trust in the consummating action of God enabled him to survive the assaults of Christendom and Islam. The loss in our time of that supernatural pride which is called the "stubbornness" of the Jew is partially responsible for the loss of contact with the legacy of tradition and the passion to give witness to the incomplete sanctity of the natural order; moreover, the immolation of European Jewry in this century has exploded the last vestige of Jewish mythology—an eschatological trust which was indifferent to the course of world history and culture.

The supernatural Jew, defined as he is by those concerns and preoccupations which form the historic consensus of the Jewish mind, is the last of the eschatologists, for the Jew, more than any other man, lives on the

---

No. 6 (June, 1956), pp. 24–28; "Three We Have Lost: The Problem of Conversion," *Conservative Judaism*, Vol. XI, No. 4 (1957), pp. 7–19; "Semite According to the Flesh," *The Christian Century*, Vol. LXXIV, No. 38 (Sept. 18, 1957), pp. 1097–89; "The Jewish-Christian Contradiction," *Worldview*, Vol. 1, No. 2 (1958), pp. 3–5; "The Natural and the Supernatural Jew," in Philip Scharper, ed., *American Catholics: A Protestant-Jewish View* (New York, Sheed & Ward, 1959), pp. 127–57.

recollection of first things and the anticipation of the last. Each moment comes to the supernatural Jew full of unrealized meaning, for each moment is abundant with the unrealized possibility of God in history. Every moment is potentially an eschatological moment; every moment collects the history of the past and portends the unfulfilled future. There is no such thing for the supernatural Jew as the denial of history, the repudiation of its meaning, the despair of its justification. Where the natural Jew may know despair, the supernatural Jew knows only trust.

But the natural and the supernatural Jew are joined in every Jew. The supernatural Jew may occasionally forget that he is also flesh and blood; he may detach himself from the world and disengage himself from history that he may pursue a path of self-denial and private illumination. Such a Jew is as much in error as is the natural Jew who forgets what links him to eternity. The natural Jew, enmeshed in the historical, cannot help but despair; destiny disappears for him and only the hard and implacable fatality of his life remains. The despair of the historical is but the consequence of fate obliterating destiny; while the ecstasy of the mystic, no less an example of fate, is centered exclusively upon the actuality of God, indifferent to his involvement in the contingent and dangerous war of history.

The religious dilemma which makes the unity of the natural and the supernatural so imperative for the Jewish mind is that the representation of God in history is not pure actuality but actuality committed to the unfulfilled possibility of history. The eschatological consummation toward which Judaism turns its face is history with God, the actual God realizing new creation, and new concreteness. As such, each moment of the present may become a redemptive moment, a moment in which the new possibility of God and the renewed sensibility of the Jew may meet and sanctify.

The renewal of the historical, the reunion of the Jew

with general culture, the reassertion of the catholic claim of Judaism depend upon the rediscovery of the implicit polarity and dialectic of the Jewish nature—that it is natural, participating in all the forms and events of history and culture, and supernatural, transforming those forms and events into bearers of ultimate and consummate meaning. God is not an eschatologist nor is God a messianist. God does what can be done—this is indeed part of the tragedy which we may sense when we speak of God, for God cannot compel history to fulfillment; he can but enrich the moment with those possibilities which become the bearers of meaning. It is man who victimizes God. God maintains freedom and the free destiny; it is human obduracy and folly which refuses such terrifying freedom and finds consolation in the refusal of destiny and the comforting delusion of fate.

The historic moment that bears ultimate meaning is always at hand. But when the argument is done and the historic precedents of the Jewish mind have been adduced and displayed and the consensus of Judaism has been recapitulated, the same question recurs: Can the testimony of all truth compel human decision? Is it possible that the sense of supernatural vocation—lost as it is in the abyss of natural fate—may be renewed? This question still remains, and only Jews can answer it.

Bibliography

Bibliographies are sometimes useful, more often not. In works such as the present one, where the emphasis falls upon the history of general ideas and movements, a bibliography serves less to document the author's sources than to introduce the interested reader to traditions of thought with which he may be unfamiliar. This bibliography will be confined therefore to the Jewish literature available in the English language, supplemented by occasional comments which may help to guide the reader. Bibliographic citations in languages other than English may be found in the footnotes. Many readers, undoubtedly familiar with French, German, and Hebrew—the foreign languages upon whose literatures we have drawn—will know that certain crucial works are as yet unavailable in English translation. This is lamentably true of important books by Mendelssohn, Krochmal, Cohen, Rosenzweig, and Kaufmann. (pb) appearing after a citation indicates that a paperbound edition of the work is now available.

AGUS, JACOB, *Modern Philosophies of Judaism.* New York, Behrman House, Inc., 1941. Useful and reliable introduction to the thought of Cohen, Rosenzweig, Buber, and Kaplan.

AGUS, JACOB, *The Evolution of Jewish Thought.* New York, Abelard-Schuman Limited, 1959.

AHAD HA-AM, *Essays, Letters, Memoirs,* trans. and ed. by Leon

Simon. Oxford, East and West Library, 1946. Excellent collection.

AHAD HA-AM, *Essays on Zionism and Judaism*, trans. by Leon Simon. London, George Routledge & Sons, Ltd., 1922.

AHAD HA-AM, *Selected Essays*, trans. by Leon Simon. Philadelphia, Jewish Publication Society of America, 1912.

ALTMANN, ALEXANDER, "Franz Rosenzweig and Eugen Rosenstock-Huessy: An Introduction to Their 'Letters on Judaism and Christianity.'" *The Journal of Religion*, Vol. XXIV, No. 4, Chicago, 1944.

ALTMANN, ALEXANDER, "Franz Rosenzweig on History," in Alexander Altmann, ed., *Between East and West*. London, East and West Library, 1958. Very suggestive essay.

BAECK, LEO, *Dieses Volk: Jüdische Existenz*. Frankfurt am Main, Europäische Verlagsanstat, 1955, 1957, 2 vols. (Eng. trans. to be published by Holt, Rinehart and Winston, Inc.). Baeck's most mature and passionate avowal of Judaism.

BAECK, LEO, *The Essence of Judaism*, trans. by Victor Grubenwieser and Leonard Pearl. New York, Schocken Books, Inc., 1948. (pb) Primary source for Baeck's view of Judaism.

BAECK, LEO, *Judaism and Christianity*, trans. by Walter Kaufmann. Philadelphia, Jewish Publication Society of America, 1958. (pb) Collection of five of Baeck's most important essays.

BAECK, LEO, "Types of Jewish Understanding from Moses Mendelssohn to Franz Rosenzweig," trans. by H. C. Stevens. *Judaism*, Vol. IX, Nos. 1 and 2.

BAECK, LEO, "Unifying Philosophy, Science, and Prophecy: Moses Maimonides: The Man, His Work," trans. by Irving Pfefferblit. *Commentary*, April, 1955.

BARON, SALO, *A Social and Religious History of the Jews*. New York, Columbia University Press, 1937, 3 vols. An indispensable work now in the process of considerable expansion and revision. The notes are particularly valuable.

BARON, SALO, "Ghetto and Emancipation." *The Menorah Journal*, June, 1928.

BARON, SALO, "Newer Approaches to Jewish Emancipation." *Diogenes*, Spring, 1960. Tightly constructed and brilliant summary of Baron's view of the problem.

BARZILAY, ISAAC EISENSTEIN, "Moses Mendelssohn (1729–1786)." *The Jewish Quarterly Review*, July, 1961.

BARZILAY, ISAAC EISENSTEIN, "The Background of the Berlin *Haskalah*," in Joseph L. Blau, Philip Friedman, Arthur Hertzberg, Isaac Mendelsohn, eds., *Essays on Jewish Life and Thought*. New York, Columbia University Press, 1959.

Bibliography

BENTWICH, NORMAN, *Solomon Schechter*. Philadelphia, Jewish Publication Society of America, 1938. Excellent and comprehensive.

BERGMAN, SAMUEL H., *Faith and Reason: An Introduction to Modern Jewish Thought*. Washington, D.C., B'nai B'rith Hillel Foundation, 1961.

BERLIN, ISAIAH, *The Life and Opinions of Moses Hess*. Cambridge, W. Heffer and Sons, Ltd., 1959.

BIALIK, CHAIM NACHMAN, "Jewish Dualism," trans. by Maurice M. Shudofsky. *The Jewish Frontier*, July, 1961. An almost miraculous essay.

BUBER, MARTIN, *Between Man and Man*, trans. by Ronald Gregor Smith. New York, The Macmillan Company, 1948. (pb) Major developmental essays on the theme of dialogue.

BUBER, MARTIN, *Eclipse of God*. New York, Harper & Brothers, 1952.

BUBER, MARTIN, *For the Sake of Heaven*, trans. by Ludwig Lewisohn. Philadelphia, Jewish Publication Society of America, 1953. (pb) One of Buber's most revealing books and his only novel.

BUBER, MARTIN, *Hasidism and Modern Man*, trans. by Maurice Friedman. New York, Horizon Press, Inc., 1958.

BUBER, MARTIN, *I and Thou*, trans. by Ronald Gregor Smith. Edinburgh, T & T Clark, 1937. With new postscript, 1958. (pb) Indispensable.

BUBER, MARTIN, *Israel and the World*. New York, Schocken Books, Inc., 1948. Collection of some of the very best and most enduring of Buber's shorter writings.

BUBER, MARTIN, *Moses*. Oxford and London, East and West Library, 1946.

BUBER, MARTIN, *Paths in Utopia*, trans. by R. F. C. Hull. London, Routledge & Kegan Paul, Ltd., 1949. (pb)

BUBER, MARTIN, *Pointing the Way*, trans. by Maurice Friedman. New York, Harper & Brothers, 1957. (pb)

BUBER, MARTIN, *Two Types of Faith*, trans. by Norman P. Goldhawk. London, Routledge & Kegan Paul, Ltd., 1951. (pb) Subtle and convincing comparison of Judaism and Christianity.

COHEN, ARTHUR A., *Martin Buber*. New York, Hillary House, 1958.

COHEN, ARTHUR A., "Revelation and Law: Reflections on Martin Buber's Views of *Halachah*." *Judaism*, Vol. I, No. 3, July, 1952.

COHEN, ARTHUR A., "The Natural and the Supernatural Jew: Two Views of the Church," in Philip Scharper, ed., *American Catholics: A Protestant-Jewish View*. New York, Sheed & Ward, 1959.

COHEN, ARTHUR A., "The Past and Future of Eschatological Thinking," in Harold Stahmer, ed., *Religion and Contemporary Society.* New York, Collier Books, 1963. (pb)

DUBNOW, SIMON, *Nationalism and History: Essays on Old and New Judaism,* ed. by Koppel S. Pinson. Philadelphia, Jewish Publication Society of America, 1958. (pb) Essays of genuine and unfailing power.

EISENSTEIN, IRA, AND KOHN, EUGENE, eds., *Mordecai M. Kaplan: An Evaluation.* New York, Jewish Reconstructionist Foundation, 1952. Illuminating in its praise and its omissions.

FACKENHEIM, EMIL, "Jewish Existence and the Living God." *Commentary,* August, 1959.

FRIEDMAN, MAURICE, "Abraham Joshua Heschel: Toward a Philosophy of Judaism." *Conservative Judaism,* Winter, 1956.

FRIEDMAN, MAURICE, *Martin Buber: The Life of Dialogue.* Chicago, The University of Chicago Press, 1955. (pb) Most complete and useful introduction to Buber's thought.

GLATZER, NAHUM N., *Franz Rosenzweig: His Life and Thought.* New York, Schocken Books, Inc., and Farrar, Straus & Young, Inc., 1953. (pb) Indispensable English source.

GRAETZ, HEINRICH, *History of the Jews,* trans. and/or rev. by Bella Loewy. Philadelphia, Jewish Publication Society of America, 1895. 6 vols. Translation of the most literate, contentious, and stimulating general history of the Jews that has been written.

GUTTMANN, JULIUS, *Ha-Pilosophia shel Ha-Yahadut.* Jerusalem, Bialik Institute, 1952 (Eng. trans. to be published by Holt, Rinehart and Winston, Inc.). Standard work on history of Jewish philosophic thought from Biblical times through the German Jewish renaissance.

HERBERG, WILL, "Athens and Jerusalem: Confrontation and Dialogue." *Drew Gateway,* Vol. XXVIII, No. 3, 1958. Very important essay.

HERBERG, WILL, "Discussion of Milton Steinberg's 'The Theological Issues of the Hour.' " *Proceedings of the Rabbinical Assembly of America,* June, 1949.

HERBERG, WILL, "From Marxism to Judaism." *Commentary,* January, 1947. Impressive autobiographic essay.

HERBERG, WILL, "Has Judaism Still Power to Speak?" *Commentary,* May, 1949.

HERBERG, WILL, "Historicism as Touchstone." *The Christian Century,* March 16, 1960. Reprinted in Harold E. Fey, ed., *How My Mind Has Changed.* New York and Cleveland, Meridian Books: The World Publishing Company, 1961. (pb)

HERBERG, WILL, *Judaism and Modern Man.* New York, Farrar,

Straus & Cudahy, Inc., 1951. (pb) Herberg's major theological work.

HESCHEL, ABRAHAM JOSHUA, *God in Search of Man*. New York, Farrar, Straus & Cudahy, Inc., 1955. (pb)

HESCHEL, ABRAHAM JOSHUA, *Man Is Not Alone*. New York. Farrar, Straus & Cudahy, Inc., 1951. Introduction to Heschel's central religious categories.

HESCHEL, ABRAHAM JOSHUA, *The Earth Is the Lord's: The Inner World of the Jew in East Europe*. New York, Henry Schuman, 1950. (pb) Moving and lyrical introduction to Eastern European Jewish piety.

HESCHEL, ABRAHAM JOSHUA, "The Last Years of Maimonides." *National Jewish Monthly*, June, 1955. Chapter from longer untranslated work.

HESCHEL, ABRAHAM JOSHUA, *The Sabbath: Its Meaning for Modern Man*. New York, Farrar, Straus & Cudahy, Inc., 1951. (pb)

HESS, MOSES, *Rome and Jerusalem*, trans. by Meyer Waxman. New York, Bloch Publishing Co., Inc., 1918. One of the most exciting prodigies of modern Jewish thought.

HIRSCH, SAMSON RAPHAEL, *Judaism Eternal*, trans. by I. Grunfeld. London, The Soncino Press, 1956. 2 vols. Excellent collection of Hirsch's apologetic and exegetic essays.

HIRSCH, SAMSON RAPHAEL, *The Nineteen Letters of Ben Uziel*, trans. by Bernard Drachman. New York, Bloch Publishing Co., Inc., 1942. Classic source of modern Orthodox apologetics.

KAPLAN, MORDECAI M., *Judaism as a Civilization*. New York, The Macmillan Company, 1934. Early, but important.

KAPLAN, MORDECAI M., *Judaism Without Supernaturalism*. New York, Jewish Reconstructionist Foundation, 1958. Highly tendentious.

KAPLAN, MORDECAI M., *The Future of the American Jew*. New York, The Macmillan Company, 1948.

KAPLAN, MORDECAI M., *The Meaning of God in Modern Jewish Religion*. New York, Behrman House, Inc., 1937. Decisive statement of Kaplan's theological views.

PETUCHOWSKI, JAKOB J., "Faith as the Leap of Action: The Theology of Abraham Joshua Heschel." *Commentary*, May, 1958.

ROSENZWEIG, FRANZ, *On Jewish Learning*, ed. by Nahum N. Glatzer, trans. by William Wolf. New York, Schocken Books, Inc., 1955. Correspondence of Buber and Rosenzweig on Jewish law is most important.

ROSENZWEIG, FRANZ, *Understanding the Sick and the Healthy*, ed. by Nahum N. Glatzer. New York, The Noonday Press, 1953.

ROSENBLOOM, NOAH H., "The 'Nineteen Letters of Ben Uziel.'" *Historia Judaica*, April, 1960.

ROTH, CECIL, *The Jews in the Renaissance*. Philadelphia, Jewish Publication Society of America, 1959. Although concentrating on the Italian Renaissance, introduces a world with which general reader is usually unfamiliar.

ROTHSCHILD, FRITZ A. (ed.), *Between God and Man: From the Writings of Abraham J. Heschel*. New York, Harper & Brothers, 1959. Valuable introductory anthology.

SCHECTER, SOLOMON, *Studies in Judaism*, First Series. Philadelphia, Jewish Publication Society of America, 1945. (pb) Essays on Krochmal and on the dogmas of Judaism to be found here.

SCHECHTER, SOLOMON, *Some Aspects of Rabbinic Theology*. New York, The Macmillan Company, 1909. (pb)

SCHOEPS, HANS JOACHIM, *Juedisch-Christliches Religionsgespraech in neunzehn Jahrhunderten*. Munich and Frankfurt am Main, Atharva-Verlag, 1949 (Eng. trans. to be published by Holt, Rinehart and Winston, Inc.). Somewhat tendentious, but invigorating, history of theological dialogue between Judaism and Christianity.

SCHOLEM, GERSHOM, "Martin Buber's Hasidism: A Critique." *Commentary*, October, 1961. Telling, but possibly irrelevant.

SCHWARZSCHILD, STEVEN S., *Franz Rosenzweig: Guide for Reversioners*. London, The Education Committee of the Hillel Foundation, no date. Excellent introduction.

SCHWARZSCHILD, STEVEN S., "Rosenzweig on Judaism and Christianity." *Conservative Judaism*, Vol. X, No. 2.

SCHWARZSCHILD, STEVEN S., "Samson Raphael Hirsch—The Man and His Thought." *Conservative Judaism*, Vol. XIII, No. 2. Somewhat too understanding.

SCHWARZSCHILD, STEVEN S., "The Democratic Socialism of Hermann Cohen." *Hebrew Union College Annual*, Vol. XXVII, 1956.

SILBERNER, E., "Moses Hess." *Historia Judaica*, Vol. XIII, April, 1951. Splendid introduction to Hess's life and thought.

SILVERMAN, DAVID, "Current Theological Trends: A Survey and Analysis." *Proceedings of the Rabbinical Assembly of America*, 1960.

SPIEGEL, SHALOM, *Hebrew Reborn*. New York, The Macmillan Company, 1930. (pb) Moving and brilliant history of Hebrew language and literature *redivivus*.

STEINBERG, MILTON, *Anatomy of Faith*, ed. by Arthur A. Cohen. New York, Harcourt, Brace & World, Inc., 1960. Collection of Steinberg's major theological papers.

STEINBERG, MILTON, *A Partisan Guide to the Jewish Problem.* Indianapolis, The Bobbs-Merrill Company, Inc., 1933.

STEINBERG, MILTON, *As a Driven Leaf.* Indianapolis, The Bobbs-Merrill Company, Inc., 1940. Important and revealing novel of a first-century Jewish apostate.

STEINBERG, MILTON, *Basic Judaism.* New York, Harcourt, Brace & World, Inc., 1947.

STEINBERG, MILTON, *A Believing Jew.* New York, Harcourt, Brace & World, Inc., 1951.

STEINBERG, MILTON, *The Making of the Modern Jew.* Indianapolis, The Bobbs-Merrill Company, Inc., 1933. Steinberg's first and most characteristic book.

WALLACH, LUITPOLD, *Liberty and Letters: The Thoughts of Leopold Zunz.* London, Leo Baeck Institute, East and West Library, 1959.

WELTSCH, ROBERT (ed.), *Yearbook I–VI,* Leo Baeck Institute. London, East and West Library, 1956–1961. Invaluable source books for any serious study of German-Jewish intellectual and religious history.

Index